WOMEN FIGHTERS IN THE KURDISH NATIONAL MOVEMENT

Kurdish Studies Series

Series Editors

Zeynep Kaya, Middle East Centre, London School of Economics and Political
Science, UK & Department of Development Studies, School of Oriental and African
Studies, UK
Robert Lowe, Middle East Centre, London School of Economics and Political
Science, UK

Advisory Board

Sabri Ateş, Dedman College of Humanities & Sciences, USA
Mehmet Gurses, Florida Atlantic University, USA
Janet Klein, University of Akron, USA
David Romano, Missouri State University, USA
Clemence Scalbert-Yücel, University of Exeter, UK
Güneş Murat Tezcür, University of Arizona, USA
Nicole Watts, San Francisco State University, USA

Titles

The Kurds in a Changing Middle East: History, Politics and Representation,
edited by Faleh A. Jabar and Renad Mansour
Kurdish Nationalism on Stage: Performance, Politics and Resistance in Iraq,
Mari R. Rostami
The Kurds of Northern Syria: Governance, Diversity and Conflicts, Harriet Allsopp
and Wladimir van Wilgenburg
The Kurds and the Politics of Turkey: Agency, Territory and Religion, Deníz Çifçi
*Kurds and Yezidis in the Middle East: Shifting Identities, Borders and the
Experience of Minority Communities*, edited by Güneş Murat Tezcür
*The Formation of Modern Kurdish Society in Iran: Modernity, Modernization and
Social Change (1920-1979)*, Marouf Cabi
*The Political Representation of Kurds in Turkey: New Actors and Modes of Participation
in a Changing Society*, Cengiz Gunes

WOMEN FIGHTERS IN THE KURDISH NATIONAL MOVEMENT

Transforming Gender Politics and the PKK

Mustafa Kemal Topal

I.B. TAURIS
LONDON • NEW YORK • OXFORD • NEW DELHI • SYDNEY

I.B. TAURIS

Bloomsbury Publishing Plc, 50 Bedford Square, London, WC1B 3DP, UK
Bloomsbury Publishing Inc, 1359 Broadway, 12th Floor, New York, NY 10018, USA
Bloomsbury Publishing Ireland, 29 Earlsfort Terrace, Dublin 2, D02 AY28, Ireland

BLOOMSBURY, I.B. TAURIS and the I.B. Tauris logo
are trademarks of Bloomsbury Publishing Plc

First published in Great Britain 2024
This paperback edition published in 2025

Series design by Adriana Brioso
Cover image: Women Fighters, Rojava © Mustafa Kemal Topal

A catalogue record for this book is available from the British Library.

Library of Congress Cataloging-in-Publication Data
Names: Topal, Mustafa Kemal, author.
Title: Women fighters in the Kurdish national movement: transforming gender politics and
the PKK / Mustafa Kemal Topal.
Description: London; New York: I.B Tauris, 2024. | Series: Kurdish studies |
Includes bibliographical references and index.
Identifiers: LCCN 2023029232 (print) | LCCN 2023029233 (ebook) |
ISBN 9780755648368 (hardback) | ISBN 9780755648405 (paperback) |
ISBN 9780755648375 (pdf) | ISBN 9780755648382 (epub) | ISBN 9780755648399
Subjects: LCSH: Partiya Karkerên Kurdistanê. | Women, Kurdish–Political activity–Turkey. |
Women, Kurdish–Political activity–Middle East. | Kurds–Politics and government. |
National liberation movements–Kurdistan.
Classification: LCC HQ1726.5 .T66 2024 (print) | LCC HQ1726.5 (ebook) |
DDC 305.48/8915970561–dc23/eng/20230712
LC record available at https://lccn.loc.gov/2023029232
LC ebook record available at https://lccn.loc.gov/2023029233

ISBN:	HB:	978-0-7556-4836-8
	PB:	978-0-7556-4840-5
	ePDF:	978-0-7556-4937-5
	eBook:	978-0-7556-4838-2

Series: Kurdish Studies

Typeset by Deanta Global Publishing Services, Chennai, India

For product safety related questions contact productsafety@bloomsbury.com.

To find out more about our authors and books visit www.bloomsbury.com
and sign up for our newsletters.

To my daughter Awasin

CONTENTS

PREFACE

Women Fighters in the Kurdish National Movement: Transforming Gender Politics and the PKK is an academic contribution to understanding entangled, contextual factors behind Kurdish women's decisions to join the PKK and engage in militant combat. A key methodological inspiration for inquiring into the situatedness of their decisions was the insistence of biologist and feminist Donna Haraway that knowledge is situated. Accordingly, I have presented the women fighters' motivations as situated by focusing on contextual details in the individual narratives. However, an implication of Haraway's concept of 'situated knowledge' is also that my inquiry is situated.[1] A book like this, despite – or rather because of – its ambition to meet academic standards, therefore has to propound its subjective dimension.[2]

The book is a revised and edited version of a PhD dissertation that I submitted in 2020 to Roskilde University, Denmark. Since 1996, I have lived as a refugee in Denmark. I was born and raised in Turkey, where my family and I always identified as Kurds. On a daily basis, I was exposed to the conflict between the PKK and the Turkish state through news of the struggle, through Kurds of my age who sympathized with the PKK or through initiatives by the Turkish state to frame the PKK as a terrorist organization. Enrolled as a student at a Turkish university, I met fellow students and other young people who assembled in the Patriotic Youth Movement (YCK). I took part in some non-violent student activities such as celebrating the Kurdish New Year (Newroz), collecting signatures to call for the release of political prisoners and collecting books for political prisoners. While I deemed these activities peaceful and democratic, the Turkish authorities considered them illegal, claiming that they threatened the 'indivisible integrity of the nation'. I was therefore twice detained, tortured and accused of 'damaging the indivisible integrity of the state and the nation', risking a prison sentence of up to twelve years. To avoid a long prison sentence, I decided to leave Turkey for Denmark to live an ordinary life. All charges against me were dropped after I came to Denmark, so I was never convicted of anything in Turkey.

As a Kurdish refugee in Denmark, and as someone with roots in an oppressed population group, I am politically engaged. This engagement inevitably has a hand in my personal motivation for writing this book; yet, it was never my intention to write the book to legitimize the Kurdish liberation struggle. Instead, it was driven by my wish to understand what motivates Kurdish women to become women fighters. This wish originates in past friendships of my childhood and youth where I looked on as many female friends chose this path – and in many cases died because of it. Another predisposition that interacts with the choice of theories for the book pertains to 'otherness', as I am affiliated with an oppressed group where members do not enjoy democratic rights of representation whether in political life or in the history books controlled by the dominant culture. This does not mean, however, that I try to compensate by using this book to give a voice to 'the other', in this case to Kurdish women fighters, because these women are, as the book will show, well-articulated and enjoy respect within their own society and region where they are active. Instead, I have been drawn to theories of 'otherness' as tools to help me understand the dynamics and multiple factors that fuelled their decision to pursue a radically different lifestyle.

When preparing the fieldwork, I wanted it to be characterized by 'democratic conditions' where the women fighters could challenge my questions and observations, just as I had to question if they revealed what they saw as the truth or withheld information.[3] Yet, such democratic conditions for fieldwork were challenged because it took place in a highly politicized field, full of ethical dilemmas. Being in a war-like struggle creates an atmosphere of distrust and suspicion affecting all parties involved. The women fighters had their misgivings. Their leader, Dersim, told me, before deciding whether to allow me to interview her unit, that researchers like me always described Kurdish women with 'an orientalist and marginalizing gaze' (Interview with Dersim, 27 March 2018), so she did not know whether to believe if I would be different from those researchers or not. What probably made a difference to the PKK, and made it possible for me to carry out the fieldwork, was undoubtedly the fact that I myself am Kurdish. I have a number of acquaintances, such as former fellow students from Turkey, who are still part of the movement. The movement probably made inquiries through its own channels as to who I was and for whom I might be carrying out the study. Once reasons for mistrusting me had been ruled out and Dersim had approved of me, the movement never treated me with suspicion.

With regard to the ethical dilemmas, the movement hesitated to grant me a travel permit until it felt assured that I could carry out my fieldwork without coming to harm. After all, the PKK has no fixed main base. Its training camps are situated in the mountains in Iraq, but never in the same place for long, as it is forced to be mobile at all times to avoid the Turkish military's searchlights and assault plane overflights in the mountains. The movement therefore did not want me exposed to risk. They often said to me, 'You have young children and family. So you mustn't take any risks!' Above all, they were no doubt aware that any accident befalling me would show their cause in a bad light.

I wanted to combine my trip to Iraq with one to Rojava, as I also wanted to observe what position Kurdish women fighters were adopting under 'democratic confederalism', which is Rojava's new political system and political experiment. With good reason, the management of Roskilde University was concerned about my journey because Rojava – despite its autonomy and political experiments – still counts as a warzone. The PKK also hesitated, especially because Turkey, at the natural point in the project for a trip to Rojava, blocked entry to Rojava, just as the Iraqi army mounted a military attack on the Kurdish autonomy, capturing a number of cities and closing the international airport in the Kurdish city of Arbil, to which I had planned to travel. After lengthy deliberations and dialogue with the movement, I therefore decided to travel first to Rojava and from there to Iraq, as according to the movement it would be easier in that order. My journey to Rojava had to go via the airport in the city of Qamişlo. The city is under Kurdish control and serves as the capital of the Rojavan autonomy. The airport itself, however, is controlled by Assad's forces and the paramilitary forces supporting his regime, which made the passage through the airport perilous. Accordingly, I coordinated my journey with a woman from Rojava whom I will call Döne. As with all informants in this book, I have pseudonomized her identity. She lived in Europe, had a Syrian passport, and was going to Rojava to visit her family. We passed ourselves off as a couple. Although there were no major challenges getting through passport control itself, it was distressing to witness the way our fellow passengers were treated by Assad's forces. It took nearly three hours to get out of the airport and throughout that time somebody was being stamped on, beaten, restrained and having their life threatened. There was utter chaos in the airport; children were crying and screaming in fear. I was concerned that the Assad forces might decide to send me on to the intelligence service in Damascus for questioning, something that had happened to somebody earlier because the Assad forces suspected their motives for entry. With much help from Döne, who was courageous and extremely patient, we managed to leave the airport and arrive in Kurdish-controlled Rojava.

Once I arrived in the area of PKK's training camps, I met Zagros, my escort. By agreement with the movement, I will not go into the details of my first journey to Rojava and from there to Iraq and back, as doing so might have consequences for the movement's mobility in the local area. Yet, I do not compromise them by mentioning the tremendous help that I received from Zagros, a long-time man fighter in the PKK. For ten days, we lived together in a small hut in the mountains. While he was in civilian clothing when he met me, once we reached the hut, Zagros immediately changed his clothes and put on his guerrilla outfit and his Kalashnikov. During those ten days, he and I had long, deep discussions on everything, but mostly politics and life in the mountains. I was also thoroughly briefed on what to do and what not to do for safety's sake – ours but mostly my own. For example, I was not to move around freely outdoors, as there was a risk of being attacked by wild animals, drones and planes. There were also landmines in some places. I do not know by what criteria the movement chose Zagros to act as my escort. They probably thought it would be easier for two men to be together. Zagros was in his late thirties; he seemed very calm and ideologically aware, maybe because he had spent twelve years in prison before he was able to come to the mountains to fight. He spoke both Kurdish and Turkish, which was another advantage. Despite being younger than I am, he seemed very solicitous towards me and did his best to ensure that I slept well, had time to rest, ate well and was protected. My access to his narrativizations has, as it will become apparent in the book, added nuances to my understanding of women fighters and conceptions of gender within the PKK. All the steps taken by Zagros and the interviewed women fighters to keep me safe made it clear to me that my presence added an extra risk to their activities. In an ongoing war, there is no such thing as an ideal and safe zone for doing fieldwork and protecting my informants. Research ethically, proper conduct was not just about pseudonymizing the informants' identities; it was also about complying with their orders with regard to safety to ensure that my presence did not put them or me at any unnecessary risk. In many ways, it was also my responsibility as a guest in the women fighters' unit to look out for our common survival.

Partway through my first visit to Rojava, I was forced to break off because a Turkish invasion of the area was imminent. The women's movement in Rojava advised me to leave the area immediately to stay out of harm's way. This explains why I did not manage to carry out all the interviews I had planned. I managed to return home without any physical harm, thanks to another Kurdish woman, Xazal, who was proficient in Arabic. In the airport, we entered a 'mutual survival relationship' to get safe through the chaos of the airport in the midst of screams, panic, harassment and fear, recognizable from the inbound journey. We both managed, but the experiences at Qamişlo Airport still haunt me. In retrospect, I realize that luck and my willingness to take chances played their part in enabling me to complete parts of the fieldwork during my first visit to Rojava. I deemed this risk-taking necessary to access information crucial for academic scholarship. However, from a research ethical perspective, my willingness should never be expected of others. It always comes down to an individual decision.

In December 2019, I had the opportunity to go back to Rojava for three days by a different route to carry out the interviews I had not managed to hold during my first trip. This time, the journey was via Iraq, and it went as planned and without problems. The airport at Arbil had been reopened, and it was also possible to get a permit from the Kurdish autonomy in Iraq to cross the border into Rojava.

It is inevitable that the researcher and the field of investigation will come to influence each other. I was affected by the interviewees' personal narratives, in which they talked openly about traumatic details of their lives. I learnt about lifeworlds to which the participants may not previously have admitted others, and I humbly enjoyed a unique and special relation to them. The thought that they might have come to harm or died in the fighting after my field visit is therefore a painful one. For example, I briefly met my escort Zagros in Iraq on my second journey to Rojava. He told me that Zelal was now back in the mountains, that Bese and Gulesor were killed in the fight and Zin had been excluded from the movement for, according to Zagros, not fitting in with the ethical and moral values of the movement (fieldnote, 18 December 2019). I felt sorry for her. She had not had a particularly easy life in the movement as a woman fighter, but, as I will examine in Chapter 6, life after the movement is not at all easy for those who chose to leave. Zin is also probably the woman fighter most often quoted in the book, because, as an intellectual woman, she was good at talking and reflecting on things as well as of great help during my field trip.

Between 9 October and 17 November 2019, the Turkish armed forces invaded parts of Rojava together with the Syrian National Army consisting of Sunni Muslim jihadists. The areas invaded included the women's village of Jinwar, which I had visited on my first field trip to Rojava. The invasion had enormous consequences in terms of civilian and military casualties on the Kurdish side, and up to half a million civilians were forced to flee from their homes. Among them were families I knew from my fieldwork. Along with the fates of the interviewed PKK women fighters, I was also affected by these upheavals in Rojava. News about someone's death, torture, oppression, massacres and so on have caused mental and physical stress that affected my work rate. One thing, however, that is important for me to stress is that the empathetic and sympathetic effect the project had on me does not mean that I do not acknowledge losses, suffering and sorrow among the other parties in the war. I have tried to the best of my ability to eliminate any *parti pris* from the data production and the subsequent analysis.

ACKNOWLEDGEMENTS

This book would not have come to fruition without contributions from many people. First, I would like to thank all the informants, especially the women fighters who chose to tell me about their reality of life with openness and trust. You chose to participate in this book, with interest and curiosity, and words cannot describe how thankful I am for your hospitality and openness, and the respect you showed towards the book, but also towards me as a person. Also, a deep thanks to those people, who sit on different posts in the leadership of the PKK. Without your permission to do the fieldwork in Iraq, Rojava/Syria and Europe, the book could not have been completed. I would also like to extend a special thanks to 'Döne' for making my first trip to Rojava possible and 'Xazal' for making my return possible.

I owe my gratitude to Marianne Schleicher – not only because she functioned as an external supervisor for my PhD dissertation but also for her commitment towards my work, her kindness and the personal investment in me as a person. I am greatly thankful for everything she has done for my academic career since also with regard to making this book a reality. During the writing process, she has been a constant discussion partner and help in revising the PhD dissertation into a book.

Situated as this book is, my workplace, during my doctoral studies as well as now, Roskilde University, has been of great importance. My primary supervisor, Rashmi Singla, has supported me through all the years of work, and I owe her my gratitude for our many academic and inspirational discussions. Thank you for being there and caring for me, Rashmi! I also owe a big thanks to Linda Lundgaard Andersen and Charlotte Højholt, and more non-mentioned colleagues who have supported me in many different ways and who have always shown an interest in my work, while backing me up with their experiences and commitment during the process. However, a special thank you to Drude Dahlerup and Kariane Westrheim for their inspiring interest in my project and their contributions.

My warm thoughts are also extended to Güneş Murat Tezcür – not only because he was the first to set this book in motion by setting up contact with Bloomsbury but also for discussing the content of the book with me while I edited it. I am certain that his deep insights into Kurdish matters have strengthened the book's substance and sharpened its focus. In line with this, I would like to thank the editors from Bloomsbury for their kind and respectful cooperation, just as I am grateful for the constructive feedback from the book's three anonymous reviewers.

From the context of friends, I would like to express my deepest gratitude to Ditte Stilling Borchorst, Jesper Nissen, Ibrahim Benli, Lola W. Thorsteen, Anne Sofie Schøtt, Özlem Has, Aviva Bernstein and Janus A. Madsen. As friends, you employed your wonderful minds to read parts of the book and gave me highly valuable feedback – Thank you for your support, which I greatly value.

Finally, yet importantly, I want to thank my family – my beloved wife, Meryem, and our two wonderful children, Awasin and Bahoz, for their support in making daily life work, for keeping with me and for being able to cope while I was traveling for long and hard periods. I love you!

ABBREVIATIONS

HDP	Peoples' Democratic Party (*Halkların Demokratîk Partisi*)
HEP	People's Labour Party (*Halkların Emek Partisi*)
HSBN	Bethnahrain Women's Protection Units (*Ḥaylawotho d'Sutoro d'Neshe d'Beth Nahrin*)
IS	Islamic State (*ad-Dawlah al-Islāmiyah fī 'l-ʿIrāq wa-sh-Shām*)
KCK	Kurdistan Communities Union (*Koma Civakên Kurdistan*)
KJB	High Women's Council (*Koma Jinen Blind*)
PAJK	Kurdistan Women's Liberation Party (*Partiya Azadiya Jin a Kurdistan*)
PJA	Free Women's Party (*Partiye Jinên Azad*, PJA)
PJKK	Kurdistan Women's Workers' Party (*Partiye Jinên Karkerê Kurdistanê*)
PKK	Kurdistan Workers' Party (*Partiya Karkerên Kurdistanê*)
SDF	Syrian Democratic Forces (*Hêzên Sûriya Demokratîk*)
SNA	Syrian National Army (*al-Jayš al-Waṭanī as-Sūrī*)
TSK	Turkish Armed Forces (*Türk Silahlı Kuvvetleri*)
YAJK	Free Women's Union of Kurdistan (*Yekitiya Azadiye Jinên Kurdistanê*)
YCK	The Patriotic Youth Movement (*Yekîtiya Ciwanên Kurdistan*)
YJA-STAR	Free Women's Units STAR (*Yekîneyên Jinên Azad ên Star*)
YJÊ	Êzîdxan Women's Units (*Yekîneyên Jinên Êzîdixan*)
YPG	People's Protection Units (*Yekîneyên Parastina Gel*)
YPJ	Women's Protection Units (*Yekîneyên Parastina Jin*)

Map 1 The Kurdish-dominated areas.

INTRODUCTION

Why do some Kurdish women join the Kurdistan Workers' Party (*Partiya Karkerên Kurdistanê*, abbreviated as PKK) to become fighters?. Do their political and militant involvement in the PKK subvert local gender norms? Does the materiality, for example, of mountainous landscapes, bodies and food practices matter to how Kurdish women fighters do their gender? These questions govern the focus of this book, which examines the personal, sociocultural and material factors at play when Kurdish women engage in political and militant struggle.

Scholarly literature already exists on how women since the end of the nineteenth century have come to the fore as active in armed ethnic and national movements. Women fighters are known from, for example, Latin America as members of the Mexican Zapatista movement, Northern Ireland as IRA members, Sri Lanka as members of the Liberation Tigers, Syria in the Women's Protection Units (*Yekîneyên Parastina Jin*, YPJ) and Turkey as members of the *Hêzên Parastina Gel* (People's Defence Forces, HPG).[1] Literature on these women offers important information on how they assumed roles in armed movements that differed from women's roles in the often highly patriarchal societies they came from.[2] In a later section, relevant scholarly literature shall be properly introduced. Here, it is suffice to mention that scholarly literature has not addressed the extent to which the last century's ethnic and national movements have influenced gender positionings within the movements and their surrounding societies, and how new gender positionings in such movements have affected the movements' ethnic and national self-understandings, strategies and norms.[3] The primary aim of this book is to mend these knowledge gaps by inquiring into the reciprocal effect that follows from the entanglement of an overall movement like the PKK and its women fighters.

With regard to knowledge gaps in academic literature, the book also intends to contribute to a rather limited literature on how women's motivations in war are multifactorial.[4] Existing research has mainly been concerned with studies of ethnicity, gender, culture *or* politics, while attention to the interaction and entanglement of these categories is lacking. There is a general lack of qualitative accounts for how women experience and think about these interacting categories as subjects while navigating their everyday lives and life choices.

A few scholarly contributions on Kurdish women fighters and gender claim that the PKK engage only in a symbolic support of women's involvement in politics and militant activities, and that the PKK in this way exploit the women fighters' loyalty and engagement in the national struggle.[5] For this reason, the book will openly inquire into interactions between official PKK discourse on women and the expressed ambitions of the women fighters themselves, just as it will assess whether the PKK discourse on women has adapted to the increased involvement and motivations of women over time or if it has tried to limit women's unfolding within the movement.

Other perspectives of the book are to counter some misleading media portrayals of women and war. Most media stories and analyses of war focus on men and their contributions. Unaware of a possible patriarchal bias, such war portrayals construct men as empowered and courageous, fighting for something of great, often national, importance, while women are ignored as fighters or described as left behind, taking care of the less important, safer domestic tasks.[6] Women are portrayed as victims of war, powerless and unable to change their own fate. When the media do cover women who fight, they focus on their overall association with victimhood without commenting on their agency. For example, Western media have described the Kurdish women fighters who fought against Islamic State (IS) as 'Angels from Kobane' who saved local women in Iraq and Syria from sexual slavery in IS, while completely ignoring the Kurdish women's political and ideological struggle to survive and change their own and other women's living conditions.[7] Another problem in media portrayals is that women are often represented as a homogeneous group, united in their disempowerment, while their diverse reasons for involvement are ignored. Public knowledge lacks a more nuanced perspective to understand why women in social, political, militant and other ways operate in global and transnational formations. A third problem in media coverage that this book tries to counter is that Kurdish women are treated in the same way as all other women from Middle Eastern Muslim countries: as a homogeneous unit. Political debates about Muslim countries, if they mention gender at all, do not consider women as situated in a particular historical and geographical context.[8]

Based on these motivations, the book seeks to identify diverse voices among Kurdish women, to gather knowledge of them and to seek an understanding of these women's own views of their becomings, identities and choices in order to explain why some Kurdish women decide to become fighters.

The Turkish-Kurdish conflict and the PKK

To understand some of the factors motivating Kurdish women fighters, I shall briefly give an overview of the history of the Turkish-Kurdish conflict and its sociopolitical background, leading to the establishment of the PKK as a national resistance movement and eventually to the movement's view on women.

When Mustafa Kemal Atatürk founded the Republic of Turkey, Kurds supported him in the so-called liberation struggle against the Western powers, but were surprised to see that the republic's first constitution of 1924 did not mention any special protection of the Kurds as an ethnic minority. Article 88 of the constitution states that '[c]itizens of Turkey with Turkish nationality, regardless of religious conviction or ethnic origin, shall be regarded as being Turks'.[9] The multi-religious, multi-ethnic and multilingual Ottoman Empire was replaced by the new nation state, the Republic of Turkey, whose founding watchword was 'one fatherland, one people, one language and one flag'. The constitution and its subsequent legal restrictions not only kept silent about the Kurds but also insisted that Kurdish ethnicity should be supplanted by a Turkish identity.[10] In this way, the constitution brought an end to the more than 500-year-old Kurdish-Turkish Ottoman brotherhood, which had been sealed with the Treaty of Amasya in 1514, where the Kurdish lords were considered an autonomous part of the Ottoman Empire. The treaty implied that Kurds had to pay taxes to the Ottoman Empire and make troops available if the Ottomans went to war in return for Turkish protection in case of enemy attack. References to Islamic religiosity as a common identity were made on both sides to legitimize the treaty.[11]

The majority of the Kurds lived under Ottoman rule until the First World War. During the war, the Allied Powers against Hitler's Germany offered the Kurds the prospect of independence if they helped fight the Ottoman Empire. They did, and the Ottoman Empire was divided under the 1920 Treaty of Sévres into a number of countries, among them the state of Kurdistan.[12] Yet, the new republic of Turkey reconquered some regions, resulting, after another round of negotiation, in the 1923 Treaty of Lausanne, which meant that the region, which Kurds today regard as their own country, was divided between Turkey, Iran, Iraq and Syria. Because of this and of the abandonment of the Treaty of Sévres (which was never ratified), the Kurds were divided and became minorities in all of the four new nation states.

On 21 June 1934, the new republic of Turkey enacted a resettlement law, authorizing the state to relocate Kurds to Turkish-concentrated areas by force if necessary. The Kurds were forbidden to establish Kurdish-dominated villages, districts and communities. Kurdish resistance groups appeared in this period but for different reasons. Some reacted to the abolition of the Muslim caliphate on 3 March 1924, while others were spurred by Kurdish nationalism.[13] The Turkish state cracked down hard with massacres carried out on the orders of the Kurds' former ally, Kemal Atatürk, and his army. The last and biggest resistance was the Dersim resistance of 1937–8, followed by the Dersim massacre, in which thousands of Kurds were killed or forced into exile.[14]

In the years following the Second World War, Turkish-Kurdish relations became relatively stable until the early 1980s when the PKK began its political struggle. In the stable period, most Kurds lived far from the cities and were slow to notice the various measures of the new republic to create a homogeneous Turkey. Kurdish women did not pay much heed to the replacement of Sharia family law with legislation inspired by Swiss family law to promote Western ideals and legal reforms for women. The legal reforms included a ban on polygamy, men and women's equal right of divorce, custody rights and rights to vote. Still, these reforms benefited only a minority of women, typically middle-class Turkish women. In line with this, the identity of the new republic's iconic woman had to rest on her Turkishness, not her identity as a Muslim, which made many Kurdish women feel excluded.[15] In effect, patriarchal norms continued to exist in the parallel societies of the new republic's provinces.

Historically, Turkish and Kurdish women have not cooperated on the political level. The challenges facing Kurdish women have never evoked the interest of women academics, including Turkish feminists. On the contrary, Turkish women often problematize Kurdish women's identity as different from those of the Turks. This is one reason why Kurdish women decided to organize separately from Turkish women from the 1990s onwards. Whereas Turkish women's activism was primarily topic-based and universalist in its discourse, and while they may have ignored the important part played by their nationality in their activism, Kurdish women chose deliberately to organize along ethnic lines because, as Kurds, they could not see themselves reflected in Turkish women's identity.[16] Turkish feminists continue to emphasize the alterity of Kurdish women. Some have even supported the Turkish government and its military campaign against Kurdish women activists.[17]

In 1978, the PKK was founded with a political and militant wing under the leadership of Abdullah Öcalan to resist various restrictions, to strengthen a Kurdish national consciousness and to establish a united and independent Kurdistan.[18] In 1980, Öcalan and other leaders set up military bases and a command centre in Lebanon. Locating the leadership out of range of the Turkish military made the organization more resilient, for example during the military coup of 12 September 1980, which was aimed at the then government, but also led to a severe crackdown on PKK members still in Turkey. Ideologically, the PKK drew on Marxism-Leninism as well as Maoism. In Maoism, the aim is to assume power through armed struggle in which liberationists wage guerrilla war and simultaneously work to win the support of the rural population to bring about a revolution. The leadership in the PKK agreed that only through a revolution carried out by the Kurdish proletariat, villagers and peasants would it be possible to liberate Kurdistan.[19] In line with this ideology, the PKK began a guerrilla war in 1984 against the Turkish government, initially to attain independence.

In 1999, Öcalan changed the movement's stance on independence as an objective. During the court proceedings on the island of Imrali in *the Marmara Sea*, where Öcalan was and still is detained, he said in his defence that in view of the brotherhood that had existed since the Battle of Manzikert in 1071, Kurds and Turks should not be divided. Instead of a separate Kurdish state, he believed that, as a democratic republic, a united Turkey should grant the Kurds their rights as an ethnic minority.[20] This change in the movement's objectives to an ideal of self-government and equal rights for Kurds in all of the four nation states mentioned earlier was related to the socialist, anti-nationalistic leanings of the PKK. Many first-generation PKK members were active in the Turkish-Kurdish socialist student movement and did not define itself as an ethno-nationalist movement, despite its strong Kurdish character and its appeal for a Kurdish national struggle.[21] Instead, they argued for cooperation with Turkish socialists to avoid the 'feudal' connotations of Kurdish identity to appear modern. Öcalan has never concealed that he was indeed inspired by the struggle of the Turkish left wing. Still, the

PKK was critical of most Turkish left-leaning movements of the time, accusing them of being blind to the way Kurdistan had been treated as a Turkish colony to serve Kemal Atatürk's Turkish nationalist ideology with no room for minority rights.[22] The tendency in the PKK to prioritize socialism over nationalism is also evident from how the PKK in the course of time has distanced itself from other Kurdish nationalist movements linked to particular tribes or elite Kurdish groups.[23] Typically, PKK members did not come from powerful, feudal, wealthy or noble families, and soon, the movement won the support of ordinary Kurds, many of whom were peasants or workers by occupation. One of the PKK's greatest achievements at its foundation was to circulate the ideal of uniting the Kurds from all the four nation states, rather than fighting only for local causes.[24] The ideal of uniting all Kurds implied the promotion of an 'us and them' attitude among Kurds in disidentification up against the hegemonic ethnic groups, from whom Kurds were encouraged to distance themselves physically and emotionally.[25]

Internally, the PKK promoted solidarity between secular and religious members. The PKK is a secular movement but not one that rejects religion, and therefore many religious Kurds were able to identify with it. This pragmatic approach to religion also made it possible for the first time for women from secular and religious families alike to fight together in a shared liberation struggle.[26] As I shall show in my analysis, PKK's education and training programmes even make claims about a matriarchal goddess religion of the Neolithic past to legitimize the movement's ideals for gender.

The ongoing military battles between the Turkish army and the PKK, which at times have resembled civil war, have had major consequences for both parties, and the civilian population on both sides has suffered badly. Although accurate figures are almost impossible to find, over 40,000 people from both camps are estimated to have died in these battles, most of them Kurds. Since the 1980s, according to unofficial NGO figures, Turkish security forces have burnt down up to 5,000 villages, and over three million people have been forced out of their homes. Official Turkish government figures peg the number of people who have left their homes at 387,000.[27] Most killings of Kurdish civilians and activists have not been processed or prosecuted in the Turkish judicial system. These killings and other 'disappearances', which were especially frequent in the 1990s, are recorded as 'killed by persons unknown'. It is therefore difficult to give an official number of the dead, but according to several human rights organizations and NGOs, the number of people who were connected with the PKK and are now dead is nearly 17,000.[28]

On the PKK's part, there have been several ceasefires, often in order to initiate a dialogue with the Turkish government on finding a peaceful solution to the conflict. The first took place in 1993 but failed to initiate dialogue, as have all subsequent attempts to date. The most recent dialogue, known as the 'Turkish-Kurdish peace process', took place between the Turkish government, the pro-Kurdish People's Democratic Party of the Turkish parliament (HDP), Öcalan from prison and the PKK leadership from the mountains. However, the dialogue collapsed in 2015 after two years of negotiations. The military conflict between the parties subsequently escalated. Many major Kurdish cities in south-eastern Turkey were completely burnt down and destroyed, and over half a million civilians had to leave their homes.[29] The civil war in Syria, during which the country's Kurdish minority has since established an autonomous self-government, has only heightened the tensions, as the Turkish government claims that the PKK operates in and from Rojava.

While the PKK carries on an armed struggle against the Turkish government, it has also been involved in establishing a legal political movement in Turkey that may help secure recognition for the rights of Kurds in the country. It includes the People's Labour Party (HEP, founded in 1990), which is regarded as the first Kurdish political movement in the Turkish parliament and whose ideological orientation, like the PKK's, has been described as Kurdish nationalism. In 1993, however, the Turkish constitutional court decided unanimously to shut down the party, accusing it of 'damaging the indivisible integrity of the state and the nation'. The Kurds have since continued their legal fight with support from left-leaning Turks. They set up several parties in order to fight politically for the Kurdish cause in the Turkish parliament. They have succeeded in gaining codetermination over Kurdish-dominated towns, for example by filling mayoralties.

Öcalan was the driving force behind the People's Democratic Party (HDP, established in 2012), which comprises several left-leaning Turkish and Kurdish movements. Despite its strong Kurdish representation, the HDP wishes to be a political party for the whole of Turkey, not just the Kurds, and attaches great importance to values such as democratic participation, minority rights, feminism and young people's rights, collectively termed 'radical democracy'. With strong support in the Turkish population, including ethnic Turks, Armenians and other religious and ethnic minorities, the HDP became the third largest party in the country in the parliamentary election of 24 June 2018, winning 67 of the 600 seats in the parliament. However, the co-leaders of the HDP, Selahattin Demirtaş and Figen Yüksekdağ, were imprisoned in 2016 and 2017, respectively, on charges of spreading terrorist propaganda and undermining the indivisible integrity of the nation. As for the sixty-five mayoralties won by the HDP in the municipal elections of 31 March 2019, most of the mayors were either never installed in office or removed from it. Despite these enduring challenges, Kurdish academic Cengiz Güneş claims that by investing in legal political parties, the PKK succeeded in transforming the struggle for 'national liberation' into a struggle for 'democracy' that involves all of Turkey.[30]

The socialist leanings of the PKK do explain not only its anti-nationalist developments but also Öcalan's anti-capitalist orientation. Öcalan argues that capitalism promotes the nation state as the only viable system of government with no room for alternative forms of autonomous organization of people's life and customs.[31] As an alternative, he argues for a system called 'democratic confederalism' under inspiration from the American anarchist and social philosopher Murray Bookchin. The PKK's support for democratic confederalism only dates from 2005 and is known internally as the 'paradigm shift'.[32]

The aim of democratic confederalism is to bring about a more equal and just balance between 'individual and society', 'man and woman', 'human being and nature' and 'society and state'. Its supporters claim that capitalist modernity has damaged the balance of these pairs in order to bolster its power and thereby rule them. Democratic confederalism is, therefore, both a critique of capitalism and an alternative to it.[33] According to Bookchin, democratic confederalism differs from capitalist society in that it is based on a shared humanity liberated from capitalist dominance, nationalism and material exploitation. It deliberately creates space for human creativity, direct democracy and municipal autonomy as a new social structure and government system to enable ethical life. Bookchin's new system is 'direct democracy' driven by women and young people and not requiring any form of state control, but based on women's liberation, a green economy and grassroots democracy.[34]

According to Öcalan, the self-administration in democratic confederalism affords an opportunity to understand democracy more as a method than as an end in itself. In this way, democratic confederalism allows people to establish a conscious political system that draws on ancient forms of social organization. He may be referring to a tribal Kurdish lifestyle of ancient times, even to the alleged matriarchal societies of Neolithic times, which inspire him. Öcalan assumes that these cultures were based on a shared social contract and consensual ethical principles aimed at meeting the needs of every individual in the community. Öcalan appeals to the Kurds' history of statelessness when people lived in tribes, as nomads or in villages. At that time, tribes traded with each other as required, so they already had a form of confederalism. This form of confederalism underpins Öcalan's idea of operating with collectives, municipalities, cooperatives, councils and grassroots movements as local 'municipalist' solutions without a need for a centralized government. In this way, Öcalan maintains that Kurdistan's democratic confederalism should draw on social history and the cultural reservoir of ancient Mesopotamia.[35]

The Marxist-Leninist part of PKK's ideology dictates that society cannot be liberated without first liberating women, because women constitute the lowest-ranking and the most oppressed social 'class'.[36] If women are free, the land is free. On this understanding, any liberation, also of Kurdistan, will have to begin with women's liberation. This line of thought appears to have resonated with Kurdish women. Since its foundation in 1978, the PKK has succeeded in mobilizing thousands of Kurdish women from all social strata.[37] Experts are puzzled about how PKK has succeeded in recruiting so many women and in benefiting from their potentials and emergence as popular agents in Turkish public debates on the Kurdish question. In addition, it surprises that women in the PKK often come from traditional patriarchal families in which Islam is normative.[38]

From its inception, the PKK argued that women's liberation from not only Turkish but also Kurdish patriarchal norms had to rest on new understandings of gender and gender positions. It was a general expectation that Kurdish women should break free of capitalist values and the Turkish government project of building a homogenous nation. In addition, the PKK idealized three roles for women: 'patriotic mothers', 'politicians' and 'guerrillas': as 'patriotic mothers' because they were to sacrifice their children for the Kurdish cause by accepting and supporting their involvement in the PKK; as 'politicians' because they were to engage in the legal political struggle as mayors, parliamentarians and activists working to find a political solution to the Kurdish conflict; finally, as guerrillas because they were to engage as women fighters, that is, around a third of PKK's 15,000 guerrilla fighters are women. As such, these three roles position women as crucial in the 'struggle against oppression' and for a better future. [39]

The PKK's goal of mobilizing women as politicians has been partly achieved in that women perform a significant part of legal Kurdish political work in Turkey. In Kurdish organizations, parties and initiatives linked to the PKK, there is a quota stipulating that 50 per cent of the governing body must be women. The HDP has the largest share of women candidates in the Turkish parliament (according to the elections in 2018) and of women mayors throughout Turkey: 39.34 per cent of the HDP's members of parliament are women, while women's average representation in the rest of the parliament stands at 14.77 per cent.[40] At the same time, the HDP is active in all councils, including in mayoral positions. In addition, some women fighters decided in 2004 to supplement their engagement in the PKK by founding the Kurdistan Women's Liberation Party (*Partiya Azadiya Jin a Kurdistan*, PAJK) to fight for women's rights and other democratic and secularized values in the entire Middle Eastern region in addition to PKK's focus on improving Kurds' rights in Kurdistan.

Kurdish women's enrolment in the PKK seems to have inspired more Kurdish women to take part in the legal political activities in Turkey. This is due not only to an overall political agenda but also to the fact that Kurdish women have skillfully taken advantage of the opportunities at hand to advance their cause. For example, the Kurdish academic and feminist Necla claims that every time since the 1990s the Turkish state has closed or suspended a Kurdish political party, women have managed to raise the quota of women in that party.[41] At the beginning of PKK's existence, the female quota of women in Kurdish parties was only 25 per cent, but this figure has risen to 50 per cent. In terms of practical politics, these numbers strongly indicate that Kurdish women have obtained equal representation with access to shaping the movement's gender composition.[42]

The PKK's success in recruiting women cannot be isolated from sociopolitical developments in Turkey[43] or from global developments. For example, the civil war in Syria and the establishment of IS in Iraq and Syria significantly strengthened the PKK, and encouraged the influx of women to the movement. This influx has made it a transnational women's movement where Kurdish women from Turkey, Iraq and Syria come together despite major religious, linguistic and ideological differences between the Kurds in these countries. In addition, women from other ethnic backgrounds, including Arabs, Syrians and Turkmens, religious sub-groupings within Islam such as Shiites and Alevis, and other faiths such as the Yezidis from Iraq and Syria, as well as ethnic Westerners of Christian cultural background, have joined the PKK. Historically, no other militant organization in the world has had the ability to mobilize so many diverse groups of women. In continuation hereof, the Kurdish women's movement with its ideological and organic framework has become a source of inspiration for other non-Kurdish women in the region in their political and militant struggles.[44] In other words, cultural factors unique to

Kurdish society cannot sufficiently explain why the PKK appeals to women. This is one of the knowledge gaps that this book intends to mend with consequences for how scholarship can come to understand how transnational movements, geography and colonial experiences and/or statelessness influence the way identity is formed across national borders.

Existing research on women fighters in general

In the 1980s, researchers like Kumari Jayawardena (1986), Cynthia Enloe (1989) and Nira Yuval-Davis and Floya Anthias (1989) begin to address the phenomenon of gender in relation to nationalism, ethnicity and identity. Jayawardena points to how women's activism in national revolutionary, sometimes anti-imperialist, movements at the beginning of the twentieth century in, for example, China and India helped increase their chances of improving their own conditions, even if women were only positioned as secondary forces in less prestigious places away from the front.[45] Enloe (1983) argues that women were indeed active in war, but their efforts became invisible because they never had equal roles with men in professional armies.[46] In *Beaches and Bases* (1989), Enloe writes that 'power' and 'masculinity' are often synonymous with both men combatants and men historians. The history of national and ethnic movements reflects men's experiences. It is founded on masculine memory, masculine humiliation and masculine utopia. Enloe claims that the history and ideology of nationalism could be read differently if one started from women's experiences.[47] Focusing on women's participation in national arenas as cultural and biological producers, Nira Yuval-Davis and Floya Anthias's edited book *Woman-Nation-State* (1989) examines how gender and nationalism work together to influence women's religious, economic and historical lives in different societies. The contributors claim that women's active participation in civil society and in politics has redefined ethnicity and nationality, and they show how discourses on nation and ethnicity are built around gender and on the gendering of nationalism. They find that women's roles in national and ethnic practices can be grouped into five categories, where women are seen as biological reproducers of members of ethnic groups, as bearers of culture who transmit the values and norms of the population group, as signifiers of ethnic and national diversity indicating ethnic and national differences in connection with the reproduction of ideological discourses, as symbols used in the transformation, reproduction and construction of population groups and as active participants in national, economic, political and military struggles.[48] Critics have asserted that Yuval-Davis and Anthias end up defining women as passive players in national and ethnic practices, reducing them to symbols.[49] Later in her own book *Gender and Nation* (1997) on women's access to national arenas, Yuval-Davis applies an intersectional approach. She examines how women have gained access to the army, what challenges they have faced in doing so and what roles are imposed on them in war processes. Her work illustrates the complex interplay of gender, ethnicity and nationalism, and the need for more work on political feminist mobilization.

Yuval-Davis argues that understanding differences between women from different ethnic groups and affiliations is a way of understanding their identity formation.[50] However, Yuval-Davis does not specifically address women in ethnic militant movements against a state. Neither does she include a first-person perspective, in which women relate their own experiences of being involved in war.

Yuval-Davis has also contributed with perspectives on how modern wars have changed character. With technological developments, it has become increasingly difficult to use physical differences as an argument for exempting women from military duties. Technological development has increased the number of women in the military and so has political contexts. The American army needed women to quell American opposition to the Vietnam War and to limit the presence of Black men in the army. Yet, women rarely serve on the same terms as men. Armies often put women soldiers into roles such as secretaries, nurses and teachers, which mirrors the gendered civilian labour market. Women's association with care and decent behavior has led the Israeli army to establish a unit called 'Chen', Hebrew for 'beauty', with the purpose of raising other units' morale and providing care for men soldiers.[51] Recent research has added a focus on the complex relationship between womanhood and victimhood, also mirroring the larger society. Reports from the US military, where separate women's corps and missions have largely been abolished, show that a third of women experience rape and sexual harassment from their men 'comrades'.[52]

Outside professional armies, findings show that hierarchical and organizational frameworks such as command, control and reporting are much less formal in national liberation movements than in state armies. Liberation movements are organized around a shared ideological position that can help to prevent violence against women and other gender tensions, as these movements see women's emancipation as a symbol of popular liberation.[53] Still, it has been necessary in some places to introduce stricter regulations such as the execution of rapists to prevent men soldiers from assaulting women soldiers.[54] Yet, fear of sexual assault and rape by security or paramilitary forces can also lead women to volunteer to join rebel movements in search of protection and revenge.[55] Men's assaults on their women colleagues are a well-known argument in military discussions for the establishment of separate women's units.[56]

The sexual assaults of men soldiers on non-combatant women in local areas are another topic that scholarly research has dealt with. Enloe (1983, 1989) describes how the establishment of brothels next to a military base in the Philippines affected local society because the relationship between the military base and the civilian population was one of political and economic dependency. Yuval-Davies argues that the military is organized around principles of aggression and obedience, and factors such as dominance culture and ideals of masculinity can spread to civil society when the military increases its influence. She claims that researchers often overlook the ultimate function of the military: to fight in war in sharp contrast with the civilian labour market, as wars cause massive destruction of human life, social relations and physical environments. Regardless of where military conflicts and wars take place, Yuval-Davies concludes that the great violence perpetrated in wars and their effects are always gender-based and thus have major consequences for society.[57]

Similar to the purpose of this book, Sandra Gilbert (1983) investigated women's motives for enlisting in armies. During the First World War, women participated mainly because they saw an opportunity to build their physical and emotional strength, and because they found war exciting.[58] Studies by Bennett et al. (1995) and Zerai (1994) complicate the picture. Based on interviews with women soldiers, they show that personal situations also contribute to women's choice to join the army, as it offers them an opportunity to create new skills and respectable social positions.

Nobel laureate Svetlana Alexievich's work *The Unwomanly Face of War* (2017/1985) is one of the first works to articulate women's experiences of war. Alexievich writes about ordinary people's experiences of war, courage and suffering. Forty years after the Second World War, she interviewed more than 500 Soviet women about their participation in the Red Army, from conscription to homecoming. These women were at the front as active fighters, but also carried out less dangerous logistical missions. Alexievich writes about the history of the war but as 'women's history' and 'emotional history', regarding herself as a historian of souls split between suppressed experiences and truth claims dictated by the zeitgeist. She notes that the first can seldom hold firm against the dominance of the second. The book's most significant contribution is that it helped change views of the war from a preoccupation with Russian bravery, love and faith in the fatherland to a concern with women's post-war disillusionment and bitterness.

Research has also dealt with wars between antagonists within the same state, sometimes involving large ethnic groups that are politically excluded from the state or underrepresented in it.[59] Such ethnic national wars typically result directly or indirectly from colonialism or the end of a war, for example the Cold War. Scholars therefore refer to them as 'postmodern wars'.[60] In such wars, women can be allotted different gender positions from those in professional armies because there is no obvious difference between being in the combat zone, on the home front or behind the supply line. In such cases, Yuval-Davis believes that women's choice to assume active roles, no matter what position, is not necessarily a conscious act but rather an adaptation to new conditions. She also claims that such women, no matter their active contributions, will nevertheless be confronted with images that emphasize how unnatural it is for women to be fighters by appealing to general conceptions of femininity and masculinity in the society the women come from.[61]

Relevant to this book's project is also research on women's roles in revolutionary movements, including armed resistance/terrorist attacks directed at the state or some hegemonic power. Valentine Moghadam (1993) has studied women's roles in such upheavals from the 1700s to present-day liberation struggles in the so-called MENA region (the Middle East and North Africa). Moghadam asserts that as implementation of new gender roles in society is a lengthy and demanding process, one must wait and see whether these upheavals have a real effect on women's liberation. She states that the revolutionary changes in the social and institutional structures of involved countries at first created rights for women and new conceptions of gender in their societies, but these were later rolled back. Moghadam therefore believes it is important to wait for a period of stabilization and normalization to see whether new conceptions of gender succeed over the traditional roles involving the oppression of women.[62]

Research shows that women enjoy proportionally more access to political participation and representation in ethno-nationalist and anti-state movements than in institutionalized states.[63] The political ideology of the movements seems key to the scale of women's participation. Marxist-oriented ideologies are comparatively more likely to include women combatants.[64] According to Yuval-Davis, one reason for this is that the less formal, yet robust, shared ideological positions of ethno-nationalist movements or national military liberation forces enable some gendered prejudices and tensions to be transcended, especially where women's liberation is seen as a symbol of national liberation.[65] Unfortunately, such an ideological position is often fraught with the risk of women's gender struggle being sacrificed or sidelined in favour of the national struggle that is given priority.

Existing research on Kurdish women fighters

There is very limited academic literature on Kurdish women fighters, let alone on Kurdish women fighters in Turkey, who are in focus in this book. Attention has been paid to the PKK's political agenda[66] with these women often portrayed from a Turkish nationalist perspective as passive actors exploited by the Kurdish national struggle.[67] Others describe politically active Kurdish women as 'liberated women' because of women's increased public visibility and their social and political commitment. While existing research positions Kurdish women fighters between these different poles either as victims or as emancipated, there is a lack of research exploring how Kurdish women define themselves.

Among the few ethnographic studies based on fieldwork in PKK camps in the mountains and on interviews with numerous Kurdish women fighters, mention should be made of Westrheim (2008), Käser (2021) and Dirik (2022). There are also a number of journalistic publications by Bejan Matur (2011), Arzu Demir (2014), Gülçiçek Günel Tekin (2014), Serdar Akinan (2014) and Frederike Geerdink (2021) that include important portrayals and interviews with numerous Kurdish women fighters in PKK camps. Since the outbreak of the civil war in Syria, where Kurdish women fighters have played a special part in the fight against IS, more academic attention has been paid to women fighters. These studies have, however, been primarily concerned with the Western media's portrayal of Kurdish women fighters and the implementation of democratic confederalism in Rojava than with the women's own accounts of their experiences.[68]

Two studies on Kurdish women fighters will serve as discussion partners in this book. Handan Çağlayan (2007) is one of the first researchers who investigates the dynamics underlying Kurdish women's mobilization in social and political movements in Turkey in the 1980s and 1990s. She tries to establish if Kurdish women are political objects or subjects and if women's participation in politics will change politics or not.[69] Çağlayan claims that the part that Kurdish women play in politics and in constructing a new political discourse enables them to move away from the traditional feminine roles that were imposed on them. With this, I agree. I do not agree, however, that the political subjectivization of Kurdish women is a consequence of the development of capitalist modernity in Turkey. Çağlayan claims that mass migration to big cities to find work or education has contributed to the emergence of a Kurdish middle class and elite in urban centres.[70] She ignores the fact that because of the role played by the military in the country's history, Turkey has not undergone a typical capitalist economic and societal development. Kurdish nationalism is related more to the country's homogenization policy, its dictatorial government[71] and the colonization of the Kurdish minority than to capitalism. Çağlayan claims that the Kurdish movement[72] has 'beforehand' created a Kurdish female identity which Kurdish women attempt to live up to: 'in many nationalist construction processes in a similar situation, the 'new woman' constructed as a symbol of the new society is constructed as a genderless identity'.[73] Çağlayan thus treats Kurdish women as passive recipients of a new 'degendered' identity, which is something against which this book will argue.

Another difference between Çağlayan's book and this book is that this book focuses on women fighters operating from PKK bases outside Turkey. Çağlayan studied women who had chosen to remain in Turkey, limiting their activity to participation in various political parties and associations. Çağlayan takes no account of the fact that legal Kurdish political work in Turkey is intimately linked with PKK's armed and ideological struggle in mountains, which have created a strong Kurdish identity and nationalism. This link has had a decisive influence in relation to that Kurdish parties and movements have been able to invest in legal political work in the civil society in order to implement its ideology and politics in Turkey.[74]

One of the most recent ethnographic studies of Kurdish women fighters in the PKK is Isabel Käser's book *The Kurdish Women's Freedom Movement: Gender, Body Politics and Militant Femininities* (2021). The book deals with the implementation of democratic confederalism in Turkey, Iraq and Syria, and with women's motivation for participating in the PKK. Käser examines personal trajectories and everyday processes of becoming a militant in this movement. Based on in-depth ethnographic interviews in Turkey and Iraqi Kurdistan with women politicians, martyr mothers and women fighters, she looks at how norms around gender and sexuality have been rewritten and how new meanings and practices have been assigned to women in the quest for Kurdish self-determination. Käser's main argument is that the PKK practises militant feminism. To a large extent, I agree with her when she writes: 'I conceptualize militant femininities as the dominant femininities desired by the party leadership and ideology' (Käser 2021: 10). Yet, many questions remain. Käser does not explain why women argue that militant feminism enables them to achieve their ideals of women's emancipation in a future society. The militant feminism in the PKK did not emerge out of nothing, nor was it simply imposed by the PKK's men leadership on Kurdish women. As I shall argue, their militant feminism grew not only out of several years of struggle against the Turkish state but also out of women's internal struggle against men in the PKK and Kurdish patriarchal norms. In this respect, my long, in-depth interviews, reflecting the women fighters' life courses, give the analysis of this book an advantage, which is why I do not conclude, as Käser and Çağlayan do, that women are merely symbolic actors or instruments of the PKK's ideology.

Another important matter that Käser does not explain is how Kurdish women fighters differentiate themselves and their liberation ideals from Turkish and Western women. This explanation is necessary in order to specify Kurdish women's perspective in comparison with that of other women, especially Turkish and Western feminists who have even perceived them as third-world women.[75] Kurdish women fighters have a critical, postcolonial approach to feminism associated with the West and with Turkey. Accordingly, universalizing feminism like Çağlayan and Käser have done would be to miss some highly significant developments in the world of gender.

Designing the project behind the book

The main objective of this book is to understand why some Kurdish women join the PKK to become women fighters. To counter previous research on women fighters that had not inquired into their motivations or expected these motivations to be multifactorial and diverse, it would be crucial to set up democratic conditions for interviews and field observation to allow different Kurdish women fighters to tell their own stories. This implied a self-critical stance on how the narratives of the interviewees to some degree were responses to my questions and told in relation to me as a person. Any interviewer's entry into a field affects the knowledge produced. Well knowing that this is a condition in fieldwork, I designed the questions for the semi-structured interviews in a way that would invite nuances and enable the interviewees to challenge any of my questions formulated in a limiting way.[76] A movement like the PKK encourages a strong collective identity, while I wanted to enquire into individual motivations. Once, a woman fighter that I refer to as Berfin told that the individual did not exist in the PKK. I asked her, 'Who is Berfin?' Can you say a bit about yourself? She answered:

> It's a bit hard to talk about yourself in the PKK. What characterizes the PKK is that there is nothing called the individual or anything special about oneself. So it isn't easy for the individual in the PKK to say 'I'. We don't say that in the PKK. Because our life is collectivist. So the personal isn't emphasized. So the individual in the PKK doesn't know how he or she can talk about himself or herself. (Interview with Berfin, 22 March 2018)[77]

The interviewees used 'we' more than 'I'. The designation 'we' had different meanings depending on the context. For example, it could mean 'the Kurds as a nation', 'all women' or 'all members of the PKK', but it could also be a compound of 'people and nature'. The interviewees spoke more as representatives of a group than as themselves. After the first four or five interviews, I found that the narratives of the interviewees resembled each other more and more and that the interviewees were keener to talk about their ideology and to romanticize their own history and that of the PKK than to talk about their own lifeworlds, where personal narratives could emerge. Here, my hermeneutics of suspicion clashed with the democratic conditions that I had wanted to set up. Should I take the collectivism for granted or should I adjust the interview format by asking direct questions and turning the questions around, to challenge the interviewees and create interruptions to take their focus away from the ideological and collective, and lead them towards answers that provided insights into their individual lifeworlds? I chose the latter, but became conscious and remained cautious about an individualistic bias in the project.

Doing fieldwork in a war zone also complicated matters.[78] On first meetings, distrust and suspicion would only be natural. My own Kurdish ethnicity was an advantage, but no guarantee to them; I was a man wanting to enquire into women's motivations in gender-segregated camps;[79] and as a civilian with no combat experience, I could put the interviewees at risk. Even if I only put myself at risk, any accident befalling me would reflect badly upon them. These challenges were constant reminders that required me to relate critically to my own positioning, including the extent to which I influenced my field of investigation. This required me to let them specify the terms for interviews and observation, just as I had to prepare for these in ways that attended to nuance and diversity in answers and that created a space where the interviewees could always challenge me back. Yet, here I also had to apply a hermeneutics of suspicion. The interviewees would always present their personal version and sometimes, given the context of war, I had to be attentive to what they wanted to achieve with their narratives and listen for systematic exceptions, silences, deviations, inaccuracies and denials in their narratives. In addition, the interviewees might also withhold information.[80] Because of this, I needed to be aware of what was said and also, importantly, what was not said. This involved a methodological triangulation of their narratives with field observations and related research.

Based on these methodological considerations, the book came to consist of semi-structured qualitative interviews with Kurdish women fighters individually and in groups, supplemented by participant observations of their training and education programme to gain insight into their everyday life. A first round of interviews and observations were carried out in March 2018 in northern Iraq, where the PKK has its main base and training camps. Here, I conducted individual interviews with thirteen women figures, three men leaders and two focus group interviews – one with two women and one with three men. I conducted interviews with men to investigate their expectations of the opposite gender as fighters, spouses, colleagues and social rescuers, understanding that women do not have a monopoly on producing knowledge about their gender identification.

After my field trip to Iraq, I carried out one week of interviews and observations in northern Syria, in the area known as Rojava (Kurdish for what Kurds understand as Western Kurdistan), which is under the control of Kurdish forces who have the same ideological framework as the PKK. In Rojava, I conducted interviews with five women fighters from the YPJ, one elected political representative and the two women who had launched the initiative for the women's ecological village of Jinwar. This visit allowed me to observe how women assume a role in the new system of 'democratic confederalism'[81] and to gain insight into how the PKK's ideals regarding gender positions can potentially be implemented after a revolution. The visit also enabled me to conduct interviews with women from non-Kurdish ethnic groups and with non-Muslim religious backgrounds. This, I believed, would be important in establishing the complexities, especially with regard to multiple interacting factors that affect the motivations among many ethnically different women for participating in Kurdish women's armed struggle. In this way, it was possible to achieve an empirically and analytically based approach to understanding how a political movement that was originally rooted in a particular ethnic group could become a transnational movement influencing the whole of Mesopotamia.

A second round of interviews and observations were conducted in December 2019. I returned to Rojava to carry out one interview with an Arab woman who had chosen to join the YPJ and one focus group interview with three women of Armenian and Syrian origin from Bethnahrain Women's Protection Units (*Ḥaylawotho d'Sutoro d'Neshe d'Beth Naḥrin*, HSBN), a Christian-oriented military movement.[82]

The data gathered in Iraq and Syria were supplemented with various interviews conducted in Europe. Interviews were conducted with six operating women PKK members stationed in Europe, one-man ethnic Westerner who fought with the all-men People's Protection Units (*Yekîneyên Parastina Gel*, YPG) against IS in Rojava from 2016 to 2017 and one Kurdish woman, born and raised in Europe, who was about to join the PKK. This interview was held a couple of days before she left for her training. I was in dialogue with her until her enrolment and I met her again one year later for a follow-up interview, when she had completed her recruitment procedure in the mountains and had returned to Europe. This gave me the opportunity to interview and observe her before and after with a focus on continuities and changes in her orientation after her participation in the movement. Finally, I also interviewed a woman ex-member of the PKK in Europe to learn why she had left the movement and what experiences and challenges she was encountering in civil society after leaving the armed movement.

In addition to all the interviews conducted in Europe, I also observed countless demonstrations, seminars, conferences, workshops, public meetings and other events in Europe arranged by associations linked to the PKK. This was partly to gain an understanding of how the PKK extends its national struggle to Europe to implement its own ideology, also for women's liberation, among Kurds in Europe by assigning special tasks to women in these activities.

Overall, based on a total of thirty-six interviews, this book is to date the biggest ethnographic study, based on qualitative data, on the PKK and Kurdish women fighters.[83]

Behind this book's focus on the motivations of Kurdish women to become fighters lies an understanding of identity as something processual, something that changes in the course of one's life as an effect of various doings and interactions. Accordingly, the data are sequenced into six chapters, not because this decision will ensure anything exhaustive about the informants' life courses, but they will provide insights into how the informants perceived the effect of specific interacting factors in their life courses.[84] The book analyses the women fighters' narratives about themselves from clashes with patriarchal norms and colonization in their childhood experiences to the period from 2017 to 2019, when I met them and when they spoke about their combat experiences and their expectations for the future in terms of improving conditions for women. Each chapter's focus was chosen to represent significant transitions in their lives where they account for intense interaction between various factors, sometimes clashes, that generated a reorientation and new life course possibilities with which they explain their decision to join the PKK and take part in its militant political struggle.[85]

Chapter 1 enquires into how the women fighters narrate their childhood experiences and explain the effects of these experiences. They all emphasize experiences of state violence, including the loss of family members, the burning of villages, and the persecution of family members or acquaintances and how they resulted in disidentification with Turkish culture and a concomitant orientation towards identifying as Kurdish. Yet, the chapter also explores how Kurdish parents' gender-based differential treatment of their children forms another significant memory that established the foundation of a lay critique against Kurdish patriarchal norms. The women thus narrate about early experiences of double otherness, in the sense of being both Kurds and women.[86]

Chapter 2 examines women fighters' strong desire[87] to resist both colonial and patriarchal powers from their teenage years towards their decision to become active members of the PKK. In order to highlight variations in the women's motives for joining the PKK, I have divided the women fighters who have played an active part in the PKK's almost forty-year history into three generations. The generational division of the women shows that issues of gender have increased their importance as a factor in the women's choice to enter the fight from the launch of the PKK to the present day.

Chapter 3 provides insights into the way that gender and other aspects of identity are affected in the PKK from the moment young women and men enrol in the movement's training camps in the mountains. Upon arrival, Kurdish women are confronted by a discourse and embodied practices that link women to nature in an obligating way. They undergo a powerful and gender-specific course of ideological instruction in which they are re-socialized. Instruction and training are combined with self-criticism and an almost ascetic self-discipline to curb individual needs and prepare oneself to become a 'cadre'.[88] The chapter explores how bodily practices and material phenomena such as cliffs, food, clothes, menstruation, others' bodies and weapons are used to subvert the women newcomers' identity.[89] The chapter includes a critical deconstruction of how the PKK operates inconsistently with notions of both a biological sex and a sociocultural gender. On the one hand, the PKK claims that women's biology contains the potential for an especially strong attachment to the natural environment, including the mountains in and from which the PKK conducts its campaign. On the other hand, the PKK speaks of constructed gender and the heteronormative discourse on love and sexuality arising from it, which the men and women of the movement must repudiate in order to focus on their warrior identity to engage in the struggle.

Chapter 4 goes through official PKK statements on gender and enquires into the reactions among the interviewed women fighters to PKK's discourse on how and why gender difference should be cultivated in the PKK, including separate organization for men fighters in the mountains. The women describe this separation as a necessary disruption, just as they take the establishment of their own party, their own military units, women quotas in the leadership and the development of their own ideology, *jineoloji*, as a matter of course if PKK's matriarchal ideals for the future should ever be realized.[90]

Chapter 5 focuses on various clashes in the process of becoming and operating as women fighters. Over the years, there have been major challenges for the women fighters, especially when life in the mountains was being established in the 1990s before they were permitted to take part in the war on an equal footing with their men comrades. Clashes include battles with their own patriarchal and liberal mentality, a physical battle to adapt to the material aspects of life in the mountains, a battle with their men comrades who for long did not want to accept or value their engagement in armed combat and finally an armed struggle against the colonizing powers. The chapter shows how women fighters' unique battles lead them to position themselves differently from their men comrades when they are at war. In drawing a distinction between themselves and the men, they even define the phenomenon 'fighter' as gendered, monopolizing the most ideal aspects of that identity. When the interviewees talk about women fighters' combat experiences, they emphasize that their contribution to the development of the war and warfare is more important than that of men. They claim to be stronger-willed, more ideologically aware, more empathetic and better able to wage war, including a readiness to die as a *fedai*[91] (Kurdish: suicide action) if necessary.[92]

Chapter 6 describes women fighters' personal and collective expectations for the future with a view to improving conditions for Kurdish women and women in general. Part of the chapter is based on interviews with women in the women's village of Jinwar. Here, I enquire about the women fighters' reception of democratic confederalism as an ideal for direct democracy, just as I probe the women fighters' handling of challenges in the transition from service in the mountains to service in civilian life. The chapter also shows how the women's armed resistance and their striving for freedom have affected their visions, revealing difficulty in imagining a life outside the PKK. The Jinwar interviews are supplemented by one interview with one woman who has left the movement, now having trouble reacclimatizing to civilized life. The chapter will also examine the women fighters from Rojava and the YPJ who are inspired, ideologically and historically speaking, by the women fighters of the PKK. The chapter analyses how, in the shadow of the PKK, the YPJ has become a transnational movement influencing not only Kurds but also other ethnic and religious groups in Rojava. This makes it possible to understand how the women's movement's socialist ideology enables Kurdish women to form an anti-colonial coalition with other women in Rojava and inspire them with a view to improving future conditions for all women.

The book concludes with a general reflection on how gender can be affected by political and militant conflicts such as the one in which the PKK is active and how women's access to ethnic and national movements can provide a platform from which they can influence, and even redefine, the strategies and norms of those movements.

Chapter 1

WOMEN'S CHILDHOOD EXPERIENCES OF DOUBLE OTHERNESS

Childhood is one complex field among many that affects everyone's process of becoming. When explaining why some Kurdish women decided to join the PKK, the Kurdish women fighters that I interviewed often referred to childhood and family life in their region of origin as the context where they first realized that they were not boys but girls, not Turks but Kurds.

1.1. The significance of mother tongue and school life

Except for Evin who was born and raised in Europe, all the women fighters said that they had not gone to nursery or kindergarten. Instead, their parents looked after them at home until they were old enough to attend primary school. At home, they were not faced with requirements to learn Turkish. They also recounted that even if they had not been brought up with a strong Kurdish national consciousness, they somehow knew that Kurds and Turks were different. In this early phase of childhood, they did not know that being Kurdish in Turkey could be a problem. For example, they found nothing problematic in the fact that they spoke Kurdish with their parents at home, while life outside the home went on in Turkish. In this context, school became not only a place where they were to start some academic learning but also a place where they encountered and were confronted, for the first time, with Turkish as a language as well as what they described as a Turkish colonial discourse. Most of the women fighters recounted how they gradually realized the significance of their Kurdish identity at school, as they found themselves being bullied, discriminated against or subjected to traumatic experiences, as can be seen in Avasin's narrative:

> How did I first experience my Kurdishness? Through a slap! I was in Year 3 [of primary school]. The head teacher asked what my mother tongue was, and I said 'Kurdish', because it was Kurdish. He gave me a slap. He was a fascist head

teacher. While slapping me, he said, 'Next time, look at your identity card before you answer. It says there what your mother tongue is!' [. . .] That woke me up. I mean it seriously woke me up! I've never forgotten that feeling. It's always with me. (Interview with Avasin, 21 March 2018)

The price of Avasin's honesty was a slap. She gave a straight answer to the head teacher's question, saying 'Kurdish' because that was the language she had learnt from her parents. The head teacher's reaction taught her that her legitimate mother tongue was not the one she spoke at home but the one shown on her Turkish identity card.[1] In this situation, Avasin was reminded of her otherness. It 'woke' her and remained in her consciousness as a traumatic event. According to Avasin, this awakening produced a change in her. It affected her process of becoming by establishing a ground for resistance. She indicated that she was proud of that feeling and grateful for the awakening that the experience had set off in her. Here, Avasin indicates that her Kurdish identity was not a random phenomenon but a logical and natural product of a transformative experience, in this case from her early life story.[2] Becoming aware of one's own identity often presumes a meeting with a significant other – in this case, an unpleasant one where contradictory discourses of the home and the school clashed.[3]

The realization of being Kurdish arose for Berivan when she found herself being bullied and discriminated against at school by other pupils:

What happened to me there [in the Turkish city] because of my Kurdish background was that one day I was called 'filthy Kurd' by one of my classmates at school. Before that, I hadn't felt I was Kurdish. [. . .] When I say 'felt', I mean I realized that Kurds have a different status. I knew I was Kurdish, but I wasn't clear about the difference between being Kurdish and being Turkish. I wasn't all that old, after all. But when this person called me that, I realized. I thought about why the person called me that. But later on you become more conscious, when you understand those kinds of division in society. You feel an exclusion. For example, there are a lot of things you don't understand at first. You can't really define them. [. . .] But the difference between Kurds and Turks first became clear to me with that remark [filthy Kurd]. That affected me a lot. (Interview with Berivan, 21 March 2018)

Berivan, who grew up in a Turkish city far from Kurdistan, was aware from infancy that she was Kurdish. She also knew about the Kurdish struggle but did not really understand its significance until she experienced being subjected to bullying. From that point, she began to reflect on the dilemmas of her position as a Kurd in a very Turkish context. She was an 'other' defined in contrast to a colonial norm as Turkish. Berivan also indicates that her consciousness of her Kurdishness was formed as part of a gradual process of becoming which did not make sense to her in the beginning – for example, the bullying – but which, over time and in interplay with other societal factors, ultimately led her to the conviction that Kurds and Turks were different.[4]

Most of the women fighters indicate that their limited Turkish vocabulary affected them negatively when they started primary school. Especially in the first years of school, they were often unable to follow the lessons. This challenge did not get any easier when their parents insisted on Kurdish as their everyday language at home and as a part of their culture. Zeri therefore had many dilemmas to manage:

> It was awkward to speak Turkish in the family. To show respect and love to them [her parents], we [siblings] didn't do it. This [being Kurdish] didn't particularly affect me at the start of my schooling, but it made a big difference in middle school. You start to be ashamed of your own identity. So you start to be reticent about it [one's own identity], and you think, 'What will happen if I reveal it?'. That was a fear! I can actually remember that, the first time I had to say I was an Alevi and a Kurd, I was shaking with fear. I was worried what reactions I'd get. I knew perfectly well that they [her classmates] knew, but I was afraid I'd end up losing my friends. [. . .] Of course, we also 'broke' it [the fear], because you can follow your concerns and your fear to a certain extent. At the same time, you have inner searches that get deeper and deeper over time. Your identity goes with you. It's the basis of your existence. So, in the end I revealed it and thought that those who stayed must be my friends. The rest could get lost. (Interview with Zeri, 26 March 2018)

Zeri's narrative indicates that she underwent a process that was initially dominated by fear of showing her school friends who she 'really' was, but that she eventually countered and overcame it. Since her parents spoke Kurdish at home and wanted to preserve their Kurdish identity as part of their cultural heritage, they wanted Kurdish to continue being spoken at home, even after the children had started school. Consequently, Zeri felt that going to school and facing the demand to learn to speak Turkish implied a break with her family. Her parents considered dialogue in Turkish as a kind of disavowal of their origins and cultural heritage. At the same time, Zeri was worried about losing her friends if she revealed her ethnicity and religious affiliation. As Zeri saw it, these identity-confusing experiences of exclusion that forced her to assume different roles and walk an obligatory tightrope between her parents' values and what she experienced in school led her to the solution: to embrace her otherness. According to Zeri's narrativization of her childhood, identity was something that she could not jettison and that would be discovered eventually whether or not she revealed it herself.

To 'break one's chains' is an expression often used in the movement as another way of describing how one liberates oneself from something. The expression by Zeri, 'Of course, we also "broke" it', is very likely an allusion to Karl Marx's famous statement that the workers have nothing to lose but their chains when they are called to resistance, as they have nothing to lose by it but a world to win.[5] The point here is that Zeri proudly said 'we' with reference to the Kurds, especially the Kurdish women's liberation struggle in which she takes part. Zeri's account is an example of what Gergen calls 'a progressive narrative',[6] in that Zeri describes how she developed herself and converted her fear into strength.

It comes out through the interviewees' narratives that the encounter with Turkish norms was more confrontational for children with politically active parents, such as Zelal, who moved from Kurdistan to Ankara as a four-year-old because of her father's political work. However, her father was fired from his job after three years when he was accused of conducting propaganda for the PKK. Consequently, her father had to flee to Europe to avoid a prison sentence. Zelal perceived this as harsh:

> In Ankara, you don't start school until the age of seven, so I was lucky compared with my siblings [. . .] But I was thrown out of school [because of my father]. At the same time, we [the family] were labelled as terrorists. We couldn't even buy bread from the grocer. We couldn't go shopping. The neighbors said, 'stop giving bread to these terrorists' [. . .] Dad was out in Europe. They [the authorities] were angry about it. We [siblings] were afraid, although we didn't understand everything. The enemy wanted to take revenge on us, the family, instead of our father. We were scapegoats [. . .] It was a hard time, when people called after us, 'You're the terrorist's children, you're from the PKK' etc. The first defense starts here. We aren't terrorists! What can you do as a child, anyway? (Interview with Zelal, 17 September 2017)

These traumatic experiences became Zelal's daily life in the years that followed until the family moved to Europe to be united with the father. The interesting thing here is that she began by describing herself as lucky in comparison with her elder siblings because she started school late. In saying this, she indicated that she was less subjected to Turkish assimilation. One can understand Zelal's account to mean that the stigmatizing incidents, to which the family was subjected by the school, neighbours and authorities, produced a form of defence in her that enabled her self-preservation. The appellation that she and her family are terrorists is a threat to their intelligibility as normal; however, in that light, their flight out of Turkey is also a resistance to abjectification – that is, being cast off as outside the norm.[7] The noteworthy thing is that she called it 'the first defence'. With her pride in her 'first defence', Zelal indicates that it was a break that produced a becoming – a process involving other similar defences. The first defence laid the ground for Zelal's anti-colonial struggle where she resists appellations such as 'terrorists'.

1.2. *The becoming of otherness*

The foregoing analytical section has illustrated how the Turkish state used the school system as a 'prop and anchor point'[8] in an attempt to socialize Kurdish children into being Turkish – yet, with the opposite effect: the school's demand that they give up their Kurdish mother tongue intensified their affinity with their ethnic culture. In extension of that, this section will explain how the experience of being subjected to oppression and processes of colonization was a contributory factor in the women fighters' acquisition, as early as their childhood, of what I will call 'an early form of ethnic alterity position' as becoming of otherness.

Zelal, who has always had a politically active family and described herself as someone who grew up in the movement, said that she was later induced by these circumstances to engage in a resistance practice rooted in her anger:

> I always saw the fear in my mother, for example. The fear as to whether my father would come home safely today. [. . .] Although you're a child, you can feel when something's wrong. You notice the risk and the danger. Because there was always persecution by the Turkish police and Turkish soldiers, for example. Always! Maybe I didn't feel it on my own body then, but people in my community did. But we felt it especially in the time after the 3 March coup [. . .]. Mehmet Sincar was killed. That had a big effect on us, because Heval [comrade] Mehmet's son was my childhood friend. It was close up and intense to see his grief. My first anger was created in this way. Also because my uncles fell as martyrs in the struggle. That's why you grow up with an anger. (Interview with Zelal, 17 September 2017)

By the 3 March coup, Zelal was referring to the period in 1994 when a number of Kurdish politicians and members of the Turkish parliament were imprisoned after their immunity was revoked. They were accused of carrying out illegal activities on the PKK's orders. Mehmet Sincar, whom Zelal mentioned in the interview, was a Kurdish politician, a member of parliament, who was 'killed by persons unknown' in 1993. The early 1990s were the period in Turkey when the armed conflict between the PKK and the Turkish army developed into a kind of civil war with far-reaching consequences for the civilian population living in the Kurdish districts. Turkish military and security forces burnt down many Kurdish villages, forcing hundreds of thousands of people to leave their villages, only to find exilic alternatives in slum areas of big cities. Zelal grew up in this period, and she understood and empathized with her mother's fear. Everything happening around her contributed to the emergence of her resistance that was, by her own account, rooted in 'anger' and empathy with her friend's painful loss of his father. It is relevant here to point to Sara Ahmed, who maintains that anger cannot be separated from an associated pain, be it one's own or another's. In highlighting the driving forces of emotion, Ahmed maintains that emotions and associated readings of the world affect the individual's process of becoming a politicized subject.[9] Following Ahmed, one may say that anger, as an urge for action, awoke the resistance in Zelal. Anger helped initiate a movement in which she created for herself a subject position to protect herself, thereby making sense of what was going on around her. Zelal indicates that she viewed the emergence of anger as inevitable and processual, hence her remark: 'you grow up with an anger'. This indicates that Zelal understands anger as something formed and changed through relationships in various contexts. In other words, the first anger lays a ground for future ruptures and new movements towards new understandings that in this case points forward to Zelal's enrolment in the PKK.

Other women fighters describe the genesis of an inner anger in a similar way. Zin, who was born and raised in a Turkish city, said:

> I was aware from childhood that I wasn't a Turk. I actually grew up in a fascist Turkish town. They are all ultra-nationalists. I've 'never' said I was a Turk. That was one of the first things I learnt. I never wanted to be a Turk, either. On the contrary, in that society it was a privilege for me to be a Kurd. How shall I explain it, because I saw myself as superior. Yes, I have to say it straight out: I saw myself as superior, because most Turks in the town were retarded [laughs]. I say that from a conviction that a fascist head is not well developed. It's scientific. I read an article about it recently. (Interview with Zin, 23 March 2018)

Zin's accusational choice of words envelops her clear conviction that being Kurdish is better than being Turkish. By ascribing sovereignty to inner Kurdish qualities and by asserting an essential Kurdish consciousness, Zin positions Kurds as more intelligent than Turks. The essentializing strategy contributes to establishing a self-image that allows for something positive despite the fact that Kurds like her do not have their rights recognized due to the attempts of the Turkish state to impose uniformity. Using Gergen's understanding of the individual's self-narrative,[10] it may be said that Zin created a stable self-narrative in that she framed herself as a person with a harmonious and positive self-understanding so as to appear stable in her relationships with others.

What is remarkable about Zin's narrative is that she used 'the science' to support her own views. As many of the following interviews will show, science is often evoked to legitimize the positionings of the women fighters. Rhetorically, they often refer to articles, books, authors, other revolutions around the world, philosophers, and so forth, to attach themselves with a science discourse. As a result, they appear well-versed in theories on sociopolitical and economic developments in the world, which add to their authority in conversations.

1.3. *The effect of the ongoing liberation struggle*

While Turkish attempts to colonize Kurdish subjects have had the opposite effect, according to the early childhood experiences of the interviewed women fighters, their motivation to join the PKK was also affected by PKK's rather successful attempt to create a national consciousness. According to the PKK, the Kurdish national consciousness should be based on the Kurds' own history, culture, language and so on as written, sung and told by the Kurds themselves, so as to lay a solid foundation for the awakening of the 'new Kurd' who is to serve as a model for future generations.[11] In general, the interviewees said that their parents sympathized in various ways with the national struggle. Some of their parents were also involved in the struggle on some kind of activist level. Due to these sympathies and engagements, the PKK's values and norms were already present in the women fighters' homes, where parents directly or indirectly transmitted them to their children. With the new normative basis of alternative understandings and ways of living came new subject positions and possibilities of becoming that differed from those of the colonizing Turkish state. Zelal recalled how she was told as a child that once a real Kurdistan existed, but it had been stolen from their people:

> I knew that we [the family] were Kurds. We lived in a Turkish town, but I wasn't a Turk. My mother tongue was Kurdish. I also knew, despite my young age, that we had paid a price. That's why we'd come here [to the Turkish town]. But we didn't understand it all [. . .] but there were conflicts with Turkish children, who reminded us that we were Kurds. They [the Turkish children] said, 'No! There is no such thing as Kurdistan'. But as small children we were told that Kurdistan existed. But we were told that it was under occupation. My mother didn't say occupation then; she said it was stolen from us, so that we as children could understand it. (Interview with Zelal, 17 September 2017)

When Zelal said the family had paid a high price, she referred to the family's forced migration away from the areas that once were Kurdistan. In the same interview, Zelal also explained how her mother mentioned family members who had been martyred, imprisoned and wounded in anti-colonial responses to the Turkish state's persecution. The family often told stories about martyrs and resistance to colonization, which reinforced a sense of alterity that corresponded to Zelal's experiences at school.

Bese, who joined the PKK at the age of thirteen, said that news of the PKK's struggle spread to her province far from the urban areas and influenced her when she was still a child:

> I can remember the story of the PKK being told when I was a child. Maybe we didn't know so much about who they were, but we knew their story. We knew them as Kurds fighting for a revolution in Kurdistan. [Interviewer: like a fairy story?] Yes, exactly! We didn't know them, but they were impressive, and they generated an enthusiasm inside us. It was an oral narrative. Maybe there was no one who knew them originally, nor any young people. But it was a narrative and a reality different to the state's. It was like another door. I mean a way out of the confinement we'd been in. An alternative door. It was like a call to us. So it got everyone's attention. As time went by, the PKK gained more and more influence in our province. Young people started to enlist. State killings [carried out by persons unknown] started to happen, too. Because of that, we began to see the true face of the enemy. So you saw that the system that was supposed to be your protector, wasn't. Because it was killing people. Innocent people. Because we knew those people. Innocent people were being killed by 'persons unknown'. People who hadn't been involved in anything political at all, but they were killed anyway. By the state. By traitors working for the state. These things made our searching keener and stronger. And they also led me to this life and brought me here [laughs]. (Interview with Bese, 22 March 2018)

Bese grew up in an ordinary Kurdish family in a mountainous area that enable people to stay away from the Turkish authorities as much as possible. The Kurdish population live in small villages where men often work as shepherds, tending their sheep and their fields, while most women help out and take care of the household and the children. Bese spoke of stories about PKK's resistance against the state, how the stories circulated and how these stories contributed to scorn as well as hope for a way out of Turkish oppression. The hopeful narrative up against experiences of state persecution, Kurds working as traitors for the Turkish state and a disrupted world intensified her inner searching for something new that gradually emerged as the 'call' that made Bese join the PKK.

In this context, mention should be made of 15 August 1984 when the PKK first engaged in an armed struggle. Incidents associated with this date are known as the 'first bullet' and are regarded by the PKK as a collective 'call' that woke all Kurds from their death sleep. That the PKK took to arms after the military coup of 12 September 1980, when all democratic forces and left-leaning resistance groups had been eradicated, surprised because no one had foreseen a new insurrection against the state. Following this collective 'call', many Kurdish civilians became involved in the PKK, some as fighters and logisticians in armed struggles, but many also in legal organizations as volunteers who helped carry out cultural, political and social work in accordance with the PKK's values and national consciousness. Accordingly, almost all interviewees would have family members with some degree of PKK involvement, which had affected them. This also goes for Zeri, who recalls seeing with her own eyes how the Turkish military carried out a government-sanctioned persecution of her family:

> There was a police search of our home in '93. They suspected my father of smuggling weapons for the PKK. That was why. But it wasn't true. My father was a smuggler, but not of weapons. The weapon that was found in our home belonged to my father's friend. It was really hard for the family. My father and brother were interrogated and tortured. (Interview with Zeri, 26 March 2018)

Stories of innocent Kurds subjected to state torture and of how victims resisted through 'prison revolts' loom large in the PKK's narrative of the movement's heroic history. The resistance narratives have greatly influenced the Kurdish population's respect for the PKK. The notorious Diyarbakir Military Prison is a place where gross abuses have taken place. Yet, it also hosted the first resistance to the Turkish military, which explains why the PKK defines itself as a 'prison movement' in which young PKK members, with their bravery and their ability to withstand systematic torture, have written the 'history of the resurrection'.[12] Cane was born during the early 1980s and was not far off coming into the world in prison. She recounts her story as follows:

> My father learns about the party in the '80s, while he's a student at university. He was with the leftist Turks originally, but later with the PKK. While my mother is pregnant with me, they end up in jail together. I came close to being born in

prison. My father, mother and big sister end up in jail. Dad's plan was to move to Lebanon together with most of the other PKK groups, but it didn't work out [. . .] My mother is released after a month, but my father stays in prison. About a month after my mother's release, I'm born. [. . .] After being released, my father gets sent straight to do his military service. I didn't actually know him until I was 8-9 years old [. . .] In this way, I grew up in the struggle. (Interview with Cane, 25 March 2018)

Berfin's story does not differ much from Cane's. As a child, Berfin and her mother went to the notorious Diyarbakir Prison to visit her elder brother, who was condemned to death. They waited for up to several days outside the prison to see him for just four to five minutes:

> Everything that happened to us in connection with visiting the prison is still so vivid before my eyes [. . .] We didn't know so much about the prison revolt that had taken place inside. They [the prisoners] told us nothing. They had no opportunity to, either. But there were some houses near the prison. It still affects me. We went there once because we needed to use their toilet. We were thirsty, too. We were exhausted. It was also raining. We wanted to wait there. [. . .] While we were waiting, we talked among ourselves and happened to laugh. The woman who lived in the house told us, 'You may well laugh, but we can't even sleep at night for the screams, prayers and sounds that come from the jail. It's not our children, but we often sit and cry in the morning.' We were horrified. (Interview with Berfin, 22 March 2018)

Many of the interviewees told similar traumatic stories from their childhood – stories that influenced the recognition of their ethnicity and their later active decision to take part in the PKK's struggle. Avasin recalls growing up with a yearning for revenge because of the frequent raids carried out by Turkish soldiers in her town – raids that ended with the family having to travel to another town after Turkish soldiers burned down their village for a second time (Interview with Avasin, 21 March 2018). Berivan describes how she had witnessed the police breaking her elder brother's arm and how Turkish soldiers killed her grandfather and uncle when they resisted military service (Interview with Berfin, 22 March 2018). Moreover, Bermal, who was born and raised in Europe, describes how her father instructed her to ignore and suppress her mother tongue to conceal her ethnic affiliation when they visited 'Kurdistan' (Interview with Bermal, 21 March 2018).

As mentioned in the 'Introduction', the PKK began as a movement with a primary aim to fight against Turkish colonization in the Kurdish districts of Turkey. Over time, however, the movement's national consciousness and ideology, along with rumours of its heroic resistance, spread to other parts of Kurdistan and to Europe, where a large population of diaspora Kurds lived. Here, there are two narratives which are actually different but to the same effect. The first narrative about oppression, atrocities and persecution visited on Kurds by Turkish military forces stoked anger among Kurds outside the Kurdish districts of Turkey. The other narrative about heroic acts of resistance and struggle generated hope. Both anger and hope helped to 'awaken' diaspora Kurds and Kurds in other regions outside of Turkey and to mobilize support for PKK's cause. In time, PKK became a transnational movement and united Kurds with common experiences of colonial experiences of statelessness, discrimination and oppression, which again led to shared feelings of affiliation and identity formation in a transnational social,[13] anti-colonial field.

For example, Ronya's childhood recollection shows that even if someone was born in Aleppo in Syria, far from the Kurdish districts, it was impossible for them to avoid being affected by the PKK's ongoing struggle, as they lived within its transnational field:

My mother is an Arab. Dad is a Kurd. So, at home we mostly spoke Arabic. Me and my siblings couldn't speak Kurdish. But we had a feeling for Kurdish. We knew that we were Kurds, that we lived together with Arabs and that our rights had been taken from us. There was only teaching in Arabic at school, so we spoke Arabic, too. However much we were among Arabs and couldn't speak Kurdish, we still had a strong affinity with our Kurdishness, because my father was patriotic and politically active. He had been in jail twice. We had an affinity, although it was secret. Although we were children, we knew it. We celebrated Newroz. (Interview with Ronya, 27 March 2018)

With reference to Levitt's and Glick-Schiller's (2004) understanding, the affinity described by Ronya can be seen as the experience of a 'symbolic bond', where a form of affiliation or relationship between people emerges, without the need for direct contact. The symbolic bond bypasses and is independent of national borders and national identity. Accordingly, the formation of people's identity is not linked solely to their location but also to the transnational and global processes of which people are a part. This is expressed in Ronya's strong affinity with her Kurdishness in the form of an adherence to norms and traditions, for example celebrating Newroz, when possible. However, the symbolic bond does not arise only in parts of colonized Kurdistan where the national struggle is actively going on but also in geographical areas far from Kurdistan. Evin, who was born and raised in Europe and who had never been to Kurdistan, told me that it suddenly occurred to her that she was affiliated in a Kurdish cause against the Turks:

I had no problem [being a Kurd]. I lived in [Europe], right? [. . .] For example, before we moved to Turkey [. . .], from the time before, I can remember when Abdullah Öcalan was imprisoned. I could remember that there were a great many problems there. We [children] couldn't really understand it, but we went out on the street and shouted 'Biji Serok Apo' [Long live Abdullah Öcalan]. I mean, we didn't know what it was supposed to mean. But there were lots of us children who went out and shouted 'Biji Serok Apo'. And the children who were older than us told us, 'You must beware of the Turks, and if they say anything to you, we'll hit them'. So, suddenly I was in the middle of a Turkish/Kurdish conflict that I wasn't even aware of. (Interview with Evin, 26 June 2018)

Evin was not directly subjected to Turkish colonization. Nor did her parents come from Kurdistan; her parents had moved to Europe from a Turkish city as migrant workers long before the conflicts between the PKK and the Turkish state began. However, she indicated that her Kurdishness had caught up with her despite the distance to Kurdistan, the family's lack of a national Kurdish consciousness and the fact that she was not subjected to Turkish colonization. Öcalan's imprisonment, though, affected her community and sparked a conflict between Kurds and Turks in Europe, of which she had been quite unaware. Evin's account exemplifies that despite the lack of a physical affiliation, a fluid social bond of great impact arose.

1.4. *Diversity in the relationship with parents:*
The formation of gender identity

Not only childhood experiences of colonial suppression but also early experiences of gender dynamics within the Kurdish families were mentioned by the interviewed women fighters as contributing to their later enrolment in the PKK.

Most interviewees, especially those who had experienced parental conflicts or divorce in their childhood, clearly showed in their narratives that they sympathized more with the struggles of their mothers than those of their fathers. The mothers' conflicts with or breaks from the fathers or the clan were recounted with pride, while the fathers' were described as patriarchal and domineering. Later, in Section 4.3, I shall review the political ideology that intra-acts with the women fighters' narrativization of their own experiences with patriarchy. Here, I shall focus on how the women fighters have vivid memories of their mothers' pain and oppression, of how their fathers' and patriarchal society in general hindered, even mistreated, their mothers. These memories seem to be important factors in the women fighters' attempts to strengthen their femininity and engage in an anti-patriarchal struggle. Berfin gave the following account of how her mother's struggle against patriarchal Kurdish social norms inspired her own ideas of resistance:

My mother and father couldn't agree. So my mother leaves him, takes her children with her and moves [to a Turkish city] [. . .] It was very unusual [for a mother to take her children away from her husband]. My father wanted to catch her. He contacts the police station and claims she's kidnapped his children. [. . .] I especially want to say a bit about women from Mardin Province [her Kurdish home town] [. . .] My mother was forced into marriage, just as her mother was. They grew up without men in the family [her mother's father and elder brother were killed by Turkish soldiers] It's just like a fairy story. A saga! When she recounted it, me and my siblings wanted to hear it again and again. We [women] were actually brought up with this culture of how you can stand on your own two feet. How you can strengthen your will. Even her family made circumstances difficult for her, but she put up brave resistance, even at times when she went hungry. She told us these things. We understood it as a saga. As a victory. How you could grow so strong under those circumstances. All of that helped her to become an independent woman in the marriage. Because she grew up under coercion. [. . .] It is one of the common traits of women from Mardin Province. Strong will and strength. It's hard to control them. Everything she went through, and the problems with my father, strengthened her. My father was also violent. He beat her. So my mother sought refuge with my brother one time. [. . .] He says to my mother, 'I won't allow you to go back to him. You must get divorced.' But my mother stands up to him and says, 'You're a man, too. So you'll marry me off to someone else the day after the divorce. A new man will be controlling me again. And my children will be stuck between me and their father.' (Interview with Berfin, 22 March 2018)

Berfin's mother stood up not only to her husband but also to patriarchal society as a whole. It is not easy in traditional Kurdish society for women to get divorced and be allowed to keep the children after a divorce. When women do not have economic freedom, it is also hard for them to leave their spouse and start a new life. Berfin's mother can therefore be said to have fought on two fronts: Berfin's mother and women from the Mardin Province are Berfin's role models. Berfin grew up with her mother's saga-like story, which helped to instill self-confidence in her and give her pride in being a woman. What is interesting here is that Berfin did not talk about the unreasonableness of her father or patriarchal society towards women. She chose instead to focus on her mother's resistance and, as she concluded, that will and strength are produced in the struggle against coercion and subjugation.

Berfin also indicated that her mother's struggle against coercion and against patriarchal society laid the ground for her own turn towards the anti-colonial struggle. In a way, she thereby expressed the view that the more oppression you experience, the stronger your will becomes. When Berfin talked about her mother's rejection of her brother's help, she was indirectly suggesting that women could only become themselves through their own struggle, not with the help of 'good men' who would be highly likely to end up perpetuating patriarchal traditions.

Almost all the women fighters also indicated that during childhood they had had a strong bond with their mothers and still maintained contact with them. Strikingly, the women fighters mentioned close contact with their families, yet none of them indicated that they were still in touch with their fathers. Zin is one of the women fighters, again from the Mardin Province, who enabled her mother to leave her father. Zin proudly recounted that she had never trusted men in the family. It was she who made her mother flee from her violent husband to another town where she could start a new life, while Zin's elder brothers did nothing and chose to stay with their father:

My mother was a better Muslim than my father. She was better at practising the good values of Islam in everyday life, while my father's Muslimness was more symbolic, although he read the Qur'an 24/7. But it wasn't reflected in his personality. He was patriarchal. Feudal. A typical man. A typical system man. He was actually very cowardly. [. . .] In our family, it's mostly the girls that fight. My first fight was against my father. The first man we loved in our life. The first anger. He was also the first man we fought against. [. . .] But the reality of Kurdish society was different. Women didn't have so much space. Women's scope for action was limited. Religion was used against women. The state also oppressed women. A woman didn't have much of a voice in our society. It was a disgrace. It was haram. For example, a woman couldn't wear the clothes she wanted. A woman couldn't go to all the places she wanted. As women, we didn't accept such things in our inner world. I understood these things even though I was a child. But until senior school, I was the family's ordinary daughter, with no problem. But slowly, quite slowly, I started to hate myself. Because that wasn't how I wanted to be. But when I started taking part in protests, i.e., revolutionary youth activities, I found a great inner peace. That was the place I wanted to belong. (Interview with Zin, 23 March 2018)

Zin grew up in a family where Islam was practised. By her own choice, she started wearing hijab from adolescence and continued until the day she joined the movement and became an active member. It was obvious from her narrative that her 'first anger' at her father and her inner searchings began when she noticed the difference between her father's and her mother's practice of Islamic values in everyday life, and her father's treatment of her mother. Over time, her father changed from 'the first loved man in her life' to the representative of all the oppressive norms embedded in the religion, the state and the patriarchal society. She then reflected on all the subject positions and opportunities for action that were assigned to women in Kurdish patriarchal society. Using Spivak's conception of 'subalterity',[14] one can see in her narrative that Zin describes three kinds of otherness that contributed to women's oppression: Islamic religion, the Turkish state and the patriarchal society intra-acted to subjugate women. She expressed the hope that these oppressive norms could be brought to an end, and this led her to take part in the political activities around her. From early on, Zin had reasons to look for an escape route or a place where she could unfold and create alternative understandings for herself.

Zeri's narrative, like Zin's, shows that when the children in the family – especially the daughters – get older, they become involved in interparental conflicts, disrupting the traditional gender positions of the parents:

My mother could be seen as the reticent one in the family, but it was she was the authoritarian one. It was actually my mother who made the decisions in the family. But it wasn't like that at first, because my father knew she was on her own. But when we [siblings] grew older and started to be protective of my mother, my father withdrew and made room for my mother. [. . .] We went through a lot. They came close to splitting up several times. My father tried being violent to my mother. I had many conflicts with him. I contradicted him and said, 'You are no longer my father if you behave like this', and [I indicated that] otherwise he should get out of our life. My brothers agreed. But my attitude was harsher. As a woman, you feel your mother's pain more deeply. I could feel how much she was suffering and how much pain she was in. On the one hand, you have a family that you don't want to break up, but on the other hand you are suffering. It's hard to be in both at once. I was the one who was closest to her, so I felt her pain more. [. . .] My mother has a big influence on me, and I'm still working on understanding it better. (Interview with Zeri, 26 March 2018)

An interesting point in Zeri's narrative is the coalition formation between her and her mother, described by her in terms of their shared gender. She claimed that there was a special biological bond between daughter and mother, which explains why she empathized with her mother. This coalition formation enabled her and her mother to stand up to the father's dominance together and, by extension, to Turkish colonization. She indicated that this coalition formation, the gender-based bond she had with her mother as the only daughter in the family, was something that she had brought with her to the movement and that was now playing a role in the way that PKK women tried to organize separately from the men. The inspiration from her mother's struggle against her father laid the ground for Zeri's anti-colonization approach and her solidarity with other women.

Similarly, Zelal recounted that her mother had brought her up almost single-handedly as her father was hardly ever at home due to his political activities. Her inner searchings and conflicts began at a very early age when she was affected by the way the women in her circle reared their children almost single-handedly because the men were either in the mountains, or in prison, or had been killed. She also said that this had forged a strong bond between the women and strengthened her gender identity (Interview with Zelal, 17 September 2017).

Correspondingly, Berivan said that the mother-daughter relationship in the patriarchal Kurdish society was stronger because the gender roles were sharply divided and women did not have access to public life on a par with men. The fact that women were alone – especially in those families where the men were absent for the aforementioned reasons or where (as in Berivan's case) someone grew up without a father – strengthened the solidarity between women. Berivan said that this had contributed to her 'feminist quest' arising very early. In fact, it arose before her ethnic consciousness. She therefore maintained that she had become a woman before she became a Kurd (Interview with Berivan, 21 March 2018).

There was a general tendency among the women fighters to describe their fathers as weak, cowardly and hypocritical, but also, at the same time, as 'system men'. This means that the man represents all kinds of oppression in the form of religion and the patriarchal society but especially in the form of the state. The father is corrupt, someone to liberate oneself from. Gulesor attached great importance to her mother as a role model in the construction of her identity. Her mother was a strong-willed person symbolizing the emancipated woman, while her petit bourgeois father maintained the part of the system that was both capitalist and Turkish. Movement rhetoric often uses a simile describing the father as the state's man who runs the family 'for' the state. He is therefore called the 'little state'. What the father and the state have in common is the need to control and dominate. According to Gulesor, though, strong-willed women like her mother do not let themselves be controlled:

> My mother had a big influence on the formation of my identity. But there was nowhere she could assert her will. She was therefore always aggressive. She stood against all the men in the village [. . .] I was proud to have her as my mother. But her later attempts to get me to leave the movement shocked everyone [laughs]. She didn't succeed, of course. (Interview with Gulesor, 25 March 2018)

What is notable in Gulesor's narrative is that she mentions her mother's lack of opportunity to realize herself or cultivate her will and anger. Although she indicated that, as a strong-willed woman, she had inherited most of her character from her mother, Gulesor saw herself as stronger than her mother was because she went to the mountains to realize herself. A similar narrative occurs in the book *My Life Was Always a Struggle*[15] by Sakine Cansız, the PKK's woman co-founder. Cansız recounts her own struggle with her mother as follows:

> My mother was a smart, clever woman with a strong sixth sense. She realised she was about to lose me to the movement. She therefore tried to stop me. But not even an engagement, a marriage or school could stop me any longer. It was actually her that taught me everything. While she was fighting with me, my combat-readiness grew greater. I was in a fight with a woman, with a mother, i.e. with the woman I had the same gender as and was a part of. Despite all the challenges, I have never said 'I wish I were a man'. When my mother told me, 'I wish you weren't a girl', I just loved my femininity even more. But she didn't realise it was her that slowly pushed me out into a big struggle. (Cansız 2014a: 100) (my translation)

Not all women, however, felt they had a strong mother as Gulesor and Cansız did. Avasin is one of those with a mother who was far from being her role model, but her mother still helped to strengthen Avasin's identity:

> Before I started to find out about the party, I always said I wouldn't be a woman like my mother. I wouldn't be such an uninspiring woman. Several times, I told my mother, 'I won't be like you!'. (Interview with Avasin, 21 March 2018)

Avasin was unhappy with her mother's victim role in the family. Avasin witnessed what her mother experienced as a woman in patriarchal Kurdish society: injustice, defeat, marginalization, sorrow, guilt and so forth. Avasin did not want to take on these values, which are characteristic of a traditional Kurdish woman. Her mother's lack of will to resist aroused anger in Avasin and forced her towards alternative understandings where she could develop and regulate herself in a different way than her mother to attain a new identity.

1.5. Gender-based upbringing and the importance of honour

Another significant theme is the differential treatment of siblings in the family and the importance of honour in a context where gender is used as a natural category to position women and men in relation to each other. Patriarchal Kurdish society is starkly gender-divided. Gender roles are well defined, and parents bring up girls and boys according to different sets of norms. This differential treatment is especially apparent to Kurdish girls and boys when they become adolescents. For example, the women I interviewed said that as children they had felt just as loved and cherished by their parents as their brothers had, but that their brothers had always enjoyed significantly more freedom than they did themselves:

> We [Zeri and her brothers] were treated very differently, for example when it came to clothes. Yes, from clothes to making your own decisions, it was very different. [. . .] I was very much affected by my elder brothers' and my father's attitude to me. To an extent, they showed me the mentality in society about not trusting women. They pretend to be protecting you, but it is actually a problem of trust. If you are a woman, you can't avoid experiencing it in society. (Interview with Zeri, 26 March 2018)

From minor everyday things like clothes and getting-home times to major decisions about such things as starting a relationship, there was a big difference in the way girls and boys were brought up and in what was expected of the children in Zeri's family. Going by her description, not only the parents but also her brothers ordered the girls about. Zeri's elder brothers were regarded as the future men and future heads of the family who would one day take their father's place, and they too were involved in deciding what the daughters could and could not do.

This meant that the women were socialized all through their upbringing to accept men's authority over them and men's right to make decisions on their behalf. The lack of self-representation and distrust contribute to Kurdish women's alterity. In patriarchal Kurdish society, for example, the word 'bêkêmasî' (Kurdish for 'incomplete') is used of women, reflecting a view of women as abnormal and unable to cope alone without men, so that men must 'first of all' define women's opportunities for action and protect them.[16] Consequently, women are subjected to a man-dominated and man-controlled social surveillance, where the men in the family strive to control the women's social lives and activities. Zeri conceived of this control as a matter of distrust, although it was framed as a form of protection or care for the women in her family.

Zin mentions how men's care became a pretext for preventing girls from engaging in 'immoral acts' that would harm the reputation and honour of the family. Zin explains:

> There was a big difference between us. My elder brothers could wear whatever clothes they wanted. They could swim in the harbour. But I couldn't even wear trousers. [. . .]My parents didn't force me to wear hijab, but I knew I had to. [. . .]

If I didn't, it was morally inappropriate, i.e. people would think I had no morals. Perhaps I had more freedom than most other girls in the family. In terms of going out and coming-home times, for example, but that wasn't down to my parents' permission, but to my own struggle. [. . .] I became myself through my struggle, not the woman they allowed me to be. The Leader [Öcalan] says: 'If you surrender to a man's conscience, you are a dead woman.' If I were to surrender to the conscience of the men of the family, they wouldn't let me study but would force me to be a traditional, ignorant woman instead. They tried to. However much you oppose it, the family still force you into what they have learnt from society's norms. (Interview with Zin, 23 March 2018)

The attempts at control that Zin describes do not necessarily operate through any kind of coercion of the women. They are taught from birth, through their socialization, to accept the family's decisions. Socialization becomes a form of discipline that aims to bring about control of women by men through the culture.

It is important in this context to mention the concept of 'honour', to which families often refer in Kurdish patriarchal society, especially as in the case of Zin, where the phenomenon is met with resistance from a woman who refuses to submit to this control. The discourse of honour, which relates to the family's status in society, is primarily directed at women and is embodied and naturalized by women when they conform to various norms through traditional ways of behaviour. In patriarchal Kurdish society, honour is understood in a broad sense as something encompassing all the property a man may have and must guard – including the family's women.[17] Women are thus regarded as objects on which the family's level of pride is based. For this reason, it is regarded as crucial for a man to have control of his honour/family, including the sexuality, behaviour and clothing of the female family members, to maintain his status in the public spheres of society. With a reference to Foucault, I should claim that the discourse of honour constructs 'a regime of repression' that aims to make the individual submit sexually and identity-wise to the regulation of reproduction that ensures the survival – in this context – of what a majority considers Kurdish culture.[18]

Brothers assist fathers in regulating the female family members. Zin recounted the following:

I have a younger brother and two elder brothers. We had a good relationship, but the more I listened to my elder brothers, the better it was for me. As I said before, I didn't have any problems with either my father or my mother, because I just had to be the well-behaved child. The nice girl. But eventually I went from being the silent one to being the one who said 'No!' my elder brothers' orders. (Interview with Zin, 23 March 2018)

Zin's narrative reflects a tension in the brother-sister relationship, typical of the patriarchal society, where the elder brother, like the parents, has to help bring up the sister and where the sister must obey him. This division of roles in the family regulates the daughter not only into obedience to the brother but also into compliance with a patriarchal system.[19] As Zin reveals, she ended up saying 'No!' to her brothers. Using Gergen's understanding of narratives, Zin's story can be described as a progressive narrative in which she paints a strong picture of herself as someone struggling to create for herself new opportunities for action and hence better conditions.

Several of the women fighters recalled that until around the age of ten, they did not find that a distinction was made between them and their siblings in terms of the freedom they were given by their parents. Their parents spoiled and loved daughters and sons to the same degree. They enjoyed almost the same opportunities for action as their brothers. Bermal said that when she was little, she was closest to her father and very fond of him. He protected her against her mother, who was occasionally violent to her and her siblings if they were naughty. In time, however, the relationship changed. Around puberty, her father began to restrict her freedom and interfere in where she was going, whom she was meeting, when she should get back home and so on. Bermal also recalled that especially on summer trips to Kurdistan, her father became more conservative:

> While I was at home [in Germany] I didn't notice that much sibling difference. It existed, but not totally obviously. Later, when I got older, I noticed it in connection with trips to Kurdistan. The differential treatment of women and men. That women have restrictions. I noticed it especially when I reached marriageable age. Because you're older, you find that your mother's family want you to marry one of them. The same with your father's family. [. . .] We have a lot of family-related marriages. [. . .] For example, your mother's family say: 'Marry your auntie's son!'. Your father's family say: 'Marry your uncle's son!'. That was the first time I experienced it [coercion]. And I was against it [marriage to a cousin]. There was someone else I loved. My parents pretended they didn't know about him. They knew it. But I kept it [the relationship] hidden, too. (Interview with Bermal, 21 March 2018)

A typical Kurdish mother functions as an anchor point for socially controlling her daughter. While the father controls the mother, the mother controls the daughter. The father hardly ever has direct confrontations with the daughter, which is an indirect way of safeguarding his authority. Instead, it is incumbent upon the mother to bring up the daughter and make her submit, as she has done herself, to Kurdish patriarchal norms.[20]

Bermal is one of the few women fighters whom I interviewed who had had a boyfriend. Although Bermal criticized her parents' norms and traditions, she nevertheless tried to keep her relationship hidden, as she had learnt from childhood, through what can be termed 'internalized socialization processes', that marriage is the only accepted frame for a man's and woman's cohabitation. Having a boyfriend would make her disloyal to the family's values. In this connection, she developed a form of 'necessary strategy', choosing to keep her boyfriend hidden from her family. She knew that a woman's premarital relationship with a man, if discovered, could have serious consequences for her. The Kurdish community would very likely brand her a whore, unclean or cheap. In other words, she would risk abjectification, and it would be almost impossible for her later on to enter a relationship that could earn the respect of the surrounding community.

Bese elaborates on how a family's esteem depends on its number of male members and how the onset of a girl's puberty comes with insights into her reduced possibilities in life:

> As a woman in patriarchal society, you are aware that the more men there are in the family, the stronger you will find yourself to be, because what gives women strength, according to society's norms, is men. I only had one brother, so I was a bit reticent in society. Of course, we were unhappy with our brother always being described as worth more than us and stronger than us. [. . .] 'Men are powerful, valuable, and know everything'. 'Men deserve love and respect' [laughs]. But our childhood was good. Until I was ten. You could play out twenty-four hours a day. Alone. You could walk around the village in groups consisting of both girls and boys. But after a certain age, it hits you like a sledgehammer. Yes, all of a sudden! When you find you've got to the age of eleven or twelve, the restrictions and the control start. These taboos were very heavy. I still have trouble understanding them. I couldn't accept them. [. . .] Although you're not all that old, you realize that women have limited opportunities in society. So you realize that your wishes are never fulfilled. Your will, your existence, aren't acknowledged. It's a life that's been defined for you. It affects you a lot, of course. I mean, you know that you must get married at fifteen at the latest. You will have a life like your mother's. The state, the system, is far away from you. But you don't know it. Perhaps you can study and become a teacher, but you are also afraid, because it's far away from you. Who is it? Which system are you to live in? Nor do you have the courage to say with relief: 'OK, I'll just go my own way'. Society is also against it. It isn't easy getting permission to study, either. When all your fear, your emotions and others' predictions are interwoven, you start to look for an alternative. You know your conditions. If you stay in society, you have to accept a life without will. Under those circumstances, I joined the movement. It wasn't so much a matter of how much you knew about the movement. Those who knew about it knew what they had to do. For those who didn't know about it, the movement was just a hope. (Interview with Bese, 22 March 2018)

Bese says that men's position in patriarchal society is not up for discussion and that she was told as a child that men were stronger than women. When men are framed in all contexts as strong and are assigned high value at the expense of women, as Bese describes it, this reflects that Kurdish masculinization of men depends on the feminization of women. The sister is forced into conformity with norms of femininity that call for the brother to protect her and through this show his strength.

Confronted with the expectation to submit to such patriarchal control, Bese points to her search for new understandings and new opportunities for action. Joining the PKK gave Bese the opportunity to opt out of the local Kurdish society, in which the patriarchal gender roles were rooted, and to embark on a nomadic journey to experiment with something new. Uncertain as a future within the PKK would be, it was better than getting married at fifteen. According to Bese, not only patriarchal family norms contributed to her decision. Bese also told me in the interview that factors such as the mountainous environment, the absence of the Turkish state and colonization, the isolation from modernity and the fascinating stories about the PKK all played a part in her choice.

To the women fighters whom I interviewed, it was a crucial factor that the PKK's struggle against Turkish colonization implied a break with Kurdish gender roles in its attempt to create a viable new Kurdish national consciousness. I met with Afrin in Rojava, where PKK's norms and values already have had great influence on the everyday life of the local population. Afrin's father had been politically active in the movement, and she described herself as someone who had practically grown up in the movement. Afrin articulates how her family differed from her uncle's family, although they lived side by side:

> Religion has never been all that important to me. Perhaps my mother tried to influence me a bit. As in, 'You are a girl, be careful, avoid rumorus, don't hang out too much' [. . .] My father treated all his children the same. Perhaps it was because he'd been in the Leader's camp [the Beqaa camp in Lebanon] several times, where he possibly learnt something new. So I didn't have a childhood with strict rules. [. . .] But it doesn't mean there weren't influences of classical Kurdishness. Women's and men's positions in society weren't the same. But there was variation from family to family, too. Our house and my uncle's house were separated by a wall. But my cousin couldn't do anything without her father's permission. She often told us if she wanted to do something somewhere. We would tell my father and he would pass it on to my uncle, and that way we got permission. I felt sorry for her. (Interview with Afrin, 13 December 2017)

The topic of religion brings Afrin to mention the strict rules within her uncle's family. Most of the women fighters interviewed described their parents as religious people. The influence of Islam on everyday life, including Islamic norms for gender and women's agency, varies from family to family. Zin is the only interviewee who has worn a hijab, while the others have never covered their hair. Periodically, some of them observed Ramadan, and some were partially practising Muslims. Yet, the strictness against which all react is related, first and foremost, to the discourse of honour and other patriarchal values that were activated to regulate women's manners, clothing style and conduct. To convince Kurds to replace the loose, tribally oriented cultivation of Islamic norms, PKK had to disseminate the movement's norms and values to the general population. The training camp in Lebanon mentioned by Afrin was used by the PKK not only to train new members or fighters but also to plan a broad dissemination of an alternative ideology, for example to Kurds from Syria, but also Kurds from Turkey who came to take part in activities and short courses for the civilian population. This explains why Afrin proudly relates how her father broke with the cultural norms, which again led to Afrin having more freedom than her cousin.

1.6. The PKK's takeover of the honour discourse

To understand why the PKK can argue for women's liberation, it is important to recognize how the movement interprets the patriarchal norms in the light of Turkish colonization. Especially during the 1990s, when the conflicts between the PKK and the Turkish state escalated, and before hundreds of Kurdish villages were burnt down and their inhabitants were forced to move to big cities, a significant section of the Kurdish population lived in small villages in the countryside and mountainous areas. Kurdish areas were hardly affected by modernity and the industrial development in comparison to the rest of Turkey, and the primary sources of economic income for Kurdish families remained crop and animal farming. Living in the mountainous districts also reduced contact with the Turkish authorities. Cultivating traditional norms was a way of protesting against Turkish colonization, and here the rhetoric and practices enforcing the phenomenon of patriarchal honour were ways to bolster Kurdish identity. Only through Kurdish women's Kurdishly regulated reproduction would the Kurdish people be able to survive occupation and continue to exist as a population group.[21] Kurdish men were obligated to protect 'their' women and ensure the continuation of the family and thereby the people by preventing both unwanted men Kurdish outsiders and representatives of the Turkish state to touch and affect their women.[22]

Since women fighters in the PKK are expected to live more or less ascetic lives and be sexually abstinent, the PKK offers a domain for women where they can both be active and still be 'honourable'. This knowledge made it easier for them not only to travel to the mountains but also to persuade their families to accept their decision. Zin recounted how she had explained to her elder brother that she would be protected in the PKK:

> Because my big brother is a patriarchal person, I told him that the PKK is the most honourable organization in the world. The most moral. And I told him I was in a movement whose concept of honour is a thousand times stronger than his own. I get more honourable treatment here than he could give me. (Interview with Zin, 23 March 2018)

In Chapter 3, I shall go into details with the PKK's view of love and sexuality and the movement's ideological arguments for forbidding members of the movement any form of intimate relationship. Yet, here I shall briefly address how this injunction is not just about preventing women from getting pregnant and having children, which could affect their combat abilities, but also about protecting women from situations that could put the PKK in a bad light with Kurds, possibly discouraging women's enlistment in the movement. This is also the reason why Zin proudly told her elder brother that he should be at ease about her participation in the PKK, as she would never be abused by her men PKK comrades or by the enemy due to the patriarchal Kurdish society's cultural heritage. Yet, Çağlayan (2007) judges that the PKK was being strategic, partly pragmatic, in tackling the honour ideology in patriarchal Kurdish society. By shifting the anchor point of honour from women's bodies to the nation's land, thereby implementing its secular ideology, the PKK strategically created a new understanding of honour that helped influence female enlistment in the PKK. Instead of engaging in a consequence-fraught confrontation with patriarchal Kurdish society, the PKK adopts the honour ideology and shapes it to fit the movement's own national ideology.

In the PKK, as in any other national movement, women therefore become part of the cultural and national heritage to be protected[23] – even though, as Chapter 4 will discuss in detail, the interviewed women fighters will insist that they self-ensure their own protection and have their own take on what counts as honour. They believed that they were not the strategic reasons of the PKK, which protected their 'honour', but they themselves through their own liberation struggle redefined the meaning of 'to be honourable'. But, according to the men fighters' narratives about their women comrades, men still feel an obligation to protect women in the movement, although they do not want to be seen as patriarchal. Firat, a man commander, recounted proudly that there had only been a couple of women who 'by accident' had fallen pregnant in the forty-year history of the PKK:

> I think it happened in '97 or '98. [. . .] That's the time when Şemdin Sakık[24] was in the leadership. A scoundrel of a man, a crony of his who later fled from the movement, gets a woman fighter pregnant. He abuses her. She gets pregnant and so she's sent to Istanbul. They [the leadership] make out she is to carry out the movement's activities there, but the reason is that she's been told by the man to get rid of her baby. [. . .] The enemy finds out about her and pursues her. She's captured before she's had time to have an abortion. Imagine, she's the victim of both the movement and the enemy. The enemy abuses her pregnancy against her appallingly. I mean, several police officers rape her while she's pregnant. Horrific! She loses the child afterwards. When she returned to us, she was almost paralysed. The police just wanted to get rid of her. They were well aware that she was guilty according to our standards. She had acted immorally in the mountains and also told the police about all our contact people. Several patriotic families were later sent to jail because of her. The police more or less sent her to us so we could kill her. But we didn't. We discussed it, because we knew that the police would also use her killing against us. (Interview with Firat, 26 March 2018)

A noteworthy point in Firat's narrative is his initial, condemning focus on the man who got the woman pregnant while the woman is described as weak and accordingly assigned a passive role in the event. Firat thus indicates that it was the job of the man leader to protect her; yet, he failed and instead the leader's male friend abused her. At the beginning of Firat's narrative, responsibility for the abuse lay with the men. The baby was the woman's responsibility. It was her child, and she had to arrange for an abortion. In this process, she was detained and ended up betraying her comrades and contacts under torture. At this point, Firat shifts into judging her weakness under torture as a treacherous matter of betrayal. Underlying Firat's narrative is the claim that the police's wish to get the movement to kill the woman rested on its knowledge about both the patriarchal Kurdish norms relating to the punishment for being dishonoured and the movement's ideological attitude to betrayal. Here, Firat proudly recounted that the movement chose not to kill the woman. Firat does not claim that the woman deserved to be killed nor that the movement, after her release, wanted to protect and take care of her. Rather, his pride relates to the movement's tactical ability to navigate in such a way that the Turkish state did not succeed in putting the movement in a bad light in relation to the norms of patriarchal Kurdish society. This end of the story testifies to the strength of the Kurdish discourse of honour also in the PKK: the woman was left to herself and punished through exclusion from the movement. The woman thus underwent a triple alteritization. First, she is sexually abused by a man PKK member, then Turkish prison personnel rape her and finally the PKK expels her, despite her initial turn to the movement to fight similar encroachments against Kurdish women. The narrative reflects that the men interviewees as well as the overall PKK movement lack the ability to acknowledge the implicit men bonding and guilt in this crime.[25]

Summary

The analysis has focused on factors and dynamics behind women's mobilization to attain collective rights, both as Kurds and as women. The chapter demonstrates how women's childhood experiences of the colonial everyday in the form of internalized oppression and resistance in their own accounts significantly frame how they understand the processual constitution of their gender and identity. The first clash with the colonial Turkish power typically related to the use of their Kurdish mother tongue in school and simultaneous challenges in mastering the Turkish language. Through emotional and bodily experiences at school, such as bullying, discrimination and harassment, the women articulated the importance of their ethnic background. Through linguistic and discursive exchanges, the women are subjected to the Turkish state's homogenization policy, including systematic attempts to assimilate them, as assimilation serves as the premise for intelligibility as a citizen in the Turkish majority culture. The interviewees also recounted a subsequent experience of 'awakening', prompting them to reorient themselves. Early on, they found that they were different from the Turks and that they had to find their identity elsewhere. This dual process of repudiation and adoption created a 'them' and an 'us'. The experience of state violence, including the loss of family members, the burning down of villages and the persecution of family members or acquaintances, resulted in disidentification with things Turkish and, at the same time, initiated a more conscious identification as Kurdish. This reorientation created a process of becoming in which different ethnic characteristics, affiliations and constructions were negotiated to create a feeling of stability in life as well as a future room for manoeuvring.

With regard to Kurdish women's gender-specific experiences, the women most often described growing up in families where patriarchal norms were dominant. Not only the parents' differential treatment of brothers and sisters but also dysfunctional relations between their parents contributed to the women's identification with the struggle and pain of their mothers. The women explained that their mothers' fight against the patriarchal society created inspiration for their current anti-colonization fight and their solidarity with other women. During their upbringing, the interviewed women found that their parents had gender-specific expectations of them involving constrained opportunities for their access to self-realization. Despite the differential treatment, the women typically felt loved by their parents on a par with their brothers. Yet, the experience of the parents' gender-based differential treatment of the children formed the women's first experience of a double otherness in the sense of being both a Kurd and a woman. The women also explained how honour and the consequences of the discourse of honour played a crucial role in relation to women's gendered body and their opportunities for action. An interview with a man fighter reflected that the discourse of honour is anchored not only in traditional Kurdish society but also within the PKK, although in a slightly different form. The women's experience of double otherness, with their own families denying them the opportunity for representation and self-realization, explains the second clash that I shall examine in the next chapter with a focus on the women's teenage years and early twenties when they acquire a strong desire to offer resistance to both othering powers.

Chapter 2

DETACHMENTS AND REORIENTATIONS IN A THREE-GENERATIONAL PERSPECTIVE

This chapter will focus on processes of reorientation during the women fighters' teenage years. While the previous chapter described a 'first clash' in the women fighters' childhood encounters with the 'colonizing society' as well as experiences of patriarchal norms in their Kurdish homes, this chapter concentrates on the women fighters' double disidentificatory processes that followed from such subaltern positions of being both Kurds and girls. The women fighters' adolescence is typically characterized by the emergence of alternative understandings and formations of identities. In other words, the chapter presents and analyses their narratives about the period in their lives when dreams of independence and quests for personal political standpoints moved them to travel to the mountains to become active members, even guerrillas of the PKK. By revealing the dynamics and processes that were significant to the women's reorientation, this chapter takes a second step to understanding how the women fighters' identity and gender were shaped. The first part of the chapter shows how the women in their narrations point to resistance against colonization and patriarchy as explanatory factors for their orientation towards the PKK. Yet, the women fighters' experiences of colonization and patriarchy are diverse and entail many variations, which is why the second part of the chapter groups the women fighters into three generations, reflecting different experiences from the PKK's almost forty-year history. This will make it possible to show how, in different ways in different generations, colonization and gender have been contributory reasons for women fighters' decision to join the PKK's struggle.

2.1. The meaning of 'waking up'

In their accounts, all the women fighters stated that various factors and dynamics had influenced the genesis of what they called the 'awakening', a reorientation that they experienced in their adolescence. According to the women's narratives, the experience of 'awakening' helped them to realize that there were alternatives to 'being Turks'. This introductory section begins with a description of when and why they left home.

2.1.1. Admission to university as a springboard to an independent life outside the family

One thing that comes out in several of the women fighters' narratives is that the starting signal for their journey to awakening was when they were admitted to a higher education institution and therefore moved away from home. Turkey is a big country with few universities typically located in the western part of the country. When young people from the Kurdish districts in the south-eastern part are admitted to university, it often involves moving away from their hometowns to the Turkish-dominated districts. This was the case for Zin, Gulesor, Cane and Zeri, who all have a university life behind them and who all first left home when they were admitted to university. Concurrently, they mentioned that initially they had seen university as the 'road to freedom'. In different ways, then, and with the wisdom of hindsight, the women described university as a springboard to new directions in life, where they could pursue their dreams.

It is important in this context to point out that on the evidence of the women fighters' narratives, they were not the only ones who saw university as a springboard. Also, their parents encouraged their daughters to pursue a higher education as a basis on which they could fight for a better life as Kurds in Turkey. In other words, the young women and their parents alike saw university as a possible route to expanding the young women's opportunities in life. However, this parental encouragement did not prevent the parents from worrying about sending their daughters to a faraway city. The parents' concern revolved, among other things, around how well their daughters would be able to manage on their own, to protect themselves and to continue living in accordance with Kurdish norms and values, as well as whether they would be able to avoid becoming part of Kurdish student politics and thus potentially coming into conflict with the authorities.

In narrativizing their adolescence, the women fighters pointed out that their parents would not have had such concerns had it been their parents' sons who were to move to another city. Zeri recounted that her parents had considered moving with her, merely because she was a woman. In the debate over whether Zeri could move by herself or not, her parents made no secret of their belief that it would be difficult for her to manage on her own in a strange town. This would prove to be true in Zeri's case, as by her own account she found that after a sheltered upbringing framed by her family, she had difficulty standing on her own two feet:

> When I was younger, my family took care of all my needs and did everything to make life easier for me. . . . It was hard for me to set off to another town for the first time. A new place. New surroundings. But my place [joining the Patriotic Youth Movement, YCK] was predetermined. [. . .] I was experiencing a separation for the first time. It wasn't easy. You have to be able to stand on your own two feet. Create your own network and life. You have a life ahead of you. How are you to do it? These worries, this fear, made it hard for me. (Interview with Zeri, 26 March 2018)

In this extract, Zeri says she found that her break with her family led to a new form of process of becoming. She also found that the passage of time brought uncertainties and possible challenges that stood in contrast to the safe life she had formerly led with her family in her hometown. In connection with university life, Zeri had to begin a new process of becoming, a kind of journey to independence, where she had to make her own decisions. As part of this, Zeri was drawn to the political student milieu, which brought the prospect of her being able to mix with other circles and forge new connections. Like most of the other women I interviewed, she had not been brought up to acquire independent skills and had not learnt to stand on her own two feet when it came to her emotional life or to coping with everyday life. In her narrativization of this period, however, she also said 'my place was predetermined', thus underlining that she perceived her joining YCK inevitable in her process of becoming.

Eventually, Zeri's parents chose not to move with her, not solely out of consideration for her decision to go alone but also because they could not afford it and worried that their moving away from the Kurdish areas would mean a life in which they as Kurds would be subjected to increased discrimination. In this context, her mother was especially important in the decision to send Zeri off by herself. On this point, Zeri said:

> Although they [Zeri's parents] weren't very keen on it, they nevertheless accepted my moving [to Ankara] as it was about getting an education. But at first they said that they wanted to come with me. They thought it would be hard for me to be alone. But my mother didn't want to leave her house and her garden, because she had worked hard for it. Because of all the energy she'd put into it, I was also against their moving with me. I said they didn't need to come with me. They were the ones who'd always made the decisions about my life. Now I wanted to decide a bit for myself. But they knew very well what I was drawn to. That I would be interested in the patriotic student milieu and that through that I would be getting close to the party [the PKK]. (Interview with Zeri, 26 March 2018)

By this statement, Zeri indicated that the move to another city was not only about moving to a new house but also about moving away from the special relationship that her mother, and thus all women, had with the local environment. The parents' decision thus rested on entangled, intra-acting factors such as ambitions on behalf of their daughter, their fear of their increased alterity as well as the daughters enrolment in the PKK, but also material things such as the house and the garden. As part of Zeri's explanation of why the decision fell out to her leaving on her own includes her belief that Kurds have a special affinity with the soil, the fields and the land, as these three elements together were regarded as one of the Kurdish people's last undefeated bases.

Other women fighters also mentioned this trinity of soil, fields and land as a means to create a shared cultural frame of reference to nature and a means not to become rootless despite colonization. Dersim assessed that it was always the Kurdish mother who defended Kurdish language and traditions against assimilation by the enemy. According to Dersim, the Kurds have not been completely assimilated throughout history, thanks to mothers being reluctant to move away from their villages (Interview with Dersim, 27 March 2018). I consider it a characteristic of the rhetoric of both the PKK and its women fighters that a special connection is stipulated between women and the villages. In contradistinction from the city, associated with men and artificiality, their rhetoric points to women's ability to preserve their authenticity by remaining in the villages. The 'special' relationship between the women and the villages will be elaborated upon in Chapter 6 that analyses the implementation of Öcalan's ideals in Rojava, where, acting on the ideology of democratic confederalism, the regional administration wants to develop the area precisely in the form of villages with a focus on Kurds' return to nature and the land.

As a significant number of the women fighters come from villages where they have worked in or related to the fields and nature, they perceive the soil as more than something that you just cultivate in order to survive. Being indigenous is thus framed as a special attachment to the rural area where one was born, but also where one's historical heritage and possible future lie.[1] In this understanding, it is the mother's responsibility to uphold the traditions and the family's sense of belonging, among other things, by ensuring that the family home in the Kurdish area and the family members' relationship with the home are preserved and perpetuated. It is precisely this role that Zeri said her mother had taken on in the family:

> My mother was in that kind of position; she was attached to the soil and to nature. The concern she showed for nature and the soil, she also showed for her children and the family. She was the backbone of the home. That the family didn't go through a split was down to my mother. (Interview with Zeri, 26 March 2018)

According to Zeri, her mother related to nature and the soil in the same way as she related to her own children. She did not distinguish between them. The concept 'home' does not refer solely to the place where the members of the family live; it also refers to material phenomena such as the house, the garden and nature that produce meaning and wholeness in relation to the family members. According to Zeri, her mother acted in this context as a sort of cohesive force also when she prevented a possible divorce between the parents and warded off a split in the family.

In this light, Zeri's narrative that positions her mother, not her father, as the main protagonist who prevented a move to the city contributes to an image of Zeri's mother as preoccupied not only with following her daughter but also with preserving the family home as an important base for the family and its members' attachment to everything Kurdish. Zeri's pride in her mother is supported by the Kurdish idea that there is a special divine connection between women and the earth, with reference to their shared reproductive capacity.

Like Zeri, the other women fighters described the landscape and nature as something especially meaningful to the Kurdish people as a whole. Helin said with pride that the Kurds are a people with a strong attachment to the soil and that Kurdish women in particular are patriotic in their love of their country, culture and nation (Interview with Helin, 24 March 2018). Zeri and Helin's claims follow Öcalan's understanding that the Kurdish nation, not as a modern people or a great empire endowed with power, wealth and great victories but as a peaceful, nomadic tribal people, has lived in harmony with nature in villages and mountain districts far from the big cities. By keeping to the villages and mountain districts, the Kurds have avoided assimilation and alienation from their own values and norms.[2]

The special relationship to the soil, or to the nation's land, also emerged in Zelal's narrative. Zelal joined the movement from Europe, where her mother always reminded her and her siblings of their origins, saying, 'Remember where you come from. You do not belong in these lands' (Interview with Zelal, 17 September 2017). In this way, her mother attempted to create an understanding that a particular relationship between ethnicity and soil/land exists that new generations have an obligation to maintain. When patriarchal Kurdish society perceives women as bearers of Kurdish traditions in a foreign country, it puts more responsibility for the perpetuation of Kurdish culture on women's shoulders than on men's. When Zelal's mother expected her daughters not to form a strong attachment to European soil because they were not originally from there, she also indicated that she saw every land as having its own children and demanding that the children return to it one day. That nature and culture exist under the same immanent conditions, where human beings, animals and the rest of nature live and interact together will be featured in Chapter 3 that analyses the PKK's constitution of the new human in the mountains.

2.1.2. University studies as a springboard to the PKK

The women who were university students before becoming fighters highlighted university life as a context of new orientations. Since the 1960s, Turkish universities have hosted highly politicized youth movements. Growing prosperity in Turkey following the Second World War led to a growing number of young people, also from the working class and rural areas, to study at university. Diverse backgrounds in the student population contributed to political discussions, for example, of the US attempted invasion of Vietnam in 1965 or the '68 youth rebellion' in Europe and the United States. Subsequent anti-racist, anti-imperialist and anti-military ideologies impacted the Turkish student environment and led to large-scale student protests against the Turkish state. This is also the time and place for the emergence of the PKK. Before Öcalan and his friends started labelling their movement the PKK, it was referred to as a 'student movement', established by a group of students in Ankara who were inspired by Marxism and the youth rebellion of the 'sixty-eighters'. Ever since, the universities have been a place where the PKK has found many student sympathizers. In 1987, the PKK established the Patriotic Youth Movement (YCK) to embrace these students.

Most interviewees recounted that they had first begun reading Öcalan's books and material about the Kurds and the colonization of Kurdistan at university after coming into contact with the YCK. The women fighters describe reading Öcalan's books as an 'eye opener'. Participating in student activities such as demonstrations, political meetings, music and festivals organized by the PKK, and covertly reading PKK material and Öcalan's books together, often led to their ceasing to attend to their studies, not least because they lost the motivation to strive for the bourgeois life of which they had previously dreamt. Ronya recounted as follows how it occurred to her that getting an education would mean being assimilated and becoming a stranger to herself and her culture:

> We read it [PKK material] because we wanted to develop ourselves. Before I knew the movement as a Kurd, I wanted to become a doctor. Have an important position in society. But I also wanted to become an aware Kurdish girl, so I just couldn't settle for having a simple life in society. After we started reading and learning about the movement, we gave up our petit-bourgeois dreams, because we said, 'We can't liberate the fatherland like that'. There were some Kurdish political figures at that time. We distanced ourselves from them, too. (Interview with Ronya, 27 March 2018)

Ronya was a university student in Aleppo in Syria. The YCK was also organized at her university in Syria. Through the movement, she became acquainted with Öcalan's books and began to have doubts about the petit-bourgeois dreams she used to have before starting at university. Although she could improve her own life by getting an education and then getting a job as a Syrian citizen, according to Ronya this choice would make no contribution to the Kurds' national struggle. Ronya wanted neither to educate herself nor to lead a petit-bourgeois life. She stated that she knew of previous generations of Kurdish academics and intellectuals who had educated themselves and achieved a political status in the public sphere, but who, rather than contribute to the revolution, pursued the fulfilment of their petit-bourgeois dreams. She therefore took a critical attitude to Kurdish intellectuals.

It should be mentioned in this context that the Kurdish intellectuals have always been considered by the PKK as a 'partial' obstacle to the implementation of the PKK's strategic plan, which aims to bring about a 'break' in young Kurds and prevent them aspiring to a petit-bourgeois, capitalist life. The PKK's scepticism is thus intended to detach young people from their families, education, civil society, capitalist interests and individual desires in favour of the formation of new values and alternative identifications, and to motivate them to abandon it all for a new life in the mountains. These alternative identifications up against significant others[3] do not necessarily arise only in a context of oppression or colonization. Significant others may also be other Kurdish men and women who do not quite fit in with or adhere to the PKK's struggle. At times, the PKK has waged armed conflicts against Kurdish emirs, tribal lords and sheikhs. Thus, in addition to the national struggle against the Turkish state, the PKK also conducted an internal class struggle against Kurdish power holders, whom the PKK regarded as colluding with the Turkish state in oppressing the Kurdish people. This internal struggle enabled the PKK to recruit several members from poor Kurdish villages and the working class, who suffered under such emirs, tribal lords and sheikhs.[4] Representing the rural areas and the working class did not suffice to secure the PKK sufficient support for its revolution. The organization also need students and intellectuals to spread its message and develop the ideology of the party. In fact, the PKK's first manifesto of 1978 states that it is a primary objective to build a patriotic, intellectual youth movement based on students. As well as helping to develop the national struggle, the students' task was to be a model for new generations of Kurds and help mobilize young people from other social strata such as unskilled workers or villagers.[5] The woman fighter Menal Bagok says in an interview with journalist and author Arzu Demir that during the 1990s, there was great respect for students who informed and raised the awareness of people in Kurdish society. When women students were among the first to take part in the movement, other young people chose to follow them as they had faith in those students' choices.[6]

2.1.3. *The PKK's struggle as a factor in the awakening*

During university studies, the women fighters experienced a Turkish double standard that contributed to the constitution of their new orientation towards the PKK. On the one hand, the Turkish state had tried to make the Kurds internalize Turkish national identity. On the other hand, university studies implied experiences where they found themselves excluded from Turkishness or treated by Turks as ignorant. Such experiences of discrimination contributed to a kind of revelation that the women fighters refer to as the 'awakening'. Zin remembers how her more mature position as a student made her see through the Turkish double standard and reconsider experiences of discrimination during her secondary schooling:

> The only thing that means anything to [Turks] is the experience of being proud of their Turkishness. Unto death! Once, a man was selling oranges who shouted, 'Hurry up and buy my oranges, because I have to do my military service and get more heads for you'. He meant comrades' heads. That's the kind of environment I grew up in. For example, when I was a pupil at Imam Hatip [the religious secondary school] I was called 'Kurd' by my classmates when I turned my back to them. When I turned to face them, they were all gone. I actually liked being called a Kurd. While they were calling me Kurd, there was also a Kurdish liberation struggle going on, and I could feel deep inside that I would end up in that struggle one day. (Interview with Zin, 23 March 2018)

Zin said that her family had moved to a Turkish city when she was small. She had therefore not been a direct witness to the conflict between Turkish military forces and the PKK or to the state persecution that many other Kurds had been subjected to in the Kurdish districts. However, she had always understood that she was a Kurd. As part of her upbringing, her parents had introduced her to the Kurdish language, norms and values. Moreover, the family watched Kurdish TV channels. However, it was not until student life when she saw through Turkish double standards that she began looking for alternative understandings. The

Kurdish liberation struggle offered her an alternative identification to her Turkish one. It entailed a rebellion against Turkish colonization as well as a pride in being a Kurd. Speaking out of her conviction that Kurds and Turks are different and that Kurds have a better inner quality, Zin inverted the Turkish condescension and said that Kurds were not primitive or ultra-nationalist like the Turks. What was noteworthy in Zin's narrative was that she framed it as though the discriminatory experiences she had been subjected to had always been present. In her narrative, she woke up one day as a Kurd and realized how past experiences were matters of discrimination in a colonial context. Zin's experiences of discrimination were supplemented by experiences with Kurds who had 'let themselves be assimilated' or who had 'los[t] their original nature'.

Gulesor recounts that she had always wanted to go to university so that she could become a journalist and convey the voice of the oppressed Kurdish women from her village. Yet, when she got to university and experienced, in her own words, a 'culture shock' from moving 'directly' from the village to the city, her sense of 'contradictions and searchings' became 'deeper'. The culture shock she experienced awakened in her a kind of conservatism or 'defence'. She did not want to be like the other Kurdish women in the city who, according to her, had lost their 'original nature' because they had not maintained the values and norms embedded in their culture of origin. She said that the combination of these challenges and her father's death brought about a kind of 'resentment' – a sort of anger directed at people who denied their original nature (see Chapter 1). On that basis, she began to resist speaking Turkish unless strictly necessary. Her reason for this was that she needed to uphold the values she had brought with her from the village. When she first met young people from YCK and began reading Öcalan's texts, she formed an alternative understanding of herself as a Kurd, rather than an identity imposed on her through Turkish state propaganda. In this context, the encounter with YCK, described by Gulesor as a 'chance meeting', was just what she needed as an answer to her resentment (Interview with Gulesor, 25 March 2018). Joining the YCK gave Gulesor a strategic opportunity to create for herself defence mechanisms against the 'chaos' that the encounter with the colonial power had imposed on her in her identity processes and her quest for understanding and stability.

2.1.4. *The awakening in the diaspora and the creation of belonging in the light of martyrs*

Women fighters from Europe who took part in the PKK describe in similar ways how experiences of being a foreigner, an outsider, of not belonging in the diaspora, had prompted their awakening. For example, Bermal related the following:

> As a child, I attended a Kurdish event with the family. There was something about the place that tugged at me. Maybe it was the music. Or the atmosphere. When you've grown up in Europe, you inevitably get the feeling of not belonging there. Maybe you don't come up against any major challenges, but even so you find there's something missing in your life. You don't belong to the place. You

feel it all the time. At school and everywhere else. [. . .] But at that Kurdish event, I felt for the first time that I belonged to the place. Maybe I didn't understand it all then, but I had the feeling. I said that 'this place belongs to me. It's a place I belong to'. When Martyr Mizgin[7] started singing, it had a terrific effect on me. It produced a happy excitement inside me. I mean, I felt a great enthusiasm. It attracted me. There was something or other that attracted me, but I didn't understand it all then. (Interview with Bermal, 21 March 2018)

Through Kurdish associations, cultural centres and other institutions in Europe that share the PKK's ideology, the PKK attempts to transfer its liberation struggle and implement its philosophy and its women's liberation values. Of the seventeen PKK members whom I interviewed, five (Bermal, Zelal, Evin, Delal and Ayten) had joined the struggle from Europe. Before travelling to the mountains, these women fighters were already active in cultural and political activities taking place in PKK-related associations. The women fighters' association with PKK activities and political circles originated back in their childhoods, when their parents enrolled them in various activities in associations and cultural centres so that they could learn to write and speak Kurdish. This introduction to Kurdish culture involved such things as learning folk dancing and singing in Kurdish. The parents sought by these means to ensure that Kurdish norms and values were perpetuated in the diaspora and that the children did not become assimilated.

Bermal spoke about such a cultural event, in this instance a big evening celebration with music, food, dancing and political talk, typically held in a sports centre. She spoke of being in two minds about her affiliation. Among other things, this gave her the feeling that something was missing in her life, making it impossible for her to realize herself. However, when a sports centre, which would not normally mean much to her, was converted into a cultural events venue, it gave her the feeling that she and the place were attracted to each other. What happened concretely was 'incomprehensible', according to Bermal, but it gave her the feeling that she belonged or had an origin, something she otherwise did not experience because of her ethnic minority background in the diaspora. Here, Bermal indicated that it occurred to her over time that, as manifest in the othering she was subjected to, she did not belong to any 'firstness', and this affected her ethnic positioning and contributed to her sympathy with the Kurdish national struggle. In connection with this, she had the feeling, after leaving the event, of no longer belonging to Europe and of Europe no longer belonging to her. The venue for the cultural event thus facilitated her joy and a positive self-concept, when she felt a social bond[8] arising in the form of a national affiliation between her, the other Kurds and the place. Bermal perceives this bond as strong enough to account for her awakening in the midst of struggling with her identity as an 'other' in everyday life in Europe.

After the evening celebration, Bermal became active in the local Kurdish cultural centre. She began admiring the guerrillas and their life in the mountains. In her account here, she explains that various 'slow' processes of becoming, in the form of relationships, interactions, networks and communities in combination, brought about the awakening and contributed to her increased Kurdish consciousness and her growing interest in the guerrilla life:

> I was enrolled in the cultural activities. They were folk dancing and music. At the same time, the friends [PKK cadres] often visited us at home. They always talked about the national struggle. That increased my interest, especially in the guerrillas. On a day when they [the cadres] didn't visit us, it felt as though something was missing in our home. There was also the magazine *Serxwebûn*. They brought it every month. I didn't understand everything in it, but I read reminiscences by the guerrillas. I could feel something gradually growing within me. (Interview with Bermal, 21 March 2018)

The magazine *Serxwebûn* (1982–present) mentioned here by Bermal is regarded as the PKK's official magazine in Europe. It is mainly addressed to the cadres rather than to ordinary Kurds, and it contains long, heavy ideological articles by the PKK leadership and Öcalan. However, the magazine is also distributed to other Kurds in order to disseminate the PKK's ideals and values, as well as news of the organization's national struggle. The magazine often contains pictures of guerrillas and their life in the beautiful mountainous surroundings, items about guerrillas who have fallen in battle and stories of their feats of courage, their life stories and memoirs. The cadres who regularly visited Bermal's family played a part in talking about martyrs and framing them as 'free and immortal people'. These cadres had themselves often just arrived in Europe from the mountains or were soon to return once their mission in Europe was accomplished. It was therefore also highly likely that they themselves might fall in the national struggle and become martyrs. On this point, Bermal said:

> I was most influenced by the comrades who often visited us at home. [. . .] There was one especially that I liked a lot. In fact, I got to know the guerrillas through him. [. . .] He talked a lot about the guerrilla life and about Kurdishness. He brought the magazine, too. The whole family liked him. Later on, he left for the mountains. Became a martyr. I happened to see his picture in the magazine. I wasn't so old, but it had a big effect on me. I told myself that I would retaliate. I had to take up his gun again, because he always said to me 'you little guerrilla'. I told myself that the little guerrilla would grow up and take up his gun. I also said it to the comrades who visited us afterwards, when they asked what I wanted to be: that 'I would be a big guerrilla!'. That's how I grew up. (Interview with Bermal, 21 March 2018)

Martyr rhetoric and the slogan 'martyrs are immortal' are often used in PKK propaganda to influence Kurds and arouse their sympathy for the national struggle. Displaying pictures of young people and telling their heroic stories enables the PKK to bring about an emotional effect in most Kurds, especially when it is also emphasized that as martyrs, they sacrifice all they have and their lives for the national struggle. The significance of the cultivation of martyr rhetoric and culture in the PKK, especially for women's combat experiences, will be elaborated in Chapter 5.

2.2. Other contributing factors for going to the mountains

Up to this point in this chapter, the analysis has shown how the conception of oneself as colonized was recognized and how it prompted the women to join the PKK to become fighters. In this section, focus will be directed at how the awakening entailed that the women took active steps to position themselves up against the colonizing power through resistance and other means to represent themselves.

2.2.1. From the meaningless to the meaningful life

Like Bermal, several of the fighters I interviewed said that the PKK martyr accounts influenced their decision to join the national struggle. Martyrs they themselves had known or had a personal relationship with, and also the great heroines who loom large in the PKK's narratives and propaganda, had been important to them and to their decision. Gulesor, for example, told how her reading of the story of Zilan and her martyr's death had fascinated and inspired her:

> Through reading [of Öcalan], my search and my contradictions became clearer and clearer to me. I also began to be more active in the YCK and moved from the hall of residence to my own place. I also switched my home over to a collective way of life. When comrade Zilan carried out her attack in '96, I began to be more critical of the meaning life had for me. What am I myself doing for the national struggle? I was also finding life meaningless since my father's death. That comrade Zilan carried out her attack to make her life meaningful, and that my mother rang straight after the attack and told me about it, and again reminded me that I should keep away from these things, all that affected me. I thought about Zilan. A Kurdish woman who made life more meaningful by her death. It all contributed to my becoming more determined, and in the end, I decided to join the movement. (Interview with Gulesor, 25 March 2018)

Moving into places of their own played a crucial role in the politicization process undergone by the women fighters, in that they all said that this was where they became ideologically prepared before going to the mountains. After a couple of years of study, during which they got to know each other and met each other in YCK circles, they moved together into a shared home where they could organize their daily lives as they saw fit. This was in contrast to a hall of residence, which normally comprises separate rooms monitored by the authorities. A shared house also enabled them to read together and build a lifestyle based on values such as solidarity, comradeship and collectivity. They influenced each other as regards opposing the values of society that they saw as capitalist and individualistic. The most important aspect of this, however, was that in the shared home they had the opportunity to cultivate the values and norms they had acquired from the PKK's ideology. At the same time, they formed a collective, which they described as a place that offered them a free life like the one they looked forward to in the mountains.

Zilan, who was mentioned in Gulesor's narrative, is beyond doubt the greatest heroine in the history of the PKK. Zilan (Zeynep Kinacı) is regarded by the PKK as the first 'woman suicide bomber'. In 1996, she carried out the 'most successful attack' in the movement's history. As well as killing herself, she killed numerous Turkish soldiers. In the farewell letter she left behind at the time of the attack, she wrote that her act was an attempt to make her life meaningful.[9] Gulesor was not alone in seeing this as a heroic feat; on the contrary, Zilan subsequently became an idol to other Kurdish women, playing an important part in encouraging women to join the PKK. Through Zilan, Gulesor came to realize that as a Kurdish woman, she could, like Zilan, make a meaningful contribution to the national struggle. For Gulesor, this meant that her meaningless life in the colonial context suddenly appeared meaningful to her by virtue of her enrolment in the national struggle.

The other cadres I interviewed also interpreted Zilan's attack as evidence that Kurdish women were no longer weak. Women could also attack the enemy on his own ground, as Zilan had carried out her attack in the city centre Tunceli/Dersim, where the Turkish soldiers were performing a military ceremony. I will describe the importance of Zilan's military action to the women fighters later, in Chapter 5, when I analyse the women fighters' combat experiences and how Zilan inspired them to associate combat with well-planned action and women's innate flair for defence.

Çağlayan (2007) reports that the Kurdish women she interviewed from the legal campaign in Turkey also look up to Western political activists such as Rosa Luxemburg and Klara Zetkin, as well as the Turk Aysenur Zarakolu.[10] However, none of these international activists were mentioned by the women fighters I interviewed. The focus was solely on martyrs from the PKK. In my judgement, the transition from women in the PKK seeing Western activists as role models to a one-sided focus on national and cultural codes/models is to be understood in relation to the PKK's amendment of its political objective. As mentioned previously, in the early 1990s, in the light of global changes, especially the collapse of the Soviet Union and its real-socialist system, the PKK moderated its campaign and began to use more cultural and moral norms aimed at a more nationalist-oriented movement. In this context, Mordem, who is a leading man leader in the PKK, also said when asked that the new focus on PKK's own national role models can be explained by the fact that after forty years of struggle in which many of their fighters had themselves become 'martyrs', the PKK has progressed and produced its own role models. This becomes apparent, for example, during training and instruction. Here, new members are asked to engage in preparations that iterate the drills engaged in by the PKK's martyrs prior to their heroic deeds. Furthermore, iterative training acts are entangled with narratives about the martyrs' actions, their names, their weapons and life stories that highlight and frame them as role models. Such exposition to the martyrs' acts help form the identity of the new members. The PKK thus ensures that the martyr culture is reinforced and that new generations of fighters always look up to the old martyrs. Because the PKK now highlights role models from its own ranks, it is now more natural for the cadres to identify with them, rather than with foreign, Western activists whom they could read about in history books (fieldnote, 19 January 2018).

The man PKK martyr most often spoken of in this context is Mazlum Dogan, who hanged himself in his cell on Newroz Day, 21 March 1982, in Diyarbakir Military Prison. He was a co-founder of the PKK and is regarded as co-author of the PKK's first manifesto.[11] He is often spoken of as a modern figuration of the saga smith Kawa, who instigated a rebellion back in 612 BCE. According to Cengiz Güneş, the PKK links the smith Kawa and Mazlum Dogan in an attempt to create a kind of Kurdish insurrectionary culture and make it part of the Kurds' ethno-cultural values inspiring the formation of the modern national struggle.[12] Here, I agree with Güneş, who emphasizes that the sort of transformation attempted by the PKK aims to strengthen Kurdish nationalism and cohesion among Kurds, including the party's own members. From the 1990s onwards, however, the PKK can be observed to mention Ishtar, the goddess of war and love, more than the rebellious smith Kawa. Öcalan's lauding of Zilan as a modern Ishtar is an example of PKK's new gender perspective emerging in the 1990s. At this time, women fighters began to have a strong voice in the movement and earned external recognition for their contribution to the national struggle, which coincides with PKK's investments in finding new symbols and narratives to help mobilize more women.[13]

2.2.2. From 'the lowlands' to the mountains

Whether students or not, the interviewees have grown up with experiences of war, persecution, oppression and conflict, and it seems that it is their involvement in the legal political struggle in Turkey that gradually instils in them a form of 'combat readiness' that drives them towards the mountains. Being political at a legal level is known in Kurdish political circles as being in the 'lowlands'. The concept of the 'illegal level' refers to the guerrilla struggle in the mountains, which is regarded as illegal by the Turkish state. The lowlands are thus the place where democratic, legal political work is performed. The struggle in the lowlands is regarded as secondary to and pointless without the struggle in the mountains. It should also be noted that the struggle in the lowlands is waged by people who are not seen as 'brave enough' to take part in the armed struggle in the mountains. The political and social activities being carried on by young people at the legal level thus act as a transition or bridge that helps determine whether young people have the will to take part in the armed struggle or whether they would rather stay in civil society and limit their agency according to the representational latitude defined by the Turkish state.

Several of the women fighters interviewed recalled that they had been active and politicized in the legal struggle while still young and living a completely ordinary daily life. Here, the legal struggle means being active in NGOs, Kurdish media and news agencies, trade unions and other voluntary organizations fighting, among other things, to improve women's conditions. Since the 1990s, there has been a significant increase in the number of voluntary organizations in the Kurdish districts,[14] which coincides with the legal Kurdish parties gaining control of the local municipalities in the Kurdish districts. This has made it easier for the legal political and social organizations and associations to carry out their work and obtain funding. This development reflects the attempt of the PKK to be recognized for its struggle in response to attempts by the Turkish state to brand the struggle as a criminal, terrorist campaign, just as it reflects the PKK's investment in finding a peaceful solution to the Turkish-Kurdish conflict if possible. The PKK depends on the legal organizations and associations to implement its revolutionary values and norms in the civil society of consequence to not only political life but also future societal and social organization, economics and gender roles. Participation in the legal struggle makes it possible for young people to contribute to the national struggle as a supplement to what the guerrillas are doing in the mountains without themselves going into armed combat.

Another incentive for young Kurds today to join the legal political and social organizations is that they inspire youngsters from the villages, from the poor urban districts and/or from resource-poor families to acquire sufficient skills to work, for example, as journalists, project coordinators and producers without any formal education. The first members of the PKK were, in reality, a small elite who had the possibility of getting an education. Today, the legal political and social organizations and associations, including political parties with close links to the movement, constitute a gateway for young people to develop themselves despite being unskilled.[15] Young people in the 'lowlands' have thus become a link between the state and the movement. They are part of what is regarded as the 'legal political struggle' in that they still live in civil society and do not carry out acts that the state regards as illegal. They do, however, act and carry out activities based on the movement's ideology in order to construct or find alternatives to the colonial system of government. Political and social activities at the legal level have contributed to more young people from all strata of society being mobilized within just a few years. A significant number of these young people have been young girls confined to the home who had no opportunity for any kind of employment or schooling. For example, Berfin said that she was one of those who never had an education, even at the elementary level, and therefore first learned to read and write Turkish in the mountains after joining the movement.

From early on, Berfin was active in the legal organizations or associations ideologically associated with the PKK. She herself describes her activities as 'semi-legal and semi-illegal'. They included sending messages between the political prisoners incarcerated in different jails in the country, arranging demonstrations and hunger strikes, and informing the public about the persecution and rights violations perpetrated by the state against the Kurds. She also proudly recounted that she had recruited several new members to the movement and ensured that they reached the free territory in the mountains. She occupied herself with these activities until she got the feeling that she had been 'found out' by the Turkish police and that it was therefore dangerous for her to continue living in the 'Lowlands'. As she had always had a strong wish to leave her life in civil society and go up into the mountains, she gladly chose at last to go there. Berfin recalled that she had hurried to join the struggle in the mountains when she turned eighteen when it was no longer possible for her anyway to contribute to the legal struggle in the 'lowlands':

> It actually started with my elder brother in prison saying, 'Why haven't you taken part [in the movement] yet'? After all, I was old enough, he said. But I'd already told the comrades several times [that she wanted to join], but they hadn't agreed to it. They said each time that I wasn't old enough. [. . .] In this period, the movement was also careful about accepting women, because there weren't many of them. [. . .] I hadn't been found out then, so they thought I was more use here in the city. [. . .] They always said, 'Wait and wait!'. I waited a year while I was active on behalf of the movement. We sent a big new group [of new participants to the mountains]. From the local area alone, there were five women among them [those who were sent away] [. . .] Afterwards, we came under great pressure from their families, although they themselves were also patriotic. [. . .] They knew about us and threatened to go to the authorities. That was a good excuse I could give the comrades. I told them I'd now been found out and couldn't carry on [laughs]. [. . .] I also told my family, 'If I don't go now, I'll be sent to jail'. So, the family didn't oppose it. They didn't even say 'Why?'. [. . .] My mother just said, 'Go, instead of staying and rotting in the government's jail'. (Interview with Berfin, 22 March 2018)

According to Berfin, when a young person is active in the legal struggle and in Kurdish political circles, they are perceived as candidates for joining the struggle in the mountains. Berfin's elder brother, who is a political prisoner in Turkey, therefore questioned Berfin's lack of 'Highland' participation. Her family was not surprised when Berfin finally informed them of her decision to go to the mountains.

Other women fighters also recount that they were met with a certain expectation that one day they would go to the mountains. They recall that their network or community exerted a kind of social pressure to get them to join the armed struggle. The expectations were particularly high in politicized families, especially if they had members in jail, members fighting in the mountains or members dead in combat as martyrs, as did all the interviewed women fighters. The members involved in the illegal activities were looked up to. Staying in the 'lowlands' would be looked down upon. Social pressure thus seems to be a contributing factor when young people decide to head for the mountains.

If the movement was less than keen on Berfin going to the mountains, according to Berfin this was not because she was not good enough, but mainly because in the 1990s, the movement was not yet ready to accept the growing participation of women. At the same time, the movement wanted to keep her at the legal level, where she would be more useful to it. This was not only because she was good at her job at the legal level but also because of the assumption that it was easier for women to carry out semi-legal work, as the Turkish authorities thought women less likely than men to be working for the movement. The interesting point here is that the movement's lack of readiness to accept women and the Turkish authorities' patriarchal view of women as innocuous merged into a strategy that kept women on the legal level to prevent their recruitment onto the illegal level. When Berfin was first found out, however, the movement could no longer risk her being imprisoned. Being 'found out' is in fact one of the main reasons given by the interviewees for deciding to travel to the mountains and not continuing their semi-legal struggle.

Avasin told a similar story of only being permitted to go to the mountains after seven years of political work at the legal level. 'Highland' members explained their refusal to let her come to the mountains with reference to the fact that the 'enemy' did not know about her political work yet, so she could be of more use to the movement at the legal level (Interview with Avasin, 21 March 2018).

If a woman gains access to the mountains, it does not mean that she can stay there forever. Women are sometimes sent back to the cities to resume their semi-legal work. Cane recalled:

> I first came to the mountains in 2002. I stayed here three or four months. Then I went back to the same work. In 2003, I came to the mountains again. That's how I got to know [life in the mountains]. In 2003 I wanted to stay, but that wasn't accepted. They said I should go back to the same work again. (Interview with Cane, 25 March 2018)

Cane indicated that she had been ideologically strengthened through her brief visits to the mountains. But the movement chose time and time again to send her back to her political work in the 'lowlands' until she was found out in 2004, after which she was forced to go to the mountains. It should also be mentioned here that another reason why women can continue doing semi-legal work for longer is that they are not subject to compulsory military service in Turkey as men are. For example, Bese recounted that a number of young men from her village had joined the movement simply to avoid military service, but there had also been a number who sought out small villages, high up and difficult for the Turkish authorities to monitor, because they too wanted to avoid military service (Interview with Bese, 22 March 2018). As Bese explains it, the mountains are a place where young men can make a new world for themselves in the PKK, but also a place, an 'escape route', where they can seek refuge if they want to avoid military service and therefore need protection from the colonizers even though they lack the will to take part in the movement. The mountains thus become a place of refuge and an alternative when they cannot remain in the colonized 'lowlands'.

A final, motivational factor among young Kurds for striving for the mountains relates to the fact that they do not believe that the legal level alone can ever give the Kurds their freedom. As arguments, they mention first that the Turkish state has blocked and closed off all avenues on which Kurds could conduct their political struggle. Turkey's constitution does not permit other ethnic or minority groups to organize in such a way as to pursue their cause within the law and without being persecuted. As mentioned in the 'Introduction', the Kurdish legal struggle has faced increasing obstacles to represent and organize themselves politically. Since the 1990s, several political parties have been suspended and several party members, MPs and mayors have been killed or sent to jail. Second, young Kurds do not have faith in the Kurdish politicians or representatives who engage in politics in ways defined by the Turkish state and who were still supposed to represent them. Consequently, young Kurds do not believe that the Turkish state will recognize Kurdish rights unless forced to. The armed struggle therefore becomes crucial to them as the only way of forcing the Turkish state to engage in a dialogue with the PKK and to accept Kurdish sovereignty in their districts. Ronya used the Kurdish proverb 'iron must be beaten with iron' to explain that the legal political struggle is pointless (Interview with Ronya, 27 March 2018). This means that if the Turkish state always chooses to fight the Kurds with weapons and does not recognize their existence, the only way for the Kurds to fight the state is by taking up arms.

2.2.3. Role models inspire a move to the mountains

So far, the analysis has sketched some of the dynamics that have awoken the interviewed women's determination and courage and prompted them to take part in the PKK's struggle as fighters. In this context, friends and family have proved to be powerful sources of inspiration to the women and have influenced their move to the mountains and hence to a new world; just as Section 2.2.1 has shown that the women were especially inspired by the 'martyrs' to join the PKK, so too are the martyrs a source of inspiration to take to the mountains.

Almost all the women I interviewed spoke at some point in our conversation of someone from their family who died a martyr's death in the struggle on behalf of the movement. Several of the women said in addition that they had grown up with stories of the martyrs, their sublime personalities and heroic exploits. To these women, the martyrs are role models whom they look up to and whom they speak of with eagerness. However, the martyrs were portrayed in the women fighters' narratives not only as role models but also as people who imposed an obligation on the women to join in the armed struggle. This came out, for example, when Zelal emphasized that anyone with a conscience would feel indebted to those who had sacrificed themselves in battle for their country. It was similarly apparent when she added that her loyalty to the Kurdish people did not allow her to have a lifestyle other than being part of the struggle (Interview with Zelal, 17 September 2017). This mentality was especially marked in those women fighters who had, by their own account, 'grown up in the struggle' because of their parents' political activities. According to their narratives, many of the women had been inspired to join the movement by (1) friends who were already members, (2) stories of fallen martyrs and/or (3) personal encounters with guerrilla soldiers or cadres from the PKK.

For example, Afrin said that when she was young and not yet politically engaged, she knew a number of cadres who were active members in her local area. At that time, she admired them very much and wanted to become like them (Interview with Afrin, 13 December 2017). Further to this, Berivan recalled something similar when describing her first meeting with a guerrilla:

> When I lived in the village, we were visited from time to time by some guerrilla comrades. I was 12 when I met them for the first time. My mother was well aware how in love I was with guerrillas. There was a knock at the door, and my mother said: 'Berivan, run'. I ran and saw the women guerrillas standing with their weapons and wearing gabardine guerrilla clothing. I mean, they radiated an impressive grandeur. To my eyes, the women guerrillas were goddesses. I was crazy about them. (Interview with Berivan, 21 March 2018)

In the interview, Berivan recalled as follows how her 'infatuation' with the women guerrillas grew over time:

> As well as the women cadres who came to visit us at home, there was also a man cadre who had a big effect on me. Heval Sait. He had a big effect on me. He was so respectful to women. All the men I knew were men from my mother's side of the family. Those men had no respect for women, but Heval Sait was different. He was the first to tell me about the Leader [Öcalan], and he gave me the Leader's books and inspired me to read them. He discussed things with me a lot, because he knew I had feminist thoughts. [. . .] He didn't treat me like a child of fourteen or fifteen. He said he respected me as an adult. (Interview with Berivan, 21 March 2018)

Berivan told me that her experience of the men in the family was that they treated the women as less bright and as people who should submit to the men. The PKK's view of women stood in contrast to this, which attracted her strongly. In this regard, with his personality, his attitude and his way of speaking to her, Heval Sait represented the PKK's view of women and its fundamental values.

Like Berivan, Ronya recounts that she was influenced by the aura, respect and authority that surrounded the cadres she met before deciding to take part in the struggle:

> The first woman comrade, I got to know was Heval Jiyan. Jiyan Durmus. They had a big effect on me. After I'd got to know them and the other comrades, I started taking an active part in student activities, carrying out activities among the people, and my desire to take part [in the struggle] grew. Of course, we looked at their [the PKK cadres'] conduct, analyzed their philosophy, tried to get an understanding of their freedom, their ideology, their attachment to the land, their will, their morality and their struggles – something completely new to us. They represented a new view of humanity, a new culture and qualities we were searching for. They were free. They were fighting for their country. First, we were influenced by their fighting spirit. The second thing that struck us was the movement's philosophy and its ideals. The third thing was the ongoing armed struggle. That was one reason why

we said we had to be involved now, too. Our existing life wasn't satisfactory for us. Young people who wanted to fight for their country had to break away from their existing life. That is a precondition for becoming a militant fighter for the Kurdish liberation movement. Anything else is just being alienated from your people. There were revolutionaries who sacrificed their whole lives to the revolution. That was moving. We saw that society accepted them and admired them. They had a certain authority, too. Everyone asked their advice. All these experiences produced a kind of love that we had to follow because it was something quite new. When someone said 'heval' then, everybody formed a queue. All the young people's eyes were on them. (Interview with Ronya, 27 March 2018)

It was the cadres' lifestyle that motivated Ronya to take an active part in the movement's struggle. Ronya saw Kurdish society as colonized and alienated from its own Kurdishness. In contrast, the PKK cadres symbolized a new philosophy, liberated from fear of losing the former life, and an invitation to a future that everyone dreamt of. In Ronya's account of her love for the cadres, she emphasized that it was a love and an impulse that she felt she 'must' pursue. Ronya's narrative can be interpreted to mean that her desire took shape and came to appear as a form of 'inner quality'. Ronya experienced this desire as a result of the opportunities given to her and as an inner quality that she 'must' follow. Ronya had to forge new connections in order to realize herself. Thus, she spoke of a desire that led her into the struggle and to her development into a new human being, even a co-creator of a new society.

Bese's desire to join the PKK was awakened by accounts of other people's engagement in the struggle. They legitimized her wish to join feel more right. Bese recounts:

There were some people from the local area and from school who were involved. That showed us that our decision was sensible, because everyone else was doing it too. It was a mysterious attraction, and perhaps a bit fanciful. You just threw yourself into it, although you didn't know much about it. These things attracted us. [. . .] I hadn't known anything other than my village. But there were many stories about the PKK that were passed on by word of mouth, such as that women and men fought side by side in the struggle. They lived and fought together. These stories, which are saga-like, attract you. That's why we took part. (Interview with Bese, 22 March 2018)

As mentioned earlier, Bese joined the movement as a thirteen-year-old. At that time, she had not yet travelled far from her village, situated in the mountains. The stories of women and men taking part in the movement and living and fighting together offered her a new world with new gender roles, different from what her village could offer. Bese added to her account about how she had to throw herself into the struggle that it quite simply felt right.

A consistent element in the women fighters' narratives of when and how they began to engage and actively participate is their mentioning of meetings with a movement representative who maybe even introduced them to a PKK-related book, film or demonstration. Certainly, other circumstances led them into political life and from there to the life of a woman fighter, but in all cases, there was some important meeting with a PKK representative. This was even the case for Arya, who is an ethnic Iranian, active today in the PKK from Iran. She admired her female Kurdish friends and beautiful Kurdish daughters-in-law, who always wore their national costume and never renounced their cultural values. It was this admiration that made her begin to love the Kurds and fight for them. (Interview with Arya, 25 March 2018)

2.3. The importance of gender for participation in the movement across generations

The individuals I interviewed have very different backgrounds. For example, they generally come from different social strata. Some come from rich, well-resourced families, while others are from very poor families with illiterate parents. Some were recruited to the movement in their villages with no knowledge of city life. Others came from big cities to which they moved when their villages were burnt down. Additionally, others came from Turkish and European cities, meaning that they grew up far away from the Kurdish districts. Geographically, the participants constitute a transnational diversity. Diversity also characterizes their educational backgrounds. Here, the spectrum is very broad: all the way from those who were illiterate when they started out in the movement to those who had a university education behind them. The women I interviewed are also diverse in terms of religious affiliation. There are one or two, such as Zin, who are still practising Muslims and observe the fast. Some are Alevis. Some, such as Berfin, describe themselves as atheists. Most, however, are non-practising Sunni Muslims. Some have been participants in the movement since childhood or adolescence. My aim with these general descriptions is to bring out the way the PKK has succeeded in mobilizing women from different social strata, religious affiliations, and cultural backgrounds and in creating a national cohesion among the Kurds. This recruitment of women succeeded for the PKK not only in Turkey, where the Kurdish district is the biggest, but also in other parts of the Kurdish districts in Syria, Iraq and Iran, and also in Europe, where the diaspora Kurds live.[16] One factor that seems to unite the women fighters across the mentioned diversities is gender. In the women fighters' narratives on why they decided to join the movement, it is mentioned repeatedly that the PKK's view of gender was a decisive factor.

2.3.1. The three generations

The women fighters interviewed are between twenty and forty-nine years old. It is therefore interesting to examine more closely how, over different generations of Kurdish women fighters, gender has been a contributory reason for their decision to take part in the militant struggle. To show this, I have divided the women fighters over the nearly forty-year history of the PKK into three generations. The first generation of women fighters were actively involved in founding the PKK and participating in the organization's struggle during its first years. There are not so many of them left in the movement, and I met only Roza from this generation. I have supplied my meeting with Roza with personal narratives from Sakine Cansız's book from 2014. The second generation are those women fighters who were admitted to the movement during the influx of women to the PKK in the early 1990s. Around half of the women I interviewed belong to this group. It is typically these women who now occupy positions of leadership, either in the PKK or in the women's own party, the PAJK. The third generation are the most recently arrived women participants in the PKK. They are the ones who joined the movement after the 2005 paradigm shift described in the 'Introduction'. Third-generation women make up the other half of the women fighters I interviewed.

My division of women fighters into three phases mirrors the three phases that the PKK under Marxist-Leninist inspiration envisaged for accomplishing the revolution.[17] The first phase is referred to as 'the propaganda phase'. It runs from 1978, when the PKK was founded, over 1984 when the PKK took up arms, to the early 1990s. During this period, the PKK worked at 'waking the Kurdish people' by influencing them and channelling their attention to the movement's national struggle. Women members were primarily responsible for spreading the movement's ideology and for building the movement's political and military bodies. After 1984, PKK women in general had to learn to defend themselves from possible attack by Turkish state representatives while going around from door to door. Women were rarely trained for combat actions. The second phase is referred to as 'the organization phase'. From the 1990s to 2000s, the PKK could benefit from widespread popular support, but the Kurdish people also had to be mobilized for an uprising against the Turkish state. Women members were once again primarily involved in mobilization. The third phase is referred to as 'the establishment phase'. It seeks to implement the final revolution and its values in Kurdish society while the war and the struggle against colonial rule continue. Once again, the women members are made responsible for the agitation for what truths to seek and the implementation of ideologies. While the PKK has given women responsibilities concerning mobilization and party ideologies, it will become apparent that for contemporary women the point is not just to be part of the PKK and wage war for Kurdish liberation but also to create and implement a new way of life for humanity in a new world.

2.3.2. *The first generation: Women in the PKK*

As mentioned earlier, I had only one meeting with a woman fighter belonging to the first generation. This meeting and my observations of her happened in Europe. What was notable about Roza, in addition to her great self-confidence, was that she was admired by the young generation of cadres. This admiration came not only from young women cadres but also from men cadres who had been in the movement for several years. Thus, it was my observation that all the young cadres craved Roza's attention and tried to find a pretext to speak to her. I also found that Roza had a sense of humour, but a big temper, too. The latter meant that she was quick to anger with everyone around her. When she got angry and bawled out one of the junior cadres, I found that they took her criticism to heart. Nobody was offended. They respected her and regarded any kind of dialogue with her as a learning situation worth reflecting on and as something that they could tell their comrades about with a certain degree of pride. With her, new members were given the opportunity to build a narrative to be recycled in other contexts in order to show that they were close to her and had not only been seen by her but also judged by her. It was thus my observation that the new members wanted to get close to respected older cadres like Roza to build networks and links of which they might be able to boast. Such a relation bestows legitimacy, similar to when someone in the movement quotes Öcalan. I found in the course of my fieldwork that much was said to invoke Öcalan in all possible contexts, from everyday life to philosophical thoughts. I therefore could not help doubting whether he had voiced opinions on all of it.

During my meeting with Roza, I saw her get angry with a young woman cadre because she had not stood up and offered her seat to an older woman who had nowhere to sit. In this situation, Roza said:

> In Europe, you mustn't forget our values of respecting them [the elderly]. You forget your morality like the young Europeans who sit on the train and the bus and forget to offer their seats to people with mobility difficulties. You should stand up and offer your seat to someone who is getting on in years. (Roza, fieldnote, 6 June 2017)

The young woman calmly stood up and showed no sign of being offended throughout the time the meeting went on, as if nothing had happened. In the movement, cadres take the view that if they criticize each other, it means that they are interested in each other and love each other. Criticism from comrades is regarded as beneficial for a person's development and ability to improve himself or herself. Young PKK members see criticism, especially from the leadership, as a matter of being valued and assisted in becoming a better member. Criticism from the first generation of comrades or from cadres who have been in the movement for a long time is therefore also perceived as a matter of caring. Young generations of women fighters state that they are unafraid of making mistakes or exposing themselves when they are with them. On the contrary, they feel safe with them, and they idolize their patience, simple life, love of the nation and way of life. Finally, it should be mentioned that Roza's criticism of young Westerners relates to a typical ethnic strategy in which she highlights ordinary consideration as something peculiarly ethnic. The idea of this is that on the one hand, the strategy helps young Kurds, wherever they live, to feel special, while on the other hand the strategy helps prevent their assimilation.

Aside from the meeting with Roza, my knowledge of the first generation of PKK women is primarily based on Sakine Cansız's book (2014a), written as an autobiography. It includes narratives of the first generation of women fighters. Sakine Cansız is one of two women who were involved in the founding of the PKK. In the book, she writes that the party did not initially have the women question on the agenda. Despite sloganizing catchphrases such as 'Women must also take part in the national struggle' or 'Women will become free through the liberation struggle', the women question was not on the movement's agenda.[18] Neither men nor women were ready to talk about the need for a separate agenda or the establishment of women units. Nor were books being written about women to inspire them.

In 1977, Sakine Cansız wrote a letter to the party entitled 'Women's place and importance in the national struggle', describing the history surrounding the Vietnam War and the establishment of women units in Bulgaria. When she gave the article to a woman comrade, Kesire Yıldırım, and proposed that Kesire should take it up at the founding general assembly, Kesire's response was that it was too early to form women's units and focus on the women question. Consequently, Sakine Cansız writes that she had many conflicts with the few women in the party at that time, as well as with her men comrades. Here, her focus was on the question of how she could get the women question included in the party program. She was, by her own account, a 'searching soul' who longed for a slightly more specific agenda for women. Her first battles were with the men comrades who, in Cansız's opinion, operated with patriarchal expectations of women comrades and assumed, for example, that the women should take care of cooking and cleaning.[19] Nor were the men comrades keen on women joining in actions out in the field, because they had no faith in women's aptitude for this.[20]

From Sakine Cansız's book, my conversation with Roza and my interview with Mordem, the oldest man informant (over sixty years of age), it looks as though gender did not play a crucial role in women's participation in the PKK in the initial period of the movement. Although some of them subscribed to some feminist ideals and wanted better conditions for women, the motivation for their participation seems generally to have been the same as that of their men comrades, that is, to be part of the national struggle and thereby contribute to the liberation of Kurdistan. During the first phase, women's potential was deployed as a secondary force, responsible for logistical work and for conveying the movement's ideology to the people while concurrently facing challenges with their men comrades. Women made up a significant part of the PKK. According to Mordem, women accounted for approximately one-sixth of all members when the movement established its first base in the Beqaa Valley in 1982. Only a handful of them are still alive, while most others have died in the struggle. A few chose to leave the movement (Interview with Mordem, 19 January 2018).

2.3.3. *The second generation: From being ordinary members to becoming women fighters*

The concept of 'woman fighter' was first adopted by the second generation of women in the PKK. These women were the first to have the opportunity to establish themselves actively in the mountains. According to Ronya, who is the supreme leader of the women's party, the PAJK, this could not have happened without the contribution of the first generation of PKK women. The first generation acted as a model for the second, thus influencing the second-generation women's decisions to join the movement. Ronya recounted:

> In that period, back in 1986–9, neither the movement nor the Leader [Öcalan] had an analytical perspective on women. But there were women who were active in the revolution from the start, as personalities, as politicians. There was a kind of female culture and ideal that created a good influence [. . .] So we said that we would also like to take part, because we wanted to be just like them. We thought about whether we could be as capable as them, because we looked up to them as our idols. We'd never known anything like it in our society. We were also searching, and we wanted to be part of the struggle and engage in politics as women. As a Kurdish woman. But there was no clear women's consciousness. But we had the ideal that we had to strengthen our will as Kurdish women, because only with a strong will could we gain the recognition of others. That was also the point. It was also what had affected society most, that there were women in the PKK. Taking the woman out of patriarchal society's constrained, feudal framework, where the oppression of women and violence against women have always been commonplace products of a masculinity mentality, and bringing her up to that level both militarily and politically, was a revolution in itself. We saw it as revolution in itself. It was important to us. That is why we joined. (Interview with Ronya, 27 March 2018)

Ronya described how women's presence in the PKK had affected her. It was within the PKK that space was first made for women to become part of society and hence be perceived by everyone as someone valuable. For women to be able to engage in politics and be part of a revolution was unheard of until then. As the image of women in the PKK perfectly matched Ronya's desire to experience something new, she realized that she was ready to embrace PKK's alternative understandings and be formed by them. Ronya went on:

> The concept of 'Kurds' didn't exist in books. In history. In geography. In politics. That is, we didn't exist at all. We had no identity. We existed as a society, but we had no name. There was a geography, but with no status. There was a body, but with no soul. With no spirit. Of course, that generated a great anger, which became the main driving force of life. That is, young Kurds realized that they had no rights or status. That brought about a quest for another life outside this captivity. (Interview with Ronya, 27 March 2018)

In Ronya's two quotations, the PKK offered her a double alternative to her subaltern identity to become both a liberated Kurd and woman. The desire to attain this double freedom had a big effect on her. Her frustrating experiences within patriarchal society as a Kurd and as a woman prompted her to the realization that she deserved something better than an ordinary life. Her narrative calls attention to the fact that she paints a picture of her development as a processual journey: from nothingness to anger, from anger to formation and from formation to the nomadic journey.

The certainty that there were women in the PKK and that they were even waging war also came as a surprise to Helin. This emerged when she described the first time she had met women guerrillas:

> It was in the late 1980s that I met the first women guerrillas. While they were telling us about their struggle, I also found the answers to my own search. I loved them. My curiosity overcame me. Listening to their stories of the prison uprising and the PKK cadres' resistance to the Turkish state had a big effect on me. As women, we'd never heard or read about women putting up resistance before. I was therefore fascinated by the women in the PKK who were fighting for their country and identity. When I started to take an interest in them, they gave me one of their little books, about the prison uprising in Amed [a Kurdish city in Turkey]. It affected me. It brought up the questions of who we were, what place we had in society, etc. A change had been set off. There was one named Berivan, who was Êzidî originally. She returned to the mountains in 1988 and became a martyr in 1989. That had a big effect on me. She was a very intellectual, very aware comrade. I said to the other comrades that comrades like Berivan shouldn't fall as martyrs. They replied that such comrades' weapons should not lie idle. That reply had a big effect on me. (Interview with Helin, 24 March 2018)

What is interesting about Helin's narrative is that similar to the other women's narratives, she indicated that she was already on her own inner quest before she met the PKK women. This meant that she was already dreaming of another world. She already had a desire for something other than what she had or was used to experiencing in her surroundings. In the encounter with the women from the PKK, she saw that it was possible for Kurdish women to break with the existing norms and engage in armed resistance. The encounter with them thus became a milestone for her. From that moment, a change in her was set off in the direction of her enrolment in the movement and her becoming as a woman fighter. She subsequently travelled to the Beqaa Valley, where the PKK had its main base under Öcalan's leadership. It was through Öcalan's narratives and analyses that she first realized how she had been oppressed for years as a woman and a Kurd. It was a great surprise for her that Öcalan valued her as a woman and thus offered an alternative assessment of her gender. Like the other women participants, she also relates that it was through Öcalan that she first learnt what it meant to be a woman and that being a woman is much more than taking care of domestic chores and being a mother. She thereby realized that it would be more meaningful for her to fight for an entire nation than merely to cook and look after a single family. This experience of having first learnt what it means to be a woman when she met Öcalan is one that Afrin also shared in her interview with me. Afrin spent three months in the Beqaa Valley with Öcalan. Until then, she had taken part in the movement without ascribing much significance to it as regards how it would affect her conception of being a woman, nor had she, before joining the PKK, been concerned with topics such as equality between men and women or women's emancipation. She therefore had no specific expectations of the revolution as a woman, until she met Öcalan (Interview with Afrin, 13 December 2017).

According to the women fighters' narratives and Öcalan's own analysis, the point is to redefine the concept 'woman' and get the women fighters to reflect afresh on the meaning of being a woman. Öcalan therefore invokes positive visions of being a woman in contradistinction from patriarchal concepts of 'woman', also in Kurdish society, which is a matter of establishing an 'imagined elsewhere'[21] that allows the subject to redefine itself.

Dersim chose to leave Europe to join the movement early in 1990 and is now one of the leading figures in the women's party, the PAJK. She recounted that the first and second generations' reasons for taking part in the PKK were very similar, although the second generation had some ideas as to how women's emancipation could be achieved. For both generations, the main objective was to decolonize Kurdistan:

> The first and second generations' participation was very similar. It was about liberating the nation. But the second generation also had its inner searchings. Especially about gender roles. But they weren't deep or well analysed or theorized. Our idea was that we should first go up into the mountains and fight the enemy and thereby liberate the country. We didn't really have a gender consciousness, a class consciousness or a revolutionary consciousness. Our participation was a result of the established national consciousness. But after our participation, we could see that things were different. We had to read. We had to take part in meetings. We had to give feedback. You had to have instruction. You had to give self-criticism. You had to stand up and give criticism to the leadership. You had to become a leader. You had to train new participants. As a leader, you had to act the part. Sometimes, we make jokes about it. We say: 'If we'd known it was so demanding we wouldn't have joined' [laughs] [. . .] Within just three to five days, we were going to liberate Kurdistan. At the same time, most of us thought we wouldn't live more than two months, because we said we've joined to become martyrs, but we'll also kill some of the enemy. Most of us thought like that. We didn't know we would live so long and face so many challenges. (Interview with Dersim, 27 March 2018)

According to Dersim, most of the first-generation women fighters were students when they joined the movement. They were therefore better equipped than the second generation to familiarize themselves with and relate to the movement's ideology. The second generation looked up to the first for the same reason. The second generation were from the period when the PKK was initiating its armed struggle against the Turkish state and gaining control of the Kurdish districts in the space of a few years. This brought major upheavals in Kurdish society and expectations of a better future for the Kurds. As members of the second generation, they felt that the revolution was right on the cusp of success and just wanted to be part of it. This sort of idealization, but also simplification, of the guerrilla life or the guerrilla struggle is also evident in Arzu Demir's interview from 2014 with woman fighter Dilan Nurhak. Nurhak says that her generation was driven by a kind of 'romantic guerrilla dream' prior to choosing to go to the mountains. They knew little of the challenges of living and fighting in the mountains; they just wanted to be guerrillas, while they were reading about people such as Che Guevara.[22]

Like Nurhak, the women fighters from the second generation whom I interviewed said that for them, being a guerrilla meant following their thirst for adventure. To them, a guerrilla was someone who went to the mountains and did not come back. They did not define their decision to take part in the movement as a considered, conscious choice aware of the challenges that go with a long struggle. At the same time, most of the second generation were from villages on the outskirts of Kurdish and Turkish cities, and they were mainly unskilled young people without qualifications. Through my observations and my knowledge of the movement, I found that this generational difference was still a source of tension between new participants with a student background and those without. In this clash, they accuse each other of not being a 'good cadre' who lives up to the movement's expectations of the individual member. For example, those without a student background (e.g. Dersim, Bese, Bermal, Helin, Afrin) were accused of being non-ideological, while, conversely, those with higher education (e.g. Zin, Cane, Gulesor, Zeri, Berivan) behind them were accused of only being theoretical, claiming activity only in words and thoughts about how the revolution is to be carried out. Should it come to actual acts of war with more work and effort required, the educated would hold back.[23]

Accounts by the second-generation women of their participation regarding their preparedness for the struggle were very much about whether, as women, they were capable of dealing with the possible challenges – that is, whether their bodies could cope with life in the mountains or whether their will was strong enough to withstand the consequences of taking part in armed combat. It was therefore more urgent for them to strengthen their will and their bodies than merely to address gender issues while participating in the struggle. This point about the strengthening of the will and the body will be elaborated in Chapter 5 where women's combat experiences will be analysed.

2.3.4. *The third generation: From women fighters to women cadres implementing new ideals*

The third generation of women fighters joined the movement after the paradigm shift of 2005 that aims at democratic confederalism as the ideology for state organization. In my interviews with women fighters of the third generation, gender issues stood out as an important factor for their enrolment. In this light, they conceived of themselves as political actors assuming new, gendered positions in order to create better opportunities for women. Zin emphasizes:

The explanation for men's joining the PKK is different from ours [women's]. I would argue that men don't say 'I need liberation, I must be liberated. I must find spirituality.' There aren't many of them taking part in the struggle for that reason. It's more because 'I must fight, I must liberate Kurdistan, I must kill the enemy.' But for women it's more about creating yourself. Reinventing yourself as a woman. [The motivation for] recreating a new being is stronger in women. [. . .] This is common to all women – to be a creator. For men, it's about eliminating the enemy, taking revenge for martyrs and Kurdistan. But when a woman is already born a slave and then has a life based on oppression, the woman sees the PKK as a place where she can have her own voice. (Interview with Zin, 23 March 2018)

In this quotation, Zin explains that women typically partake in the struggle to recreate themselves much in line with an association, typical in the PKK, of women being associated with creation, that is, their reproductive capacity. All interviewees, men and women alike, said that this capacity was the reason for women being more emotional than men by nature. Here, the PKK has succeeded in convincing their members, both men and women, of women's reproductive capacity or emotionality, which has been used throughout history by patriarchal society against women as an explanation for their weak, irrational character. Yet, the PKK reinterprets it in an essentializing way as women's strength, as a kind of sovereignty that can be used to strengthen women's self-confidence and inspire them to cultivate a positive gender difference. The PKK even promotes the idea that women are better than men at offering resistance to colonial society. Paradoxically, the insistence on women reproductive capacity and emotionality comes at the cost of sexual denunciation because this essentialized power in women has to be deployed in political and militant service within the PKK. I shall return to the ideal of de-sexualized bodies in Section 3.4.

Zin's generalizing claims about motivations among her men comrades for membership are confirmed by the men fighters whom I interviewed. They said that gender had not played a part in their decision to take part in the struggle. Here, the honour ideology mentioned earlier may play a role. It ascribes to men the responsibility for standing guard over the country and its people. To honour that responsibility, they have chosen to join the struggle to liberate Kurdistan from enemy oppression and thereby achieve freedom. However, to say that this has nothing to do with gender is to miss the point. Certainly, they are not motivated by women's liberation, but both the interviewed men fighters and Zin overlook how local gender ideals for men play an important role for their enrolment. Everyone seems to associate gender with women and even monopolize it as a motivational cause, even though it seems relevant for the enrolment of both men and women. What is worth noticing, however, in Zin's remarks is that for men, the objective of ethnic liberation is well defined, while for women, the objectives are still in a process of being defined and thus involves a lot of searching.

Another point, addressed by Zin several times, was that the third generation's participation in the struggle was different in motivation not only from the men's but also from the first and second generations of women. The third generation's motives were mainly about recreating themselves as women. For example, Berivan, the most recently arrived and the youngest woman fighter I interviewed, said that she became a woman before she became a patriot. She understood this as being the other way round for the earlier generations of PKK women. Berivan recounted that the main challenge she faced in civil society was to find herself. Her reason for joining the PKK was not that she had no opportunities for self-realization in her life, such as practising leisure activities, going to school, seeing friends and pursuing her interests. She did have these opportunities, but, whatever she tried doing, she found that it did not feel right. It was as if something was always missing in her life. Berivan indicated that her decision to join the PKK was not a choice of desperation, nor was it about seeking hope (as Bese mentioned earlier). On the contrary, it was a conscious choice, in that she expected something else of life and was at the same time aware that she could realize herself afresh in the PKK (Interview with Berivan, 21 March 2018). Berivan's exposition conflicts with Yuval-Davis's assertion, cited in the 'Introduction', that women's engagement in political and militant struggle takes place in an ill-considered and/or random way.[24] Jocelyn Viterna's study (2013) on women fighters in El Salvador supports my claim as Viterna also shows that women's decision to participate in the war was not made at a particular moment; yet, it was a series of small decisions, to engage in small tasks, which eventually led to a final, conscious decision.[25] In line with my point mentioned earlier, Viterna argues that the movement *Frente Farabundo Martí para la Liberación Nacional* (FMLN) did not force the women fighters to join, but the situation convinced them. The women fighters in the FMLN draw on their personal narratives when defining their participation: 'Each of my respondents had a story to tell about how the state military killed or tortured someone in their family or their community, and forensic evidence has now confirmed many of the most horrific massacres of civilians – including hundreds of children – on Salvadoran soil'.[26]

Third-generation women fighters were all born after 1984, when the PKK took up arms. Once they reached maturity, discussions no longer pertained to whether or not to support the PKK in the national struggle. Rather, discussions concentrated on how to implement what ideals, also for gender. Gulesor, a third-generation woman fighter, said that her primary motive for going to the mountains was not that she was unhappy at being oppressed as a Kurd, but rather that she was dreaming of another world and seeking a new way of life:

> There were women in my family who studied at university or trained as lawyers and doctors, but they didn't inspire me. I never dreamt of becoming like them. Never! I knew what I didn't want to be, but I couldn't decide what sort of woman I did want to be. A study I carried out at secondary school on women was actually about their experiences of being Kurds. They were women living in exile, and their narratives contributed to my inner searchings, where I told myself that I didn't want to be like them. But what sort of woman should I be, then? That was probably why I did it [joined the PKK]. It wasn't a very conscious act. More

emotionally driven. [. . .] Not so much for Kurdistan. It was more about my own
quest. I know that Kurdistan existed and that a war was going on there. And that
the war had to be stopped. [. . .] But I hadn't really experienced oppression as a
Kurd. We could practise our Kurdishness in the village. We lived in Turkey, but
we only spoke Kurdish when they [Turks] came to our village. We were better
off, and we were richer than the Turks. (Interview with Gulesor, 25 March 2018)

In this extract, Gulesor spoke of her inner searchings in which she felt the need to
position herself in a different way than how the women in her family had done.
She thereby indicated that it all started with her resistance to conformity with
familiar ways of living. Here, she distanced herself from two women types. The
first was the type of woman who chose to lead a petit-bourgeois life in Turkey,
get an education and strive for a career. The second type were the village women
(including her own mother) on whom she had once carried out a study for a
secondary school assignment. Both seemed unattractive, yet helped to influence
Gulesor, channelling her towards the PKK, where she could develop into the
sort of woman she wanted to be. According to her self-narrative, Gulesor first
positioned herself against educated career women and then against Kurdish village
women like her mother, and she knew that these comparisons were part of her
inner searchings with regard to her future. In other words, Gulesor, like many of
the other interviewees, presents her motivation as a course of events constructed,
deconstructed and reconstructed in her relations with the world around her. To
use Gergen's understanding of subject formation, they suggested that their current
identity and choices did not arise at random, but rather resulted from a series of
joined, interlinked experiences.[27]

This progressive narrative or positioning adopted by the interviewees signalled
that they stood by their decision to take part in the PKK. It was expressed as a
conscious choice understood to imply new self-realization possibilities, rather
than a random choice. Another instance of conscious choice was that Gulesor
concluded her account by saying that she had no direct experience of oppression
in Kurdistan. She had grown up in Turkey, where she had had a better economic
standard of living than the Turks. This made it important for Gulesor to emphasize
that it was not the sociocultural, political and economic conditions in the colonial
context that had led her to the PKK, but rather her quest for the 'sort of woman'
she should be. Similar points were made by Zin and Zelal:

It was about creating yourself. [. . .] In that context, the PKK was the best place
to be to recreate yourself. I thought it could happen in the PKK. That is why I
joined the PKK. (Interview with Zin, 23 March 2018)

My inner searchings became deeper. At the same time, I was very much affected
by the Leader's [Öcalan's] analysis arguing that Kurdistan could not be liberated
without women being liberated first. Nowadays we say that societies cannot be
liberated until women are liberated. The expression has become universal. But in
the beginning I thought about why there was so much focus on women. In time,
from my observations of my network, my own family and my mother, I realized

that the power holders will always hit women first. Women! That affected my own quest, too. Why women? In time, I also experienced the strength of women's will. (Interview with Zelal, 17 September 2017)

From Zin and Zelal's extract and the narratives of other interviewees, it seems that the women fighters perceived a connection between women's 'inner quest', contradictions in their day-to-day lives, seen from a gender perspective, and the movement's woman-oriented ideology. Further to this, it is important to mention that the PKK's outward face gradually became more and more inclusive of women. As technological developments made it easy to communicate messages through the social media, the PKK spread messages about the national struggle to all Kurds, wherever they lived in the world. The messages featured accounts of women martyrs, heroic stories of women fighting against the Turkish state and IS, and also stories about the contribution of their Kurdish mothers, such as taking part in demonstrations while wearing national dresses or taking part in hunger strikes. With such accounts, the PKK signals that the movement values women's contributions. Kurdish slogans such as 'Jin Jiyan Azadî' (Woman, Life, Freedom) also contribute to inviting women to join the struggle by emphasizing that the national struggle cannot be won without the participation of women. In other words, it is being signalled that not only do women need the movement in order to gain their own emancipation, but the movement's national struggle cannot bring about the revolution unless women are an active part of it. According to this strategic appeal, it seems that the PKK has made a virtue out of its necessity for women's engagement in the national struggle. Zelal's comment that the power holders will always hit 'women' first and that the PKK would 'save' her must be understood in this light. The movement is aware that the female sex has become a battlefield and that whoever has women on their side will achieve victory.[28]

This strategy on the part of the movement, creating a reciprocal relationship between the liberation of the country and that of women, also found expression in Zelal's narrative. She said that their women's struggle had now also become universal, because Kurdish women wanted not only to take care of the revolution in Kurdistan but also to inspire other oppressed women in the world to resist. By this, she was referring to the fact that Kurdish women fighters as a phenomenon had become world famous – especially after women fighters' role in the uprising against IS in the Kurdish city of Kobane in Rojava/Syria back in 2014–15. During fieldwork, I found that PKK women fighters were very proud that their struggle and ideology had inspired the women fighters of the YPJ in Rojava/Syria to halt IS's advance in the region. They emphasized that the revolution in Rojava/Syria was deservedly called the 'women's revolution', as it was mainly the women fighters' contribution that had prevented IS from gaining control of the region. In Chapter 6, I shall elaborate on the history of the battles in Rojava and the story of IS's expulsion, known as the women's revolution.

In their interviews with me, the women described themselves as revolutionaries searching for the truth. To them, their participation in the struggle was about finding answers to the question: 'How does one live?' Referencing Öcalan, who maintains that the PKK's struggle must define not only how the revolution should be fought but also what kind of life the free, new human should live after the revolution,[29] the women fighters indicated that their participation in the PKK was first and foremost about creating a new human. This new human was to liberate himself or herself from all forms of oppression and immoral acts, including capitalist modernity's consumer mentality and egoistic lifestyle. Accordingly, women must purge themselves of all historical influences to which they are subject by going to the mountains and returning to their original state, thus attaining 'ultimate truth' (Interview with Delal, 15 June 2017). The interviewed women fighters explained the attainment of truth as identical to a total freedom from all forms of oppression – ultimately, perfection. In our conversations, the third generation of PKK women expressed the view that the PKK is creating good conditions for this transformation towards the perfect human. Zelal said:

> Taking part in the struggle has made it possible to reflect deeply on the ways and means of attaining the way of life we want to create. We are created from our experiences and are still searching in order to attain the truth. That is, to return to an original state. We are people who continue to search for the truth. (Interview with Zelal, 17 September 2017)

Zelal told how she felt that the critical, resilient way of life, which demanded a kind of cleansing, could be achieved by joining the PKK. Here, the PKK has clearly been successful in presenting an ethos including ideals such as 'authenticity', 'ultimate truth' and the 'perfect human', arguing for its 'salvific' function for creating stability in communal as well as individual lives. It helps both to stimulate enrolment in the movement and to make members stay in. One should not overlook how this ethos rests on a questionable essentialization of 'the truth' and a retrievable 'original state' of every human.

The interviewees related that the road to attaining ultimate truth began with their breaking away completely from the system, used as a synonym for capitalist civil society. For example, Zin said that it would be impossible for her to recreate herself with a view to becoming a new human unless she opted out of the system (Interview with Zin, 23 March 2018). This need for a complete break with the capitalist civil society is entangled with the perception, which many of the women fighters had, that life in the mountains would enable them to identify with the new human from day one. Cane explained it as follows:

> As the legal level was full of contradictions and had limited opportunities for action, it occurred to me that I couldn't realize myself at the legal level. So it made more sense to go to the mountains. [. . .] It was also a reaction and an attitude to practice radical resistance, as we saw that the legal level couldn't be the answer to our inner searchings. That is why I took part. (Interview with Cane, 25 March 2018)

Cane said that joining the movement was about dedicating oneself maximally and radically to the struggle so as to feel that one was making a sufficient contribution to the struggle and to find answers to one's 'inner searchings'. For Cane as well as many of the other interviewees, her inner searchings for a more meaningful life with greater opportunities for self-realization coincided with the national struggle as a motivational cause.

2.3.5. *The generational conflict and differences between women fighters*

The three preceding sections have shown the role played by gender throughout the history of the PKK in women fighters' decision to join the party. This section will focus briefly on how the older generations of women fighters in the PKK see those who have arrived recently. I consider this important to understanding what the first women – those who helped create and implement the phenomenon of Kurdish women fighters in the mountains – make of the way the new generation has carried on the baton for them.

Dersim of the second generation of PKK women fighters said that the new members are less ideological, weaker and hence not robust. She said that the motives for her own participation were very simple. She just wanted to be part of liberating Kurdistan, but the new generations came with all sorts of different reasons. She thought the newcomers seemed inauthentic, superficial and more preoccupied with their personal needs and challenges than focused on the national struggle. She also emphasized that the challenges with the new generation were due to their having been more subject to assimilation and the consequences of capitalist modernity. Dersim and her generation often came straight from their villages to the mountains and were therefore less subject to assimilation (Interview with Dersim, 27 March 2018). This point was also highlighted by Cane, who maintained that because women fighters of the third generation are mainly from major cities, not from the Kurdish districts, they have been the generation most subject to assimilation. As children, the women fighters of the third generation had experience being forced away from their villages because the Turkish state did not want the villages to act as supply bases for the PKK. Consequently, they are not good at speaking Kurdish, and they are unfamiliar with traditional Kurdish norms and values. Cane claimed: 'They are petit-bourgeois and they have grown up with liberal values' (Interview with Cane, 25 March 2018).

The older women fighters felt that the newly arrived women fighters had not experienced the same challenges as they had and that they took many things for granted without respect and without appreciation. Arya said:

> It seems to them [the new arrivals] as though they have left home and gone to their aunt's. That's how easy it is for them. For me, it was like coming to another world. It was a shock for me. Everything was new and different. I wept, fell, felt pain, went hungry, was afraid, was violated, was treated unfairly and treated others unfairly, too. We went through a lot. It's all so easy for the new ones now. (Interview with Arya, 25 March 2018)

Arya added that she had been away from the mountains and the military campaign for about five years, and during that time she had served in a city. When she returned to the mountains, she did not recognize her surroundings, as the new members were very different from herself. They were not as skilled in military operations, causing the movement to suffer many losses. Above all, they were non-ideological and did not spend time on their personal development aimed at becoming strong-willed. Instead, they merely tried to emulate previous martyrs. According to Arya, the new members were also less moral and had been too much under the influence of the system, that is, the state and liberal values. She described them as 'digital', in that their approach to life and the norms they were fighting for were superficial, while in combat they chose to focus mainly on technology, that is, the use of weapons or weapon-handling skills. They therefore had difficulty adjusting to the challenges of life in the mountains, which required them to work more on themselves and on adapting to nature than on the use of weapons. Like Arya, Bese went on to say that the first generations of women fighters had more goodwill and were more reliable than the new generations. However, Bese also said that the new generations fought bravely and were willing to sacrifice themselves in the struggle as *fedai* when necessary. But she also underlined that the point was not to die bravely in battle but to represent a life based on the movement's ideological values, which symbolized liberty and were therefore attractive to everybody (Interview with Bese, 22 March 2018). Ronya was not quite as pessimistic as Bese. She said that she saw challenges with the new arrivals but that it was nothing they could not overcome:

New participants also have a transparent side, although they are also very influenced by modernity. By transparency I mean that they are clever, smart, dynamic, courageous and they go to war like *fedai*. They aren't afraid to go to war. But their lifestyle, their mentality development, their personal character, discipline and strength of will are a challenge for us. That's because they are products of modernity. They are individual-focused, not collectivist. They also have difficulty living up to our expectations and integrating with us. They have difficulty leading a disciplined life based on the culture of the revolution. But it's a phase of the struggle. We are bound to overcome the challenge with more focus on ideological instruction. (Interview with Ronya, 27 March 2018)

Ronya stated that society had changed since she enrolled in the movement and that it was therefore natural that the new generations were different from her own. At the same time, she also indicated that the existing power mechanisms in the movement were challenged when it came to absorbing the new participants. Here, she pointed out that the movement must perforce reform its instruction and its recruitment procedure in order to iron out the unwanted aspects of the new participants and create a more homogeneous, standardized identity in all of them.

The first-generation women fighters were certainly proud of the new generations of women fighters who were following in their footsteps and trying to live up to their ideological standards and combat prowess. But it was also clear that the first generations went in for a certain degree of nostalgic self-narrative. I consider that their criticism was affected by developments in Rojava and the fight against IS, which led to more young people choosing to join the PKK, not all of them necessarily ideologically prepared before setting out. For this reason, the first generations of women fighters have in a way taken out the patent on the phenomenon of 'woman fighter' or 'Kurdish woman of the uprising', and they believe that these concepts demand a clear ideological standpoint.

Summary

The chapter demonstrates how a significant number of the interviewed women fighters experienced the effects of colonization as they moved away from home, which made them more aware of their Kurdish identity. Those who went to the cities for university education met with fellow Kurds of their own age and with shared interests. The PKK's youth organization (YCK) appears to offer women a strong political environment in which young people can cultivate their identity and forge new links leading towards new understandings of identity. Yet, moving away from the Kurdish districts entails feelings of longing, which establishes an emotional reminder of their special attachment to Kurdish nature and culture and of Turkish districts being a foreign country. In the YCK, young Kurdish women immerse themselves in both the PKK's ideology and Kurdish culture, and on that basis they quite gradually reject liberal values and the petit-bourgeois life of both Turkish and Kurdish civil society. The Kurdish liberation struggle and the guerrillas' stories of heroes and heroines also begin to loom larger in their day-to-day life, producing the possibility of replacing their negative subaltern identities as both Kurds and women with the prospect of being able to think of their double identity as Kurds and women in a positive way through the PKK. The prospects of an alternative life lead to identifications with guerrillas and martyrs in their 'beautiful' gaberdine outfits, with their 'strong' weapons and their 'simple life' in the mountains.

It is worth noticing that many of the women fighters objected to patriarchal patterns in their families. At the same time, almost all of the interviewed women fighters have family and friends who have been or are still active in the movement. One would expect these relatives and friends to have had a return influence, with their gender ideals, on Kurdish civilian life. Here, though, it seems that it is primarily the values of the anti-colonial struggle that have influenced Kurdish civil society and not yet its gender norms.

With regard to differences between three generations of women fighters, I was able to establish that women like men came into the struggle during the early 'propaganda' phase to contribute to the national struggle without any notably strong gender awareness. In hindsight, these women noted how the PKK exploited their femininity in accordance with patriarchal expectations, reserving non-combatant tasks for them. Only few women engaged in armed combat. During the 'organization phase', women members of the PKK specifically wanted to be women fighters and went to the mountains, with Öcalan's backing, in a conscious choice of not living like traditional Kurdish women. Despite Öcalan's moral and ideological support, and despite their effort in the war to decolonize 'Kurdistan', this second generation of women fighters had an internal struggle with the men in the movement to achieve equal opportunities of representation and action in combat. As part of this internal struggle, they engaged in strengthening their will and their bodies rather than merely engaging in gender-aware participation. The third generation of contemporary women fighters are the most gender-aware women in the PKK. They wish to construct a strong, robust woman fighter personality while being curious about new understandings and perspectives. Women of this third generation have a tendency to describe themselves as women first and as Kurds second. They describe themselves as political actors assuming new gender positions in the PKK and Kurdish society in order to make both themselves and the men completely free of all forms of oppression and complicity in oppression. In hindsight, they themselves point out that as 'children of the revolution', they already had a strong ethnic and political consciousness from infancy and before they joined the PKK. The chapter therefore shows that the women fighters' battle against a subaltern identity has been in constant flux and carried out on multiple fronts.

Chapter 3

RECONSTRUCTING GENDER, LOVE AND SEXUALITY
IN THE CONTEXT OF MOUNTAINS

This chapter describes the PKK's recruitment processes and life in the training camps with the purpose of analysing if and how materiality and physical experiences have an effect on the formation of gender and other identificatory phenomena such as love and sexuality among the movement's members.

3.1. The break with civil society

The PKK designates the mountain territories, conquered from the Turkish military, as 'the free territory'. The majority of party members, approximately 10,000 men and women, live in camps within it. In Kurdish society, the young people's act of choosing to leave home and go to the free territory is referred to as a 'break'. The break marks the act of 'moving up to a higher level', concretized as the high and 'sacred' Kurdish mountains where young people become guerrillas and wage war against the Turkish military.

Almost all the women I interviewed described the break as the beginning of their new life and even spoke of it as a 'new birthday'. The break enables young people to lay out and pursue a journey of no return. After the break, a return to their old lives would be highly unlikely. First, the Turkish authorities would prosecute them. Second, the members would hardly think about returning due to PKK's efficient promotion of a free and independent life in the free territory as the only viable option. As already mentioned, the women I interviewed spoke with great enthusiasm of being positively influenced in their younger days by their first meeting with the guerrillas in their local area. The guerrillas' military equipment, their way of talking about their struggle, their self-confidence, attitude and clothing all strongly influenced the young women's decision to join the movement. This was apparent, for example, when Berivan described her first meeting with the guerrillas and the dreams she had afterwards about her future: 'I was always daydreaming about myself wearing gabardine'[1] (Interview with Berivan, 21 March 2018).

With regard to setting out on the journey, the women fighters said that clothes and other material goods played a substantial part in enabling them to break with civil society and become guerrillas instead of staying in civil society and taking part in the legal struggle. One explanation they gave for this was that in the 'lowlands' they never felt well enough kitted out to take active part in confrontations with the Turkish security services. The guerrillas' military equipment indicated effective armament. They felt that they were more vulnerable to persecution by Turkish security and to torture, detention and killing by 'persons unknown' when they lacked the sort of materiality that they associated with resilience. The fear of being the victim of sexual offences such as rape – which many of them had heard of as taking place on a large scale in Turkish prisons – loomed large in the women's minds. In addition, they did not want to waste their youth in jail and thereby risk being unable to play an active part in the struggle. It therefore seems that young people's choice of going to the mountains is also an active step to protect themselves against colonial threats.

3.2. *Abolishing the nature/culture distinction*

Those who choose to be recruited to the PKK's armed struggle are referred to as 'cadres' of the party. According to my escort, Zagros, becoming a PKK cadre entails that one is considered a loyal party member and already devoted to the struggle for revolution. In other words, one must previously have been active in the party and have shown commitment in fighting for the PKK's ideals. If so, one must pass a short training and education programme laid on for cadre candidates. Candidates must be prepared to take on a mission at any time whatsoever the party considers necessary.

According to several of the cadres I interviewed, it is a big step for a young person to break with civil society and get used to life in the 'free territory', which includes, in particular, having to 'integrate' oneself into the mountains and nature. Here, integration means becoming part of nature and feeling embraced by nature, with nature taking care of you and protecting you in a process that at the same time requires cadres to show respect for nature. The women fighters interviewed said that they already felt drawn to and connected to the mountains prior to the break. Moreover, Zagros said that the guerrillas cannot live in the mountains if the mountains do not accept them and feel them. In this account, nature and the mountains are spoken of as living beings to whom one must conform and form vitally important relationships. Berivan said:

> I've always wanted to come to the mountains [...] As a woman, I was very insistent to the party that my wish had to be met. As a woman, I 'had' to experience the mountain. The Leader [Öcalan] says that women can stay in the mountains, even after the revolution. Crossing the border and coming to the mountains was very different [. . .] I fought hard to come here. I finally succeeded the fourth time [. . .] The mountains were magic! I always dreamt of the mountains when I was in prison. Mountain! Mountain! Mountain! Missed for two and a half years. I'm very happy here. (Interview with Berivan, 21 March 2018)

According to Berivan, the mountains are a place where women can always be sure of feeling free. This understanding of the mountains and their importance to the women implies that the mountains are not to be regarded as a temporary home for the women but as a long-term one that can ensure their independence, protection and freedom not only in the present but also in the future. The idea of the mountains as a long-term home able to provide the women with an independent, protected and free life is also a guiding component of the PKK's strategy development regarding their way of waging guerrilla war. Until the 1990s, the PKK used to withdraw its guerrillas from the Turkish territory to its main base in Iraq when winter came. They did this to protect themselves from the winter cold and to avoid being killed by the Turkish military. In winter, it is harder for the guerrillas to obtain food and lodging. The long, cold and very snowy winter in the Kurdish areas of Turkey restricts the guerrillas' mobility, making them vulnerable to Turkish military attacks. According to Zagros, Öcalan therefore decided in the mid-1990s that the guerrillas would no longer withdraw to the main base in Iraq for the winter, and that the guerrillas should instead learn to live in the mountains and nature all year round. For example, Öcalan ordered the guerrillas to cultivate the feeling of the mountains and their magic so that the mountains could take them in and protect them. In the years that followed, the PKK sacrificed a great many guerrillas' lives during winter, until they learnt to adapt to nature and the winter cold.

Like Berivan, Zeri recounted how she had a relational attachment to the mountains before deciding to join the movement:

> I thought of the first guerrilla I'd meet, and guerrilla campfires. Waging struggle in the mountains! I have always loved the mountains when I was at home. I used to wander in the mountains near us, too, before I came here. (Interview with Zeri, 26 March 2018).

The extracts from the conversation with Berivan and Zeri show how they both felt drawn to and connected to the mountains. Kurds associate them with their culture and geography. The mountain districts are considered in the context of Kurdish values, ideology and needs. Throughout history, for example, the Kurds have regarded the mountains as their only loyal friends in their attempts to distance themselves from peoples such as the Arabs and the Turks with whom they tried to live together but by whom they felt betrayed. This is why the Kurds have always chosen to seek refuge in the mountains when persecuted by power holders. Yet, the mountains are more than just a context in which they act. Nature is considered agentive. The cadres relate to the mountains as living beings, with whom they expect some form of intra-action that is productive to the development of their survival skills as well as their new identity after the break.

All the women I interviewed were critical of the dualist understanding of the relationship between humankind and nature. I assess that this scepticism originates in the party's first ideological platforms, namely Marxism and Leninism, and that this scepticism gained strength with the paradigm shift to 'democratic confederalism' in 2005, when capitalism was accused of separating humankind and nature from each other. Following on from this, Öcalan has, for example, described his belief that from the beginning of civilization to the present day, humanity has constructed a wrong relationship with nature and animals. According to Öcalan, the change and destruction wrought by humans have had catastrophic consequences for nature. Nature can be sustainably preserved, but it requires that the existing relationship between humans and nature, including animals, changes. Western cultures have treated nature like an object. To liberate culture from human dominance implies an abrogation of the ontological distinction between nature and culture before sustainable coexistence can be established.[2] On the basis of Öcalan's aforementioned ideas for the liberation of nature, the cadres stress that the modern human has become alienated from his or her own 'naturalness'. At the same time, the cadres say they have relearnt that nature, animals and humans are part of a whole. They have learnt this because while living in the mountains, they have cleansed themselves of the influence of civil society.

Zelal left Europe and travelled to the Kurdish areas of Iraq because of her commitment to the PKK. She explained how her time in the mountains had changed her relationship with nature:

> The [capitalist] system separates you from nature. Makes you hostile to nature. It does the same with animals. It belittles animals and elevates humans. As though there's a constant war and competition between nature and humans. [. . .] In the mountains, we learnt to live with nature and become one with it. To be friends with nature. I'm not afraid of animals anymore. We have learnt to make friends with animals and live with them. (Interview with Zelal, 17 September 2017)

Zelal went on to describe briefly how the PKK operates with and thinks in terms of an abrogation of the distinction between nature and culture, with human beings not necessarily taking centre stage. It is a matter of not just forming a new relationship with nature but also overcoming one's former fear of animals and feeling stronger and in harmony with the mountains. The late woman fighter Gurbetelli Ersöz writes in her diary that 'The mountain gives you, and strengthens, a feeling of freedom and sovereignty'.[3] The cadres thus experience the mountains almost as a temple that the young Kurds can go to to get in touch with themselves in the process leading to their freedom. More women fighters said in a similar vein that for them, the significance of the mountains lay in the fact that most of their new understandings, such as their self-knowledge, their strength, the effects of colonization on their identity and world view, first occurred to them in the mountains.

3.3. *The constituting of the new human*

This section describes details from the life and experiences in the training camps to shed light on how the interviewed women's old self-perceptions are subverted into new perceptions and identifications in intra-action with the mountains and other aspects of nature and materiality.

3.3.1. Training and instruction in the mountains

All new cadres are sent to camps in the 'free territory' for military and ideological training. In the training camps, participants are isolated from all contact with the outside world. For reasons of security, mobile phones and internet access are forbidden. Leaving the camp, receiving visits or having contact with one's family without permission from the leadership is not allowed. The training programme for new fighters lasts from three to six months. Young people often have a longer training course, because they are not regarded as mature enough to learn everything during a short-term course. The PKK offers constant and intensive instruction and training. Attendance is mandatory regardless of whether one is new to the PKK or has been a member of the party for ten years.

An ordinary day in the free territory starts for everyone at 5 am and ends around 8 pm, including breaks for meals and relaxation. There is a lunch and relaxation break from 12 noon to 2 pm, while the evening meal is between 6 and 8 pm. Not until after 8 pm can one have a couple of hours to oneself before sleep. Morning training begins with physical activities, including military training and weapon use. The daily physical training takes no more than a couple of hours, while the remainder of the training is dedicated to ideological instruction. After morning fall-in and physical activities, they set about preparing breakfast. Morning fall-in, training and all other meetings in the movement – whether in the mountains or in civil society (including Europe) – conclude with the communal call of 'Biji Serok Apo'. This is Kurdish and means 'Long Live Öcalan'. The slogan is called out three times in succession.

In the mountains, there is always a duty roster setting out who is to do what. The division of labour is not gender-determined. Some set about collecting dry bushes and old pieces of wood for a fire, while others make bread. Pieces of fresh wood are never placed on the fire due to their great respect for nature. It is a fundamental belief that nature must not be harmed unless necessary. Women and men eat in the same place, although often in gender-segregated groups. Here, between six and eight men or women sit in a circle on the ground and eat together with their hands from the same big plate, using the thin bread as a spoon.

The reason for eating with the hands is not just limited resources, says Zagros, but also that they are always on foot, so carrying a lot of things is seen as impractical. Physically, they typically take up position under a tree or below a cliff so as not to be seen by planes and drones. They sit close together, shoulder to shoulder. They generally go around close to each other most of the time, and there is a lot of physical contact in the form of touching. The fact that everything is done collectively, such as the meal where they eat from the same plate and share the same teacup, is highlighted by Zagros as something that strengthens solidarity and their care for each other. On our journey down from the mountains, Zagros and I spent a night in a house used by the movement as a hideout. In the kitchen, there were plates, cutlery, a dining table and much more. I helped lay the table for breakfast, which consisted of a mixture of egg, tomatoes and onions fried in a pan. The pan was placed in the middle of the table. I set out plates and cutlery for each person. There were five of us for breakfast. I was the only one who used the cutlery and plate. The others all preferred to eat from the pan, using flatbread as a fork. I felt that their choice was partly a habit, but also came from a desire not to be called a 'conformist', a term used by the cadres when they criticize both others and themselves, referring to their former life in civil society, when they had 'petit-bourgeois dreams'. 'Conformist' here refers to a person who is overly concerned with his or her own well-being and care, shunning the collectivist lifestyle towards which the movement strives.

The non-conformism takes on a note of asceticism. For example, the cadres insist that they do not eat to satiety, but so as not to die of hunger. Eating is thus not seen as something done for enjoyment. The cadres' explanation for this attitude or mentality is that they are against an 'overconsumption mentality', which they see as created by capitalism. The interviewees also explain food moderation with reference to occasional shortages of food. They therefore have a fundamental rule that they are to show mutual consideration among themselves when eating and that priorities have to be made. The sick, the wounded and those taking part in an action are to have first priority. In one of my interviews, Arya elaborated this:

> Getting food was often hard. For example, I still can't eat as much as I want. Back then, we often didn't have so much food, so we ate very little. One time, we only had four olives. Nobody touched them. Nobody dared. Everyone steered clear of them. We thought we could eat them for lunch. No, for dinner. We did this [postponing the eating] for days [...] There was also a time we only had one loaf. We went hungry for two days. We thought we could eat it with the comrades once they were back from the action. We didn't go to the village to fetch food, either, because we didn't want to put the action in danger. (Interview with Arya, 25 March 2018)

Arya's narrative addresses how the cadres are trained to show consideration for each other and how food is divided equally among them. This is a form of asceticism in the concept's original meaning as training. Cadres have to train themselves by taming and strengthening their bodies in an inner fight against bodily urges, because bodily urges can divert attention from the PKK's cause and end up jeopardizing one's own life and those of one's comrades. The interesting thing about Arya's description of her and the other cadres' attitude to food and hunger was that she also made it clear that the desire to eat does not disappear, but the will does not allow her to eat more than just enough to quell her hunger, even when there is enough food. For Arya, it is about defining herself, her appetite and her desire.

After breakfast, at 8 am, ideological instruction begins. There are both Turkish and Kurdish classes, and new cadres choose for themselves which language they are best able to follow. However, the PKK intends that everyone should ultimately be able to speak and receive instruction in Kurdish. The leadership and the training cadres are in charge of instruction. There are both men and women instructors. Women and men attend instruction together. Here, the women typically sit at the front, near the instructors. Although Zin says that this placement of the women in the room seems random, she is obviously proud that the women want to be near the instructors. She goes on to stress that this shows the women to be more interested than the men in the instruction and ideological learning (Interview with Zin, 23 March 2018).

Zagros said that the PKK is a 'party of teaching' and that the aim of ideological instruction is to create the new human, to get new members to submit to the party's norms and values and to get them to show allegiance to Öcalan. The locality for teaching is typically a big cave in a cliff or underground. Conditions are simple and basic, with no facilities such as chairs and tables. They just sit on the ground. If there are tall trees for cover, instruction can take place in the open air, which Zagros said they prefer because they appreciate 'teaching out in nature' where they can feel the wind, smell the flowers, hear the sounds of animals and so on. Zagros also emphasized that it all helps to give new participants the feeling that it is important to be part of nature. It is made clear to new members that instruction in the PKK is not concealed behind high-walled institutions such as universities that, according to the PKK, produce knowledge in artificial laboratories and offices cut off from reality. In the mountains, the cadres feel the effect of nature, and they are obliged to confront this material effect in order to survive in combat. This intra-action between the cadres and nature, in which physical experiences and materiality effects become noticeable, creates a special setting for the subversive formation of identity in new cadres.

The PKK clearly intends for the course of instruction to consolidate the 'break' and set in train a subversion process leading. New cadres are subjected to strict and harsh ideological instruction for the first three months. The PKK does this deliberately to cleanse new participants of patriarchal Kurdish norms and values, including Islamic religious values, and to prevent them seeking out the Turkish and Western lifestyle that Öcalan regards as liberal, egotistical and capitalist.[4]

Instruction is largely based on Öcalan's analyses, which focus, among other things, on assessments of world political and social developments, current struggles and evaluations of the new personality that Öcalan wants to create. The aim of this is to make it possible to create the party's 'new human' by replacing the existing identities that the cadres have brought from civil society. In connection with this, party members are asked to choose a code name. The code names are meant to symbolize each participant's new identity. The code names most often refer to a Kurdish geographical feature such as a high mountain or a major river. The choice of code name is a decolonizing act in itself, because, as citizens living in the colonized lands, the members have been forced to have their names recorded in the national registry, which is not of Kurdish origin. They were not allowed to be registered under Kurdish names. A code name enables them to get rid of, for example, Turkish or Arab names that symbolize a layer in their identity that prevents access to some kind of original Kurdish nature.

Moreover, it is not only a person's name that has to be remade. The desire for change also applies to the body itself. I will exemplify this with my observations of Evin. The first time, we met before she travelled to the mountains. The second time, we met when Evin was back in Europe after spending about a year in the mountains. Before she left for the mountains for the first time, I met with her for a period to follow her recruitment process. At this point, Evin was very talkative. Her temperament was very changeable, and she conducted herself in a very attentive manner. When she returned from the mountains, she was reticent towards me and seemed reserved. She had also lost weight and got into shape. She spoke more slowly, more carefully, as if choosing her words with care. The changes in Evin clearly indicated the effectiveness of the instruction and training that the movement organizes in the mountains, particularly for new members. The task is not just to produce the new humans by changing their thoughts. The instruction and training must also affect and reshape their bodies and the bodily gestures, attitudes and speed, for example. With Käser following Foucault,[5] one could say that discipline has produced 'docile bodies', where the body is shaped to make it more biddable. When I met with her a third time, she had stayed four months in Europe. At that time, Evin was close to being the old, attentive Evin, and she seemed less militarized in speech and attitude. I believe there is a reason why the movement invests a lot in training and ideological instruction and brings its members to the mountains for long periods to adjust their bodies and personal development through performative acts. It does this because it understands that over time and through interaction with its surroundings, the body will gradually become de-disciplined and fall back on the old behaviour that it is unconsciously used to. The movement sees the body as an object and target of power aimed at tempering the individual's behaviour. It must therefore be subjected to discipline to make it obedient and hence useful to the movement. I will elaborate on this point later, in Chapter 5, when I examine the women fighters' combat experiences.

Overall, the task for the movement is to invest in personal, ideological symbolic (cf. the code names), bodily and volitional development in order to produce a dynamic process in which members experience their life undergoing transformation into something new. Westrheim examines why thousands of young people took to the mountains in the 1980s and 1990s to fight with the PKK, and how former political prisoners in Turkey organized educational activities in jails to educate themselves and their fellow prisoners. Westrheim calls this education process 'transformative'. Westrheim claims that the idea behind transformative education is to engage people in actively constructing and reconstructing knowledge, thereby transforming meanings in order to arrive at new understandings of themselves and the world. According to Westrheim, 'becoming' entails the notion of transformation and is linked to ideas about human development, growth and potential.[6] This is also what I found in the interviewees' accounts: their experience is that through participation in collective and individual learning activities, self-evaluation and evaluation by other members of the movement, they have become able to strive for something new and ultimately become a new person. Once the transformation has been accomplished, they have established a platform for themselves for a new future, but also an asset for the PKK and the national struggle. As a consequence, it seems that members cultivate a joy of learning something new. Westrheim mentions how practical educative activities and political education in the mountains, prisons, streets and communities become constant opportunities for learning and becoming something new, for being in the process of changing. Westrheim therefore claims that for each member, whatever their role in it, being part of the movement is like being part of a continuing school.[7]

3.3.2. *Öcalan's understanding of being a woman*

As all instruction in the movement, and the cadres' understanding of the world, is based on Öcalan's analyses, the following section will focus on the importance of his analyses as the conceptual basis of women fighters' self-understanding. It should be mentioned by way of introduction that it is difficult to specify who was the source of inspiration for Öcalan's ideas, as it is not Öcalan's practice to cite sources in his works. According to Andok, who sits on the PKK's Education Council, in his earlier years as a student, Öcalan was inspired by Enlightenment philosophers such as Jean-Jacques Rousseau and by the Frankfurt School and other dissident Marxists who tried to practice Marxism in a new way. The German women's rights advocates Clara Zetkin Eissner and Rosa Luxemburg were also particular sources of inspiration for him (Interview with Andok, 26 March 2018). Çetin Gürer, who provides a detailed analysis of Öcalan's ideas in his thesis, writes that Leslie Lipson, Anthony Giddens, Adorno Horkheimer, Fernand Braudel, Michel Foucault, Mihkail Bakunin, Pierre-Joseph Proudhon and Murray Bookchin were sources of inspiration for Öcalan's viewpoints on democracy, power, the state, capitalism and modernity. Öcalan is also known to be well read and have a broad knowledge. Gürer writes that during Öcalan's first fourteen years in İmralı Prison (1999–2013), he read a total of 2,300 books and periodicals. As Öcalan reads and writes on a broad range of topics, he occasionally resembles an ideologue from the time of the Frankfurt School criticizing the Enlightenment, a theoretician and critic of the capitalist system or an anarchist, who targets the relationship between power and state.[8]

When Öcalan addresses the PKK's cadres directly, imageries and memories from his personal life, including reflections on the influence of his own family, permeate his speeches. Öcalan's speeches invite interpretation and are full of ideological and moral values that apparently make it easy for the cadres, whatever their background, to see themselves reflected in his narrativization. For example, Zin recounted that the first piece of Öcalan's she read before joining the PKK had been a text in which Öcalan analysed the child marriages of his own three sisters. Öcalan's critique of patriarchal values caught Zin's attention, not least because her own siblings had had similar experiences of forced marriages when they were still children.

Zin, who wore a hijab until she joined the movement, still prays five times a day and fasts according to Muslim prescriptions. During the interview, she told me that she sees many similarities between her understanding of Islam and Öcalan's understanding of socialism. Accordingly, Zin did not find it hard to go from a Muslim lifestyle to a socialist one, because all religions and ideologies are based on the same moral values:

> In the Qur'an, the first verse is Iqra. It is the 'Read!' verse. In the Leader's [Öcalan's] defence statement, there is a sentence: to know oneself is the beginning of all wisdom. In principle, he is doing the same thing. He is saying: Read! (Interview with Zin, 23 March 2018)

The above comment made it clear how Zin has transformed one ideology into the other by finding similarities between what the Qur'an says and what Öcalan writes. Moreover, she states that her knowledge of Islam made it easy for her to adjust to the movement's ideology, because both ideologies could be seen to have the same conceptual basis. If Öcalan has a tendency in his narratives to base his ideology on his own, personal stories of his family and his childhood village, he also creates a kind of transformation strategy that implicitly urges cadres to look back on their former lives to find inspiration and shift their perspective towards the new life. Inspired by Barad, I consider this strategy a matter of diffractive positioning where the cadres are encouraged to use Öcalan's imageries and memoirs as a diffractive filter, through which they should see their own lives. The diffraction thus becomes a platform for transformation.[9] Here, Öcalan is actually suggesting that people should look to the potential in their inner tensions and contradictions, and accommodate how differentiation from the past can arise 'from within'. The cadres must always have an eye for what their inner world, their previous experiences and the sociocultural processes try to tell them. In the movement, this method is called 'self-understanding'. Öcalan developed this method to strengthen the first women in the party and support them in establishing a new self-understanding. Afrin, who joined the party in 1987, recalled that this method had great significance for the women in the party:

> It was in the party that we first learnt the significance of being women and men, and how much influence men have on us and how much they oppress us. The Leader [Öcalan] showed us this with examples [. . .] Once, the Leader said to us [women]: 'Go out and do your own instruction.' We were shocked. We looked at each other. What could we instruct each other in? Who among us could be in charge of that instruction? I mean, we had nothing to give each other. What could we talk about? We asked him. He said: 'You'll think of something.' We came back to our section and began to think. We all looked at each other. There was one courageous comrade among us. She said, 'Let's tell each other our stories of participation. Our personal stories.' We did that. It went really well. They were all unique. At first, I thought we had identical stories. For example, there was a comrade who had been locked in her room by her parents, as they wanted to stop her joining the PKK. She was locked in for days and not allowed to do anything else. But in the end she managed to find a way out, run away from home and join the party. The Leader valued her participation highly, as he

said she had made the revolution before she joined the party. The next day, we told the Leader how the instruction had gone. He praised us. He had confidence in us. In time, his confidence in us helped us to build our own self-confidence. (Interview with Afrin, 13 December 2017)

Afrin recounted that in this way, Öcalan had pushed the women to create something for themselves in the form of self-instruction via sorts of active learning, by constituting new narratives which are – as understood by Gergen – progressive in character[10] and in which the women fighters develop into something better. The women fighters' self-instruction, their joining together around a shared task, helped to establish among them sisterly solidarity which also helped them to free themselves from 'men dominance'. The self-understanding method also contributed to two important strategic personality development results: first, they attained a new self-understanding by redefining experiences from their former lives as special. This boosted their self-confidence, in part due to Öcalan's encouragement and thus authorization to react against men dominance in their past as well as in a military context. Second, once the women found out that their stories of participation were unique, it gave them a feeling of having a free will as individuals that could serve as a driving force towards a new future. With the attainment of burgeoning self-understanding, they became aware of two new opportunities for action: that they as women could produce and accommodate their own needs without being dependent on men and that they were unique, strong-willed women who could overcome all forms of resistance. In Chapter 5, I shall return to the effects of women's combat experiences on their self-understanding.

The method where women analyse their own memories and life stories to produce a new history and self-understanding is key to understanding why the women fighters engage in separate instruction without the presence of men. Moreover, the movement benefits from the women's stories as part of an overall strategy to subvert dominant conceptions of history and knowledge, formulated by men power holders. On this point, Zeri said:

During the instruction of new starters, there's a particular focus on life in the movement. There's less focus on ideological instruction, because you're new. The instruction is mostly about the history of the movement, women's history, the importance of leadership, military training, the history of Kurdistan, the organizational function of the PKK etc. [. . .] We [women] also have our separate instruction. We discuss the Leader's [Öcalan's] analyses of women. For example, what families we grew up in and how we were brought up, our inner searches and what contributed to our joining the movement. In the beginning, you focus more on yourself. (Interview with Zeri, 26 March 2018).

Self-understanding sessions often take place in the evening when women's shared activities with the men have finished for the day. According to Cane, women's separate focus on their own narratives help newcomers increase their self-confidence and strengthen their personal development (Cane in FGI,[11] 25 March

2018). After a while, men started using the method of self-understanding, too, but when men engage in it, women facilitate the process, as it is claimed that the men will be better at analysing themselves and talking about their inner worlds if women are present and support the process. With the implicit claim on women's special access to the inner world, an indirect reference is made to what is termed 'women's nature'.[12] I will analyse and discuss the meaning of this in Chapter 4, but here I will briefly mention that, to Öcalan's, the whole idea of making woman special is about freeing women from their previous conception of themselves, affected by patriarchy, and thereby allow everyone to gain access to the resources in women's essential nature.[13] Here, both Öcalan and the women fighters are convinced that they are contributing to a new identity for women that acknowledges them as something special.

3.3.3. *The importance of self-creation and self-criticism*

For the PKK, the idea of liberating Kurdistan and setting a revolution in train is about creating a new human.[14] Following Foucault's thinking about disciplining power,[15] this section will describe how the discourse on the new human pervades and regulates the members and their relations, and it will reflect on the strategies, channels and anchor points in play to constitute the new human as a cadre. According to Öcalan, to become a new human, whether man or woman, the person must achieve an 'individual liberation', achievable through a process that Öcalan calls 'self-creation'.[16] Zagros explained to me that 'self-criticism' is a central term here, intended to bring the cadres to realize that their personality is not sufficiently developed. Through self-criticism, the cadres confront the challenges they faced in renouncing their former lives, including their families and spouses, and why it is difficult for them to submit to the party's values and norms. This is not just a matter of social control exercised by the cadres over each other but also of the cadres disciplining themselves by means of the PKK's party ideology and culture, constant self-analysis and self-development. The PKK invests in processes of self-disciplining both in the lowlands and in the mountains through education and training programmes to refresh knowledge relevant to the PKK ideology and to purge the members from liberal and egotistical values, by which one is unavoidably influenced when living one's life in the lowlands.

The disciplining of cadres in the mountains is much more intense. The isolated training camps, far removed from civil society, create an optimal setting for new cadres to submit to the organized programme of instruction. All the women I interviewed considered this positive, because it provided them with the means to create what they believe is central for a new, free life as women. Mordem is a man instructor and one of the PKK's first cadres. Mordem openly admits that the PKK's intention is to produce the strong-willed and free human (Interview with Mordem, 19 January 2018). In many ways, the strict instruction that the PKK offers its new cadres, and the new lifestyle they are expected to transition to, can resemble a conversion of individuals on a par with what takes place in religious movements and other ideological traditions where participants, to transition from one world view to another, are said to be brainwashed and manipulated.[17]

The young people who join the PKK have varying backgrounds with regard to education, family, class, religious affiliation and so on. One of the crucial aims of the training is to even out the differences between the cadres and produce a more homogeneous and standardized identity to lay the ground for them to fight together for a shared objective. According to the cadres, this requires strict instruction and a disciplined, ideological lifestyle. As I illustrated with Zin's transition from the Islamic to the socialist lifestyle, many of the young cadres have childhood experiences of being disciplined and socialized into strict patriarchal moral norms and values. For example, the woman fighter Helin stated that the values her parents passed on to her as part of her upbringing closely matched Öcalan's ideas and the content of the PKK's teachings. She considered both world views a matter of producing honourable lives, being faithful to cultural and moral values, being a good person, putting up resistance in order to ensure one's own survival and so on.

The programmes of instruction in the mountains are not the only anchor points of the new human discourse. The cadres themselves also take on this task out of a desire to be prepared both ideologically and with regard to required knowledge. They spend almost all their spare time reading or having debates with each other. Here, I judge that with their commitment to immersing themselves in the ideology, the cadres are cementing their position around assuming the role of a loyal member of the movement. Most cadres carry a book in their bag, whether they are in Europe or in the mountains. This can be unexpected to a newcomer, as it was to Cane, for example, who recalled being surprised at the intellectual level she found in the mountains:

> The friends in the mountains had already read books we didn't know of in Turkey. They'd also set up groups called 'Democratic Information Units' that were responsible for organizing intellectual debates and implementing institutions. Day and night, they had long, deep debates. The read a wide range of books, from postmodern studies to critical sociology, and debated them. So it was a high-quality environment. (Interview with Cane, 25 March 2018)

Cane went on to recall that as a former university student, she was surprised that both cadres from Kurdish villages and those who arrived illiterate had learnt to read and write, and had educated themselves to be part of the Democratic Information Units.

3.3.4. *Anti-feminism as part of the anti-colonial struggle*

In my conversations with the women fighters, they repeatedly expressed their scepticism about Marxism. I find this interesting, as Marxism has been a source of ideological inspiration for the movement's thinking. The women fighters criticize Marxism for failing to establish a real alternative to the capitalist lifestyle or

Western feminism, which they regard as a white, capitalist, middle-class product. The women fighters base their scepticism on their reading and interpretation of Öcalan's writings in which he criticizes the implementation of Marxism, associated with 'real socialism',[18] for not creating better conditions for women, despite its representatives claiming to have overcome all the issues created by capitalism. Over time, rather than maintain its focus on 'human nature' and freedom, real socialism became power-oriented and preoccupied with setting the framework for a socialist state that, according to Öcalan, was not much different from the framework of a capitalist state. In its implementation, issues around the family and women's liberation were either postponed or sacrificed in order to achieve a socialist state.[19] Thus, argues Öcalan, the socialist countries have only managed to create a sort of 'physical freedom' for women, because they focused purely on women's participatory opportunities in the labour market and their social mobility in society generally.[20] According to Öcalan, Marxism overlooked the way people, especially women, are thought of as capital. Unlike Marxism, argues Öcalan, the PKK's ideology incorporates two fundamental elements: the abolition of gender oppression and ethnic oppression.[21]

In acknowledging the cause of Western feminism, Öcalan agrees that capitalist societies of the West exploit women as modern slaves.[22] Moreover, in his first book focusing on women, *The Women and Family Question*[23] (1992), Öcalan writes that although the woman appears on the face of it to be a central figure in modern Western society, in practice she is not regarded or treated as anything other than an object or a tool that society can earn money from. According to Öcalan, liberal feminism in particular is preoccupied with the question of whether it is possible to bring about equality with men, but is blind to the fact that liberal feminism is a means for capitalism to exploit women in the workforce. Accordingly, liberal feminism cannot truly secure complete freedom for women.[24]

Öcalan's indictment of Western feminism can be summed up in three overarching points. His first charge is that Western feminism defines woman based on an opposition between women and men. The second charge is that Western feminism does not provide a historical evaluation of power and its significance for the exploitation of women as sexual objects. The third charge is that Western feminism focuses exclusively on the possibilities for women of achieving legal equality and integration into the existing man-dominated world rather than striving for more, for example, the possibilities of women achieving economic freedom independently of men. From an academic viewpoint, Öcalan's critique of Western feminism is misleading and downplays the points that he actually shares with feminism.[25] However, Öcalan is an ideologist with strategic skills, not an academic, and I therefore consider that his unfounded claims about Western feminism are to be thought of as purely strategic steps with the disidentificatory aim of highlighting an 'us and them' division between feminism and the PKK's view of women, and his strategy has worked. Throughout my interviews, I noticed especially that the women fighters who have experiences of being in Europe were critical of Western feminism. They pointed to income differentials between Western women and men and the unequal representation of genders in political party leaderships. Both examples were brought to argue that women in the West are far from achieving total freedom due to the incompetency of Western feminists in bringing about real change for women. All the cadres I interviewed directed such a critique at Western feminism, so Öcalan's disidentificatory strategy seems to have worked.

As part of the disidentification up against Western capitalist modernity with everything that it entails, the women fighters blamed the West also for spoiling non-Western women's 'nature'. While Western feminism nowadays has given up speaking of woman's or man's nature, it can be seen, in line with Spivak (1988) and Mohanty's (1988) strategic essentialism, that the Kurdish women and the PKK generally use essentialist assertions about woman's nature to promote their own anti-colonial liberation struggle and to unite Kurdish women as a 'we' under the PKK banner.

3.4. De-sexualized love

This section is concerned with how the PKK invests in a de-sexualization process through strict regulation of cadres' clothing, appearance, behaviour and sexuality. This regulation is anchored in several different subprocesses, all of which are centred on the PKK's vision of producing a cultural change in cadres' way of forming relationships, across genders, within the PKK, but in the long run also in families and intimate partnerships.

3.4.1. Love without intimacy in the party family

Cadres within the PKK must abstain from entering into sexual relations with each other. This abstention includes an unwritten rule, not stated in official party documents, against declaring any romantic feelings for one another, from having sex with one another and from getting married. Nevertheless, the term 'love' pervades much of the party's use of metaphors. Cadres are to become a 'people of affections' and 'creators of love'.[26] According to Mordem, all cadres are familiar with the unofficial prohibition against sexual relations among cadres (Interview with Mordem, 19 January 2018). Underlying the unofficial prohibition lies Öcalan's ideal that party cadres do not regard each other as sexual objects or become unfocused due to undisciplined bodily drives. Instead, cadres must engage in 'free love' where they consider themselves and each other de-sexualized, complete human beings working together to build a free society.[27] Their relations must not involve romantic expectations of each other but should be of an exclusively comradely character.[28] These comradely relations can be practised in the party environment that Öcalan calls the 'party school'.[29]

The PKK's understanding of love is also founded on the disidentificatory idea that capitalism creates fertile ground for a consumer society in which everything, including relationships, is based on mutual exploitation, which again leads to the individual being damaged and alienated from himself or herself. The cadres

I interviewed said in unison that love in modern society is detached from moral norms and reduced to erotic love, and that the capitalist lifestyle permeates a love life that the cadres regard as patriarchal. Especially the cadres who had been in Europe (e.g. Zelal, Delal, Evin, Mordem, Bozo and Cudi) described patriarchal love as false, empty and contributory to a dependence on consumption rather than to freedom. They emphasized that domestic violence against women and children is widespread and that legal equality is not translated into everyday life. Following Öcalan, the women fighters repudiate the individualism of Western lifestyle in contrast to the Kurdish lifestyle, characterized by solidarity and collectivism. By drawing on such stereotypical categorizations, they seek to argue that the love of the colonized is innocent and genuine, not yet spoilt by capitalist development, while love in the West is false. They point out, for example, that Westerners suffer from loneliness because of individualism. For example, Mordem stated that love in the West is no longer unconditional love but something that couples negotiate about:

> Everything is self-oriented! Even love. When the individual enters into a relationship, the individual is thinking: 'What can I get out of it?' It is seen as naïve or stupid if you love someone else without demanding anything. [. . .] The individual thinks [when he or she is about to enter into a relationship] only of his or her own needs, drives, worries about the future, reproduction and financial worries. So you can say that love and falling in love have been liquidated, killed! (Interview with Mordem, 19 January 2018)

It is worth noting that cadres use stereotypical readings of love in the West at the same time as expressing dissatisfaction with the (stereotypical) way in which women from Muslim and colonized countries are described in the West. Like Mordem, the cadres offer assertions about love in the Western world as constrictive, individual-centred, inhibiting and body-oriented. With the following narrativization, which I see as a form of reverse orientalism, Mordem explained why more great love stories such as 'Romeo and Juliet' did not come out in our time:

> In the West, there are no more great romantic dramas such as 'Romeo and Juliet'. [. . .] There isn't even a great new saga. A poem you can read. We don't see any great romantic novel nowadays. [. . .] Love has just become a little scene in an individually focused adventure film [. . .]. It doesn't mean that everyone is like that, heartless, where they've lost their motivation to find true love, freedom or something collective. But people are searching and fighting. [. . .] And we are some of them. (Interview with Mordem, 19 January 2018)

Until the 1980s, there was no unwritten rule in the PKK that cadres could not become lovers. Some of the party's first cadres even got engaged and married after the foundation of the party or were permitted to continue their already established relationships. In time, this was altered when the PKK leaders saw that the cadres had difficulty being revolutionaries at the same time as being in a relationship. Sakine Cansız describes the problems that followed from the unregulated love:

> Several comrades did not know how to handle their relationships; they began to close ranks and conceal their relationships. There were also married couples who took part in the movement together. There were also some who were engaged. Or there were those who kept their relationship hidden from the party. They avoided each other to avoid misunderstandings, so they wouldn't even greet each other. Some said nothing out of fear of giving themselves away, while others had radical attitudes to those who were already in relationships. Those who were in a relationship criticized each other to divert attention from themselves. (Cansız 2015: 101; my translation)

Cansız describes conditions in the Beqaa Valley, where the movement had its main base in the early days. In the Beqaa Valley, it was possible for new members to be in a relationship with a member of the opposite sex, but they could not sleep together or have physical contact. The cadres knew that their relationships would be broken off when training was over, and they would leave for their new posts in different Kurdish districts where they might not see each other again. According to Mordem, party members realized over time that a free and meaningful relationship with the opposite sex could not be possible without first creating the social and geographical conditions for a free coexistence. The revolution and the liberation of Kurdistan were such conditions.

To men cadre Bozo, not even a liberated Kurdistan would suffice to allow a worldly life with children and family:

> First, you must create the right circumstances for love. For us, there is nothing called 'after the revolution'. We have dedicated our lives to the revolution. If the revolution in Kurdistan ends, we will join a new revolution in another country. We have dedicated our lives to our conviction. A worldly life with children and family is a non-existent possibility for us. We have nothing called 'after', but we do have a 'continuation'. (Bozo, 16 August 2017)

Furthermore, Bozo argued that there is as yet no free society or free country where women and men can live together without having ownership of each other. They are not yet liberated from the power holders, and they do not yet have a balanced relationship with nature. It is therefore disturbing to put emotions and attraction on centre stage and to believe that they are enough to make a couple happy. The interesting thing here is the way Bozo argues that a cadre has no 'after' but always a 'continuation'. After 'the revolution in Kurdistan', he expected to take part in a new struggle somewhere else in the world. If Butler's ideas about agency can be read as latitude to participate in iterative acts, then it is the discourse about continuing the struggle elsewhere, which Bozo refers to as the next phase of his life, that gives him intelligibility as a cadre in line with the PKK's ideology. This form of subjectivization seems naturalized and invisible to Bozo, who perceives his opportunities for action as a free decision.

When Bozo says that their lives are a continuation, he is basing this on an understanding that arose after the paradigm shift set in train by the PKK in 2005, when it abandoned its initial objective of fighting for an independent Kurdistan in favour of fighting for democratic confederalism as a system of government. In connection with this paradigm shift, the cadres' obligation to the movement became redefined. The cadres of the PKK were fighting not only to liberate Kurdish land but also to accomplish a world revolution bringing all peoples to freedom. With this as the aim of their struggle, their engagement became a lifelong dedication. I judge that this paradigmatic shift was undertaken partly for strategic reasons after realizing that accomplishing a revolution or achieving a free Kurdistan would take far longer than initially assumed. The aforementioned arrangement thus served to keep members, especially the cadres, within the PKK, also when a revolution would not happen for a long time to come.

Other cadres pointed to the challenges of having a family and children in the mountains while a war was going on. Being with them and protecting them would be extremely difficult. In line with this, Bozo explained that it is difficult in the current situation to create good conditions for a family life with children. In a similar vein, Zelal recounted:

> My two sisters got married [they were never active in the PKK]. I don't understand how they could get married, because we are facing a reality in society that is broken. Not just in a geographical sense but also in a cultural and linguistic sense. How can we give life to others without liberating ourselves? We are of the opinion that we can't create anything new and liberate others until we've recreated ourselves. (Interview with Zelal, 17 September 2017)

These statements by Bozo and Zelal support the argument that the chapter has presented up to this point, namely that the PKK's policy brings with it a de-sexualization process in which clothing, appearance, behaviour and sexuality are regulated with the aim of strengthening the PKK's power position. In his analyses, Öcalan pays considerable attention to the family as an institution and reflects on the formation of couples and families in Kurdish society. He argues that the formation of couples and families has contributed to a weakening of the Kurdish people's national identity and cohesion. According to Öcalan, the oppression, assimilation policies and massacres directed at the Kurds by the power holders over the years are among the reasons why the Kurds have been particularly focused on saving themselves and their families rather than fighting for national ideals. For that reason, Öcalan goes on to argue that it is very difficult for the individual Kurd to break away from his or her family and fight for new ideals that the family will not necessarily accept.[30] These arguments lead Öcalan to state that a new prototype of the family, the 'party family', should be created within the party school. The party family would be, in its core structure, the prototype for the big family, the nation. The aim is to reform the existing patriarchal Kurdish family, which neither works nor makes sense, and to revolutionize it with new values and norms. The family will thus become a place where new kinds of gender roles are practised and where new, free generations will grow up.[31]

Although Öcalan himself was against the idea of getting married and showed no interest in living what he regarded as a petit-bourgeois life, he nevertheless had a brief marriage with a woman cadre who was also one of the co-founders of the PKK but who later left the party. Öcalan argues from his own experience that the PKK is not against cadres getting married and starting families,[32] if they believe they can continue their revolutionary struggle unhindered.[33] However, referring to his brief and broken marriage, Öcalan emphasizes that cadres should not necessarily believe that they will be able to achieve this, given that he himself, with his strength, was unable to do so. Öcalan is equivocal here in that he says, on the one hand, that he will not prevent cadres from forming relationships, but on the other hand, he indicates that it is not really possible to balance a relationship with a life as a fighter, since not even he, the leader, was able to do so.

Öcalan's thoughts on Kurdish families and his ideals for them are based not solely on his own experiences but also on Engels's book *Origin of the Family, Private Property, and the State* (1884). In this book, Engels writes that he regards the family as the smallest unit of society. Citing Lenin, Öcalan argues that a revolution cannot succeed without the participation of women.[34] Öcalan goes on to argue that in order to liberate society, the family must be reformed into 'a revolutionary unit' able to construct society from scratch. Above all, a system change and a radical overhaul of the structure of society are required if love is to be allowed to evolve afresh. The man cadre Cudi, who is still married and a father of two, and who has very limited contact with his family in Europe – because he himself is in the mountains in Iraq – told me that if he were to go home to his family to be with them now, he and his family would be unable to avoid becoming a classic family, because the existing social norms would dominate their relationship no matter how much he and his partner fought against them (Interview with Cudi, 20 March 2018).

According to Öcalan, the solution to problems pertaining to married life is a dissolution of existing family structures, be they feudal, capitalist or socialist. Instead, people must return to the morals and spirit of Neolithic times, when woman and man first formed a partnership involving sexual relations. Their partnership was simple, based on survival, reproduction and mutual advantage.[35] Chapter 4 will describe in more detail the movement's view of the characteristics of Neolithic gender positions, including Öcalan's notion of the 'natural woman' that has inspired the movement's ideals for new gender positions.

Öcalan is critical of the relationship between the sexes in Kurdish society. He asserts that it is based solely on the desire to start a family and ensure reproduction. In Kurdish society, men and women know very little of each other before marriage. According to Sakine Cansız, this explains why Öcalan wants to change how men and women in the PKK perceive each other. Initially, Öcalan as well as Cansız encountered much resistance.

In this period [in 1991], the topic of 'Women and Family' was taboo. When the Leader [Öcalan] tried to broach topics such as the woman question, love and the question of emotions, he said, 'I am having difficulty, because you do not understand me. You are like a closed box. You cannot overcome the traditional woman/man distinctions. When you don't define the question as a political condition, a condition of war and of life, you have an attitude like the primitives. You see everything in an ugly way. You do not even know what the beautiful is or what there is to be experienced.' [Cansız continues:] I therefore had to tread very carefully in relation to this topic. When I gently broached topics related to women in my teaching, the men comrades would immediately put their hands up and ask, 'Why do you talk so much about that topic? Tell us about the war or something else. You are sowing confusion on purpose', thereby cutting me off. (Cansız 2015: 72) (my translation)

Although Öcalan is fundamentally critical of the typical Kurdish man, whom he claims to find hard to understand, he also admits in his book that he was no different from the typical Kurdish man. When Öcalan grew up, he too kept well away from women because he did not know how to form friendships with them.[36] By his own account, his upbringing as a Kurdish man in a patriarchal society made him see women only as sexual objects with whom he could not form friendships.[37]

The women fighters' narratives support Öcalan's point about men's and women's lack of knowledge of each other, in that several of the women fighters reported having had no close relationships with men before joining the movement. Even in the movement, they held back from interaction with men, as the culture of the movement set the guidelines for the separation between women and men cadres in a way that made it easier for them to avoid contact with each other than to form relationships. Moreover, most of the women fighters also said that they actually wanted contact with the men, but were inhibited by their lack of knowledge of men and by their lack of self-confidence. Arya recounted the following:

I didn't know Kurdish men. So I didn't know how to protect myself from them. [...] I don't know why we couldn't just make contact with them. Perhaps because of everything Ferhat did. There was a man friend who later fell as a martyr, the martyr Berxewadan. I loved him very much from afar, but I never allowed myself to get to know him, listen to his story and learn more about why he took part in the movement, and get an insight into what he expected of life. He was a very honest friend. I didn't really get to know him, because I constrained myself. I couldn't be a part of his world. I couldn't find out anything about him. Afterwards, I promised myself not to treat the comrades [men and women] differently. No matter if they were men and if they came from a different culture, it mustn't make a difference. I wanted to know them. (Interview with Arya, 25 March 2018)

From before joining, but also after having become a cadre, some of the women fighters knew of rumours of how some men in the movement supposedly had abused or violated women. These rumours influenced how some of the women fighters position themselves in relation to the men. For example, Arya mentions Ferhat. Ferhat is the code name of Öcalan's younger brother, Osman Öcalan, who was a high-ranking leader in the PKK until he decided to leave the movement in 2004. He is infamous among women fighters for being patriarchal, domineering and disrespectful of women. He is also much talked about for his wish to push through a kind of 'social reform' in the PKK permitting cadres to form couples, among other things. Especially the women fighters among PKK's members vehemently opposed this, arguing that they had come to the mountains to liberate Kurdistan, not to pair off.[38]

In addition to the expectations towards the women fighters to discipline themselves and exert social control as to what they may and may not do, the PKK impresses on the women fighters not to give out any wrong signals to the men fighters. Together, these experiences in the movement and the honour-related childhood socialization described in Chapter 1 made Arya stop herself from entering into what she perceives as natural relationships with both men and women. Thus, her love for, or interest in, the martyr Berxewadan remained purely platonic. When she became a cadre, Arya recalled that the aspect she found most incomprehensible was that men and women could live together in the mountains but could not form couples. I also observed this personally on my field trip. Our driver, Adnan, was a young man in his mid-twenties. He had not received full status as a cadre yet, but had previously received a good deal of ideological instruction; he worked for the movement, helping with many logistical tasks. One of the women fighters who knew Adnan and his family well once teased him that he could become a good cadre if he joined the movement, although he would have trouble giving up the idea of getting married. Adnan did not reply to her, but blushed, which may indicate that she had hit home.

3.4.2. De-sexualized and de-corporealized love

Like Arya, most of the women fighters, especially those from the first and second generations, stated that their relations with men fighters were characterized by distance during their first years in the movement and that, as women, they had mainly had to 'make do' with each other's company. This was also due to the women fighters' perception that physical desire does not disrupt women's love for and interest in each other. A certain ambiguity marks their way of speaking of desire: the women seem insecure of their own desire directed at men; the women are afraid of the men's desire directed at them, because they do not know 'men's culture'. They therefore keep their distance from the men in order to protect themselves. However, they do not think of their own homosocial bond,[39] implying love, touching and intimacy as problematic, as their mutual bond is perceived as free from desire. Women fighters thus treat their love among themselves as an innocent, feminine category that binds them together and hence creates solidarity, while love felt for and received from men is associated with a dangerous kind of desire. The good kind of love therefore becomes a feminine quality associated with women. It is understood as feminine in that it both originates in women's inner world and can only be experienced between women. This form of love is also defined as de-sexualized, as 'pure love without desire'. It is hard to ascertain from the interviewees' narratives why a woman's love is seen as 'purer' or more 'desire-free' than a man's. Love is described as protective, caring and supportive, but at the same time as challenging. Love, in their eyes, is not about sexuality, touching, physical intimacy or passion but more about the feeling that it is there and surrounds everyone in the PKK as a collective and unconditional emotion.

De-sexualized love towards men is legitimate if conceived as contributing to the greater cause within the PKK. Bese said:

> If a man is strong or brave in war, he will also attract your attention and your emotions. Your love turns towards him. The same is true of a man who is highly respected by those around him. So you think, 'I must go to war together with him. I must have the honour of waging war together with him.' You also want to be in his unit. (Interview with Bese, 22 March 2018).

De-sexualized love or – to use the movement's own word – 'comradely love' is perceived by the women fighters as a sort of admiration/force of attraction that moves them towards the movement's objectives. De-sexualized love is nevertheless difficult for the women fighters to handle, especially during their first years in the movement. But in time, through performative acts in the form of bodily and ideological training, self-discipline and reconstruction in the mountains, the women fighters become enabled to practice de-sexualized love of men cadres. De-sexualized love is a matter of achieving a state where you know that you admire how a human being incarnates the movement's collective ideals. Accordingly, comradely love is individualized or directed at one particular body. Comradely love is collectivist. It comes into being through intra-action where it is experienced as an attractive force and an emotion that connects the cadres within the collective.

It seems that the men cadres conceptualize comradely love in a similar way. Mordem told me that he is in love with all women in the PKK. The other men cadres said the same. As men, they are in love with the women's strength, their fighting spirit, their pursuit of freedom, their self-confidence and the way that women cadres affect the general PKK ideal of the free woman with their personalities. Love and women's liberation are thus linked – at least as far as their view of the movement's women is concerned. This is directly expressed in the movement's most used motto about women members of the PKK: 'She who wages war becomes free, she who becomes free becomes more beautiful, she who becomes more beautiful becomes loved.' The motto stipulates a promise to the women members that they will be loved if they just fight for freedom.[40] Mordem added that it does not necessarily refer to armed struggle and violence as a prerequisite for the movement's love of a woman. Warfare can also take the form of a woman's inner, ideological struggle in the effort to act as the ideal human being (Interview with Mordem, 19 January 2018).

Mordem's position reflects the movement's ideological standpoint, which implies that individualism should be eliminated and that bodily differences should be made meaningless. Love must be independent of bodily appearances. Nick has a Western background. Nick has fought not with the PKK but together with men YPG fighters from Rojava yet has embraced the PKK's ideology on love. Nick was surprised to encounter this different kind of love:

> I might tell my mother I love her every other year, and my partner not so often. It's not something we often tell each other. But there [in Rojava], there a heval can already tell me he loves me the second time we meet. It's very different from here [in Europe]. You form ties in a different way, and it happens quickly. You express your feelings quickly. But here [in Europe] it takes a long time. It's not something you talk about. Why should I tell my best friend I like him? [There] you watch TV and sit very close to each other. It's very natural. Nobody questions it. For example, if someone is tired and sleeping under the rug, someone else [of the same sex] can get under the rug too and share the rug. That happens all the time. It's nothing unusual. There's nothing sexual in it. It's pure love. We need each other. We're like a family. And the need to be close to other people without sexual feelings is human nature. Kisses on the cheek and big hugs are their interaction. (Interview with Nick, 12 July 2017)

Through my interviews with women fighters from Rojava, I have found that they have the same view of love, whether woman-man or woman-woman. It should not involve a romantic relationship with another person. This form of love is pure, without expectation, without desire and non-sexualized. It is not about owning or controlling another person, and in time, this comes to appear meaningful to everyone in relation to the rest of the movement's ideology. 'It's that love that keeps you in the movement', said Arya (Interview with Arya, 25 March 2018). Arya added that she had changed her attitude during her time in the movement, so that she was no longer afraid of showing her love for her men comrades. She had acquired a different ideological consciousness enabling her to intra-act with the men comrades without worrying.

During the interviews, I found it noteworthy how many of the women relished talking about love and showing their love for each other. Here, love was perceived and lived out as an undefined, disembodied, platonic and non-romantic form of love that was about transcending the constraints of individuality – not about realizing oneself through the other or finding the one and only – and thus about making the collective the central focus.

On comradely love being collectivist, Bese explained:

> Among us, love is something collective. We don't practise individual love. Of course, it may happen to someone. We don't say it never happens. There are some people who have different inner forms of searching that don't mean anything to us. For us, love is a shared goal. A shared life. A shared perspective. A collectivity. Something that makes us more alive, puts us in a better mood,

makes us happy. We have no other recipe for love. (Interview with Bese, 22 March 2018)

Bese suggests that love is something that happens and exists in the present, rather than taking the form of a fixed, unique relationship between two individuals. On this understanding, love becomes a drive that connects the individual to the comrades, to nature and to the ideological collective. It is a kind of neighbourly love in an ascetic sense. Zeri explained it like this:

> I fulfil my need for love through togetherness with my comrades [. . .] There is no need to say much: a look, a smile, doing something together. It's lovely to feel that you're together, in sorrow, in joy. . . . Believe me, it is higher than a mother's or a father's love. We become soul twins [both men and women]. We become a whole. It [love] affects me a lot. You become complete. It [love] doesn't own you. However, it is always with you. (Interview with Zeri, 26 March 2018)

From the cadres' perspective, love is understood not just as an individual emotion but as a special meaning-producing emotion that binds people, nature, animals, ideology and so on together. The becoming of love through a large number of relations is expressed, as is typical in Kurdish society, through a large amount of physical contact and caress. I personally observed that members always shake hands when they meet or part. Women always give each other hugs and kisses. I also observed women and men hugging each other, but here I found that only those who had known each other for a long time did so. This is different from Kurdish society, where physical contact is most often heteronormative. Although cadres disavow sexualized behaviour and attempt to avoid signalling anything romantic, men and women in the PKK are not reticent about putting a hand on one another's leg while sitting together. The two sexes often sleep on the ground with their clothes on, without any kind of mattress or sleeping bags. Cadres of the same sex can sleep together under one rug if there are not enough rugs for everyone or if it is cold, and they see this as a way of keeping warm.

It is notable that touching is never problematized or regarded as stimulation or as a sign of homosexuality between cadres of the same sex, although some of the interviewees expressed a form of homophobia. Several cadres say that they themselves can tell whether the intention is more than comradely when they are touched by another cadre. In these cases, or if a cadre declares his or her feelings for another, the person is asked to pull himself or herself together and is sent for retraining for 'weak personalities', which will be a shameful experience for that person. This retraining applies to everyone, no matter his or her gender, who is seen to have sexual motivations behind a gesture directed at any person. At the same time, it seems to be hard to define what touching involves and how it differs from sexual intentions. The understanding prevails among the cadres that the body has agency and hence can tell for itself whether a touch is to be perceived as being solicitous or as something erotic.

3.4.3. Self-disciplined love

During the interviews, I found that the cadres do not quite agree on how to react to the state of falling in love romantically. Some cadres agree with Arya and Zeri in emphasizing that the proper reaction is to take complete control of one's desire and eliminate it in relation to the desired one. Others say that emotions and desires will always be present, which is why becoming conscious of an infatuation, taming it and then channelling its energy into creating a better relationship would be optimal. In my conversation with the woman fighter Ronahi, I found that she was not reticent when it came to talking about emotions and love, nor when it came to saying which of her men comrades she liked best and which women comrades she found beautiful (fieldnote, 26 April 2019). Beautiful would, however, be a matter of inner beauty, which includes being brave and having a strong will and/or strong morale. During my time with the cadres, they never commented on each other's appearance and never described the physical appearance of someone as beautiful.

Despite the expectation not to give in to infatuation, Ronahi addressed the contrast between ideals and reality. She distrusted her comrades if they denied or pretended that they had never fallen in love with another cadre. Like Nick, she said that the feeling of being loved and loving others was always present. It is therefore not a question of whether falling in love happens or not but of the choice, that is, whether or not one chooses to live it out. Moreover, Ronahi explained to me that the cadres who did not talk so much about love or who were very critical of those who left the movement in order to have a romantic relationship were typically the ones who were very unsure of themselves and refused to let themselves confront their real feelings. Referring to a couple of love poems by the eleventh-century Kurdish poet and dervish Baba Tahir-i Uryan, Ronahi said that love was more complex than her comrades believed.

Ronahi and Zin's willingness to speak of the inevitable existence of passionate love among the cadres and how they themselves had once chosen not to follow through on such love indicated that passionate love was a common challenge. In this context, it is important to mention Esin Düzel's (2018) work on the deceased women fighters' diaries. Düzel implies that the diaries reveal that the women fighters missed being held and kissed by their partners, with whom they were in a relationship before their enrolments as cadres. In the diaries, it is possible to get a glimpse of what Düzel calls the women fighters 'moral subjectivities' that frame what is allowed and not allowed in the movement, and what can be spoken of, and what must be left unsaid. Düzel's work shows how the women fighters in their diaries shift between different voices – friendly, intimate and vulnerable voices, constantly self-judgmental, creating moral dilemmas between subjective sentiments and collectivist ideals, dilemmas difficult to solve while they are supposed to both live and fight.[41]

Düzel's reading of the diaries is gainsaid by the most interviewees to whom I talked. Like Öcalan, they said that falling in love is something one chooses.[42] The disciplining seems successful in that the cadres prioritize above all else their love of the party, their people, whose representatives they are, their freedom and their struggle. Unconditional, passionate love between two people requires the fulfilment of various preconditions, not yet fulfilled. Strategically, then, for Öcalan the task is to get the cadres to postpone their personal needs in favour of the movement's objectives.

Öcalan's and the cadres' observations on sexuality and infatuation show how the cadres believe that the human being has a free will that goes to explain one's own choices. They thus operate on a traditionalist mindset based on the idea that the individual can use 'common sense' to choose for himself or herself whether to fall in love or not. The issue for the cadres is therefore not about desire or emotions but about disciplining the will to abstain from pursuing the love of another person and forming a passionate relationship with him or her. According to Öcalan and many of the interviewees, only the strong-willed will experience love in the revolutionary way. Zin, however, is sceptical towards the possible extent of self-discipline:

> The Leader says that you have to be able to organize your emotions politically. To give my own opinion, I don't think you can hold a person back from falling in love. After all, it's very natural that you become interested in another person. It shouldn't be criticized. In fact, people often keep it a secret that they are fond of another person or have feelings for someone. It is experienced inside. I don't think you can stop someone from having feelings for another person. And that shouldn't happen. The actual problem must be if you can't love someone else. After all, you're a human being, and being able to love is very human. If you can't feel anything, you aren't human. We have comrades who are only seventeen to eighteen years old. They are in puberty. You can't keep them from experiencing what has to be experienced. You can't intervene in their development and affect their anatomy. (Interview with Zin, 23 March 2018)

3.4.4. A critical form of permanent abstinence

Cadres' participation in the training programmes described earlier supports a strict self-development in which the focus is on disciplining the body, mind and drives, as well as on permanent abstention from various forms of sensual satisfaction, such as through alcohol or narcotics. Following Sloterdijk, one could call it a form of secular asceticism.[43] Following Foucault, one could call it a matter of pastoral power,[44] which is discursively implemented with effects on subjectivization, including one's performance of love. Even though the concepts of 'asceticism' and 'pastoral power' derive from within the field of religion, both concepts are applicable in the context of the PKK to describe the movement's surveillance and self-surveillance in connection with love. This form of permanent abstinence, which Käser calls an unwritten 'abstinence contract' between cadres and the movement,[45] was thus described by Mordem:

> We are trying to create a new model that can fix the existing situation. [. . .] We don't expect everyone to live just like us. We don't expect reproduction to stop.

When you are going to make a change, you first make a little model or a pilot project. That's what we're doing. We are creating a philosophical and political kernel that will help to change society. But we can't stand alone. There must also be space to practice the model. What we are doing is not new. It was there in Socrates, Plato and lots of Eastern philosophers, too. It's also there in a lot of religious movements. You make a little model, and in time it's practised in the big context. If you say something new, you have to live by it. Just as Jesus and his disciples did. We aren't an ascetic movement, but some aspects of our way of life have a lot in common with asceticism. Not just asceticism but other movements as well. Some religious traditions in Islam. Christianity and Judaism, too. But not in all faith traditions. Some aspects are also found in Buddhism. The point is to be critical, ideological and philosophical about the present day and its life conditions, and to think about how things can be fixed for the future [. . .] what all movements have in common is a focus on the family and the relationship between man and woman, because that's where societal change starts. (Interview with Mordem, 19 January 2018)

When Mordem says that they, as a movement, do not want reproduction to stop, but that they themselves abstain from any form of sexual relations and from having children, the reason is that Kurds must carry on having more children so that they can continue to survive as an ethnic group. But, when they themselves do not want to bring children into a colonized society, their decision seems to be an anti-colonial act, in that they do not want their children to undergo the oppression that they themselves have experienced. They want to protect their unborn children. To have a child would be regarded as a contribution to colonization, something Bozo explained to me by saying, 'A slave will always give birth to a slave' (Interview with Bozo, 16 August 2017).

In my view, Mordem's hesitance to call the movement's view of couple formation ascetic is due to the fact that the concept of 'asceticism' in Turkish (*sofuluk*) relates only to religion and is used of traditions within Islam that are highly conservative. It signifies the act of living in isolation from the world with the purpose of salvation to an otherworldly state. In the PKK, the cadres are seen as an elite in line with how ordinary people conceive of ascetics. However, the PKK and its members are not world renouncers. Rather, they are world-affirming in that they aim to improve conditions in this world and intend to create an alternative lifestyle. In addition, the cadres feel a responsibility for the general Kurdish population and even all of the world. They do not strive towards isolation. In fact, they seek to approach the general population in order to inspire, influence and benefit as many as possible through their lifestyle and learning.

Avasin supplemented Mordem in saying that their abstinence from forming couples helped enable them to create a better societal model: 'Where some women who get married are to live free, other women must sacrifice themselves' (Interview with Avasin, 21 March 2018). It can be deduced from this statement that Avasin saw herself as sacrificing her life for others in order to improve women's agency and hence contribute to better conditions for married couples. Arya went on to say that as a movement, they were already in the process of implementing their model of love, although they themselves did not experience it:

> There were a young man and woman who were in love with each other in a village. I mediated between the families so they could get married. In principle, we ourselves are against these relationships. But society's conditions are different. I said to the young people that they shouldn't be in a hurry to get married. They were too young and had a long life ahead of them. They were affected by what I said. I also criticized them because they didn't know much about each other. They had only met each other once before. I mean, they couldn't just get married after one meeting, just because they felt a chemistry between them. (Interview with Arya, 25 March 2018)

When Arya emphasized that traditional Kurdish society was a different context, she indicated at the same time that she knew that the PKK could not expect everyone to live like a cadre. Reproduction is seminal for the Kurdish nation to survive, as Mordem mentioned earlier. In this context, the practice of sexuality within the regulated frames of married life is considered a necessity for the reproduction and survival of the Kurdish nation; yet, sexuality should not be cultivated as a source of individual pleasure.

3.4.5. Perceptions of sexuality

The interviewees stated that they did not perceive or experience sexuality as a source of individual pleasure. The sexual drive was given to human beings and animals for reproduction purposes in order to ensure that life continues. Like many other human instincts and tendencies, the sexual drive should be disciplined:

> So, it's about making a choice and then adjusting your mind and body according to it. It's about gathering all our energies and using them for a particular life where the need and the necessity of something becomes less every day. It's not only about sexual instincts and how you control them. It's about taking control of your own body and being able to define your own body's needs. We mustn't just say that the body needs sex, food and sleep. Who defines what and how much we need? Sleep, for example! You can also live on four hours' sleep or seven hours' sleep a day. [. . .] That's what we are doing as cadres. [. . .] We are trying to create a new balance between body, instinct, needs and pleasure. (Interview with Bozo, 16 August 2017)

Bozo added that the sexual energy should not and could not be repressed and must be tamed and transformed consciously into an energy that would strengthen the fighting spirit. Thus, the need becomes something not physiological but something that one can construct and govern if the will is strong. Bozo's scepticism towards unleashed sexual energy is not only because he and the PKK believe it will weaken one's focus and be a waste of energy but also because of the kind of sexual relationship that would emerge from it.

During the interviews, not only Bozo but also the other informants spoke disparagingly about sexuality. The choice of words used to address such themes as sex, sexuality, eroticism and intercourse reflected some devaluation and a lack of familiarity in addressing them. I judge that this is culturally conditioned, as sexuality is not something one talks openly about neither in patriarchal Kurdish society nor in the context of the PKK's de-sexualized conception of love – and not at all with a man stranger like me.

On the topic of taming one's sexual energy, Mordem denied that repression should be involved. One cannot repress something so strong and big without becoming mentally or physically ill from it. Yet, it can be tamed and must be so to carry out the revolution and create the new types of human beings (Interview with Mordem, 19 January 2018). One therefore needs to abstain from, or at least moderate, one's personal, sensual and bodily needs. Delal explained this as follows:

> We do not experience a sexual need. We discipline ourselves. This has nothing to do with de-sexualization. One can decide for oneself if one wants to have a sex life. And if one doesn't, it shouldn't be seen as the person having less freedom, just as the experience of a sexual life should not be seen as an expression of freedom. I myself think that sexual needs are exaggerated in modern society. Capitalist modernity uses sexuality to materialize the woman further. For example, pornography has become a gigantic market. But we study what life was like in the natural society. Everything had a context where sexuality was a part of the whole. But now, sexuality is placed at the centre of life. This is a total exaggeration that happens in the name of liberation, also by feminists (Interview with Delal, 15 June 2017)

The interviewees seemed to agree that capitalist society exploits the sex drive and exaggerates the need for it, resulting, they say, in women becoming slaves in the pornography industry. They do not deny the need to feel, to love, to give and to provide care, nor that this may happen through sexual interaction, but they believe that one should have a more natural and moderate relationship to sexuality. Supplementing Delal, Zeri noted that it is not just about sexuality but all drives in general, so that all cadres are taught and trained to moderate personal, sensory and bodily needs and to avoid expressing sexualized feelings to one another. If they form sexual relationships, they cannot avoid experiencing let-downs, break-ups, disappointments and jealousy, which can affect their combat skills (Interview with Zeri, 26 March 2018).

The PKK defines the framework of the cultural norms and gender regimes to which the cadres must submit by reference to the importance of control of life processes and relations, including self-centred love and sexuality. The PKK thereby produces a counter-discourse with regard to sexuality that closes in on itself and exercises defining power in the same way as the dominant discourse in the culture it wants to combat.[46]

Summary

The analysis shows that the PKK operates with notions of both biological sex and sociocultural gender. On the one hand, the PKK claims that women, thanks to their biological sex, contain the potential for an especially strong and attractive attachment to the natural environment, including the mountains in and from which the PKK conducts its operations. On the other hand, the PKK speaks of constructed gender and of heterosexuality/heteronormative love arising from it, which the men and women of the movement must repudiate in order to focus on their warrior identity and to engage in the PKK's struggle. This means that Kurdish women, once they arrive in the mountains to become cadres, are met with the perception that they, in contrast to men, are especially attached to nature and that this attachment carries obligations. Mountains in particular are regarded as living beings, with whom the women cadres upon arrival are expected to interact. For young women, going to the mountains may serve as an escape from life in civil society and an access to constituting themselves in new ways. Upon arrival, all new cadres undergo a powerful ideological and also gender-specific course of instruction in which they are re-socialized. Instruction and training are combined with methods of self-criticism and an almost ascetic self-discipline to curb individual needs as a means to prepare themselves to life as a 'cadre'. I found Butler and Barad's theories of performativity relevant here to point out how the subversion of the women newcomers' identity is subverted through bodily practices in which material phenomena such as cliffs, food, clothes, menstruation, others' bodies and weapons intra-act with effects on their mobilization in the anti-colonial struggle. All these disciplining, teaching and training activities on the part of the movement transform the lives of newcomers. The isolated training camps in the mountains, far removed from civil society, create an optimal setting for new members to submit to the organized programme of instruction. The purpose of it all is to produce strong-willed cadres willing to sacrifice their individual needs for the benefit of the Kurdish collective. The instruction programme also evens out the differences between the cadres, regardless of their different backgrounds with regard to education, family, class and religious affiliation, and thus produces a more homogeneous and standardized identity to lay the ground for them to fight together for a shared objective. Socializing new cadres implies controlling their life processes, easily affected by individual needs and drives. It involves social control over the members' sex and love life.[47] The body undergoes a powerful de-sexualization process where love is redefined. If love is felt passionately, it must be tamed, cleansed and re-educated, so that its energy, passion and strength can be used to overcome any self-centredness and maximize the cadres' combat skills. Accordingly, love between the cadres must be free, de-sexualized and de-corporalized. Love towards the opposite sex must be transformed into a radical love for the native land, even to death do them part.

Chapter 4

THEORIZING SEPARATION AND BIOLOGICAL BODIES

This chapter will begin with a brief account of the ideological and political motives underlying the PKK's decision to separate women fighters from men fighters in the mountains. This will be followed by an analysis of the women fighters' narrativizations that assume that a person's biological sex determines his or her character traits in specifically gendered ways. The analysis substantiates the impression that women who choose to enroll as cadres in the mountains do so to exert gender-related resistance in order to create alternative understandings and narratives of themselves as liberated subjects.

4.1. Partial segregation of men and women

When new members join the PKK, men and women are segregated as much as possible. Thus, they live in separate camps or at least sleep separately. Most daily activities are, however, performed together. The distance between the training camps is usually no more than a couple of hundred metres. In my interview with Avasin, she said that this division means that the women are allocated the distinctive place in the movement that they need in order to be themselves:

> A woman can't be at ease together with a man. That's just the way life is for a woman. You retire to your own unit. But, in the daytime, everything is done communally. The first training is shared. Breakfast is shared. Cooking is shared. Only in the evening, when you retire to your own unit, then you sleep separately. Otherwise, everything takes place communally. [. . .] But we also have our special units such as the YJA-STAR or the PAJK.[1] They are distinctive. There are only women there. No men have any influence there. You're totally segregated there. You are also alone [only women] in the daytime, not just in the evening. [. . .] the mechanism [segregation] is there to help the woman. Because the woman has become alienated from herself [over time]. She has moved far away from her gender and her body. So the point of segregation is to create a distinctive will, a distinctive consciousness and a distinctive history. (Interview with Avasin, 21 March 2018)

My feeling was that Avasin with her formulations attempted to stress the significance of separation from men by emphasizing and explaining why the movement practices a heteronormative conception of gender. She seemingly believed that women needed special treatment, as she maintained that they were distinctive. As a concept, 'distinctiveness' is probably used more than any other within the women's movement. 'Distinctive body', 'distinctive consciousness', 'distinctive defence', 'distinctive organization', 'distinctive war' and 'distinctive history': these are just some of the terms they use when speaking about themselves. Here, the purpose of emphasizing women's distinctiveness seems to be to establish a feeling within these women of being unique and special as compared with men. Generally, the PKK operates on the basic understanding that woman has always been unique, but that because of men's oppression of women and other woman-oppressing power mechanisms in society, she has moved away from understanding herself in that way, and it is therefore necessary to create space and opportunity for women so that they can recreate themselves. Consequently, it is regarded as necessary to separate the women from the men, as this is what it will take to enable women to embrace the category 'woman' and be proud of being part of it.

In contrast to the generalization of women's distinctiveness, the various women cadres articulated different views during our conversations on what would explain the physical and organizational separation and how they felt about it. For example, the woman cadre Zeri recalled her first encounter with the camp and her surprise at the segregation as follows:

> We were on our way down [this is her first meeting with the guerrillas in the mountains]. The camp was at the water's edge. The comrades were eating. Women eat together, while men eat together. I was surprised and asked about the division. [Laughs] Why are you split up? It made no sense. They said: 'That's our culture.' I'd been at university before [. . .] It was different to where I came from. (Interview with Zeri, 26 March 2018)

Here, Zeri recounted how the physical segregation did not immediately make sense to her, because she came from university life in a big city, where she had been used to gender roles other than patriarchal ones. Zeri was not alone in being surprised and uncomprehending at the gender segregation during her first days in the mountains. Ronya, who also has a university background, said it made no sense to her at first. She regarded it as downright primitive that women and men typically sat separately when attending instruction (Interview with Ronya, 27 March 2018). The man cadre Mordem explained to me that the division was introduced out of necessity in its day:

> In the 1990s, there was collective participation in Serhildans [Kurdish word for Intifada]. Thousands of people arrived [in groups at the camp] who we couldn't include. Most brought their traditional culture. We couldn't include them. We weren't prepared for it. (Interview with Mordem, 19 January 2018)

In the previous extract, Mordem articulates the understanding that the movement was not ready to receive mass enrolment of women in the 1990s where newly arrived women made up a third of the total membership of the movement. According to Mordem, men and women had to be kept apart from each other to minimize the possibility of conflicts and problems arising from their being together. Segregation was also introduced to guard against clashes between the PKK's ideology and the traditions and fundamental attitudes that the members brought with them. Against this background, segregation is a means to ensure women's possibilities of survival in the mountains and to protect them from men's lust and dominance. It was a necessary step both to avoid chaos and to make the women feel safe enough to remain in the struggle.

The segregation is presented as a means to protect women from situations giving free rein to men's lust with the risk of women being subjected to rape and becoming pregnant. Yet, I assume that it is also advantageous for the movement to avoid such situations because they could put the PKK in a bad light with the Kurds in general and reduce women's enlistment in the movement. These concerns add to an understanding of why the participants receive ideological instruction in how to act in particular ways in the PKK according to their gender. The two women cadres Zeri and Zin said of this instruction:

When we came [to the movement in the mountains], we were informed of what we could and couldn't do, in accordance with the party's morality and culture and with party organization. [. . .] For example, a woman mustn't wander alone in the mountains. Being careful is a precaution in life as well as in the party. You're a woman. So you have to be careful in your behaviour and attitude. You mustn't be misunderstood! [. . .] These rules seem irritating at first. [. . .] Then you think: don't they trust me? But everything makes sense in time, when you build up experience and come to learn that the rules have arisen out of necessity. (Interview with Zeri, 26 March 2018)

In the youth section especially, you could see that the leadership paid attention to the women and often intervened to protect them from the men's masculinity. (Interview with Zin, 23 March 2018)

Although the PKK aims to do away with patriarchal society, the aforementioned arguments show that the PKK recreates and reproduces a patriarchal categorization of women and men. Along with party power mechanisms, women are allotted a particular position with a specific gender-determined responsibility within the party.[2] Norms that define how women and men are to behave with each other and the methods mentioned in Section 3.3 on how to constitute the new human are used to establish and maintain particular gender roles. This translates into women being held responsible and put in their place if the PKK judges that they are signalling something that may be misunderstood by the men. These initiatives reflect a certain mistrust and Öcalan's view that women and men have very little knowledge of each other in Kurdish society and are therefore not used to forming friendships without the expectation of a romantic relationship.[3] This interpretation can also be read in Zeri's account of what she was told she may and may not do while a cadre in the movement:

> You are told that you're a woman and that therefore you must be careful about your attitude and the way you behave. All the time. [. . .] We were told things like that. At first, it really doesn't make sense. [. . .] Then you start to protest: Why is it that way? Am I child, or what? Or don't they trust me? (Interview with Zeri, 26 March 2018)

At first, the party's restrictions on women made no sense to Zeri, and she baulked at following them. In time, though, like the other women, she began to comply with the rules because she judged that the restrictions helped to protect the women in the mountains. This narrativization recurs among the women I interviewed: at first they did not see the point of the restrictions, but in time along the above-mentioned process of self-regulation and self-disciplining, they end up defending and appreciating the restrictions that have become naturalized.[4]

Ideally, men should be able to resist the temptations that follow some women's attitude or perhaps challenging clothing. However, due to the movement's distrust in men's resilience, PKK's women become trapped in a sort of temptress position, even leaving women as responsible for protecting themselves against some men's lust.[5] Only women are assigned a weighty responsibility in respect of the aforementioned expectations of iterative acts in the form of self-regulation and self-discipline, while men are merely assigned the responsibility of 'killing his masculinity' as Öcalan has done. Öcalan describes himself as someone who killed his masculinity.[6] This means that he is no longer masculine but nor is he feminine. He is gender-neutral as regards his attitude, his mindset and the way he sees and judges the world. Nazan Üstündağ (2007) calls this position of Öcalan's an androgynous identity, in that Öcalan has now liberated himself from the gender patterns in which both sexes are regarded as being trapped. According to Üstündağ, this position gives Öcalan two advantages: his leadership never comes up for discussion in the movement from a gender perspective; and, by killing his masculinity, he makes men and women ideologically equal. It is also possibly the explanation for why the women fighters I interviewed considered Öcalan as their Sun, who illuminated their freedom, rather than a man leader or as constituting a unifying 'institution' beyond his personality.[7]

Men's masculinity that is to be killed is the patriarchal one, which is also a 'false' masculinity. Its eradication is killed to enable men's return to their own original and innocent masculinity. From the observations I made during fieldwork, my judgement is that the men were much less focused on transforming their identity and masculinity than the women were. For the men, it was more about 'just' having to surrender something of themselves and curbing their patriarchal Kurdish masculinity, while the women were made responsible for preventing the emergence of sexual chaos.

4.2. The PKK's theory of separation as a form of emancipation

Whether physical separation was introduced out of necessity or out of ideological motives, both men and women fighters feel that segregation strengthens both sexes. Both the interviewed men and the women explained the idea of segregation in terms of what the movement calls the 'theory of separation'. The theory of separation is based on the ideal of women returning to what is regarded as their natural origin as a precondition for becoming free human beings. Delal explained what this meant in practice:

> Coming to live up in the mountains involves breaking with society. In the mountains, you have to break with men in order to get organized. So, it's a double separation. To become free, this is a necessity. Your first war is with yourself. This is the war of return, the return to your origin. This is a long and perhaps endless struggle, because it demands a mentality revolution. (Interview with Delal, 15 June 2017)

Delal said that the physical separation in the mountains made it possible for the women to work on themselves and return to their 'original state'. At the same time, she stressed that this physical separation was not enough. By this, Delal indicated that the theory of separation was more about an endless mental revolution aimed at freeing oneself of everything masculine to recreate oneself. Partly in order to achieve this, women in the PKK began to organize themselves internally from the early 1990s.

The first women's units were set up by Öcalan in the Beqaa Valley in 1990,[8] but the need for women to organize separately within the PKK was not formally discussed until 1992 at the first autonomous women's congress with around 300 women fighters represented. In general, the women fighters regard the congress as a failure, because a large part of the leadership at that time opposed a separate organization of women. At Öcalan's urging, the women's congress was reconvened in 1995. This time, around 500 exclusively women participants attended in a large subterranean room that the women called the 'women's temple'. At this congress, the women fighters decided to create the first women's army units and to unite in the Free Women's Union of Kurdistan (*Yekitiya Azadiye Jinên Kurdistanê,* YAJK). Against this background, the overarching themes taken up at the congress were 'self-will, self-confidence and willpower'. After the congress, two YAJK representatives began to attend the PKK's Central Council. This was the first time that women were represented at such a high level in the PKK, something the woman fighter Ronya described as 'a revolution' (Interview with Ronya, 27 March 2018). The congress and a raft of concurrent steps resulted in women forming both their own army unit and their own political party. They now became more specific with regard to the internal objective of freeing themselves completely of men dominance when fighting side by side with men for a common goal. Not until 1999, though, did the discussions result in the foundation of the Kurdistan Women's Workers Party (*Partiye Jinên Karkerê Kurdistanê,* PJKK), whose aim was to implement the women's ideology in practice. The PJKK was later expanded into the Free Women's Party (*Partiye Jinên Azad,* PJA) and most recently, in 2004, into the present-day Kurdistan Women's Liberation Party (PAJK), which acts as the umbrella organization for the various women's organizations in the Kurdish Freedom Movement. An incentive during the consolidation of these parties was to secure a more flexible and comprehensive confederative women's organization. The Women's High Council (*Kome Jinen Blind,* KJB)[9] was therefore established in 2005 as a new umbrella organization including women and women's organizations from the four parts of Kurdistan as well as Kurdish women living abroad.[10] Dersim said that the separate military and political organization of women in the PKK was seen as necessary for women to be able to create themselves anew:

> [Öcalan said to the woman] Go and make your own dwelling. Your training camp. Go and collect your own firewood. Fetch your own water. Find your own food. You are also a human being. You are a woman, but also a human being. Why are you dependent on the man? Why should the man make your dwelling? Why should the man fetch food and firewood for you? Why should the man do this and that? In this way, [Öcalan] sets you free from your dependence. He creates your own will and the way you can stand on your own two feet. (Interview with Dersim, 27 March 2018)

Dersim recounted with pride how good and strategic Öcalan was when he forced the women to explore their potential. From Dersim's point of view, Öcalan's greatest contribution to the women's movement (KJB) had been his assistance in the creation of gender consciousness. This had led to the PKK today becoming what Öcalan himself describes as a 'women's party'. For Öcalan, said Dersim, the task was not only to protect women but also to create the ideal woman and expand women's representation and opportunities for action. Sakine Cansız, one of the two women who were the first to attend the PKK's founding general assembly, also writes in her book, in a similar vein to Dersim's narrative, that women's involvement in the PKK can be attributed solely to Öcalan, who stubbornly resisted his comrades' mistrust of women's presence in the PKK.[11] In this context, I believe that Öcalan's support for women can also be considered a strategic investment in his leadership. In arguing the case for women representation in the political parties and for women fighters at a time when women joined the PKK with low prospects as well as low expectations, he hedged his bets. Öcalan created a loyal army concurrent with the band of men members that constituted the leadership at the time. Afterwards, his leadership has never been disputed. Despite Öcalan's imprisonment since 1999, it has never been a discussion in the PKK to appoint another leader to replace him. Women fighters have a decisive role in creating for Öcalan the eternal leadership as long as he is alive.

The women I interviewed stated that both mental and physical detachment from their men comrades was necessary if they were to succeed in becoming free, independent women. According to Delal, it was a matter not merely of escaping from their allotted role of victim in the patriarchal Kurdish society but also of creating better opportunities to secure women's rights after the revolution, which many other anti-colonial and feminist struggles around the world have not succeeded in doing.[12] Delal recounted the following:

> So what are we [women] to do? How are we to organize ourselves? How can we avoid making the same mistakes as were made in the real socialism period? Yes, we have a national problem, and many women joined this struggle because of the national problem, but at the same time, we have a women problem. The men [the men comrades] tried to make us believe that the women problem would be solved after the solution of the national question. We didn't accept that and that was a hard-fought issue in the PKK. [. . .] We didn't want also to deal with the women question after the revolution. [. . .] We didn't want to repeat the same mistakes that were made in previous revolutions. [. . .] Because of this, we went in for a form of organization that separates the women from the men and creates separate women army units. (Interview with Delal, 15 June 2017)

Going by Delal's description, the separate organization of women serves two main purposes. The first is to secure women equal opportunities for action within the PKK, that is, to prevent the men comrades from dictating to them what to do. The second purpose is to ensure that the women can maintain the rights they have fought for – also after the revolution. According to Delal, the separate organization of women has not only increased women's influence in the PKK and made it easier for them to participate in it but also made it easier for women to join the PKK. Cane, who is from the third generation, was of the same opinion; she described how it had been easier for women of her generation to join the PKK than it had been for the older generation:

> It wasn't difficult to come here [to the mountains]. I didn't encounter the difficulties that previous generations did, because it was an organized women's movement that had emerged from previous experiences. The experiences and challenges of the women who took part in the 1990s and 1980s laid the ground for today's separate organization. My generation – I came here in 2002 – didn't really experience having to overcome any kind of challenges in order to establish ourselves in the PKK. Everything had been secured and experienced. The women were organized. (Interview with Cane, 25 March 2018)

According to Dersim, it took some time and some struggle to achieve the organization of women with subsequent institutionalization within the PKK that Cane was able to enjoy when she joined. Dersim recounts that it was not only in the PKK's leadership but also among the men cadres that the women felt some resistance against the idea of them organizing separately. The men cadres attempted to talk the women out of the idea by arguing that women were fragile and weak and must therefore be supported by their men comrades and must settle for less dangerous missions and logistical tasks. Chapter 5 will examine how the debates about this led to changed conditions for the women, which will focus on the women's own combat experiences.

With regard to the theorizing of women's separation from men, the interviewed women fighters all advocated the separate organization, yet emphasized that this advocacy did not equate to their hating men. On the contrary, they see the men, too, as being, like themselves, victims of capitalist modernity and patriarchal culture. In another conversation, Delal told me that the women fighters together with the PKK's overall leadership have distanced themselves from the liberal ideal of 'equality'. Women's equality with men is problematic, when men are also subjected to patriarchal power holders' control and oppression. The women fighters' struggle is therefore about both women and men's total liberation from all forms of oppression (Interview with Delal, 15 June 2017). Like the other women interviewees, Delal is here drawing on Öcalan, who points out that women's liberation struggle is not just a struggle against men but one aimed at liberating both oppressed genders.[13] According to Öcalan, the party focuses particularly on women because they are the more oppressed gender, but men also need to be saved. The party must find solutions not only to the problems of women but also to those of men, including a redefinition of their masculinity.[14] Emancipation must, however, be taken in sequence with a focus on women first. Delal explained it as follows:

> For example, women speak and move freely at meetings without men, but, if there is one man present at a meeting of 100 women, then all the women will adjust themselves to that one man. So, we do everything alone. After that, we women act as one body and with a strong will so as then to meet the men and implement our collective planning together with them. (Interview with Delal, 15 June 2017)

Here, Delal argues for the need of a natural location, a place or a gender-delimited area, where women can realize themselves and practice their 'natural gender' before interaction with men can take place without the women falling back into old patriarchal habits. As mentioned previously, Öcalan points to the transformation of power and property relations and to the mentality revolution as a solution to the women question, which all entail that women should organize separately. Great upheavals demand the establishment of free, gender-segregated institutions and women's units if a 'gender-liberated society' is to be created.[15] In this connection, the women fighters seem to consider women's separate organizing at all levels and in all domains compulsory.

Like Delal, Bermal explained how the separate organization of women creates a kind of collective strength that enables them to resist men dominance together:

> Our separate organization goes back to the foundation of the YAJK in 1995. Before that, we gave our briefings and updates to men comrades. It was they who took the decisions. Before that, we had no real influence. Those were hard times. The men did things as it suited them. How? For example, by looking down

on you. Oppressing you. Bawling you out. We criticized them, but we weren't organized, so we couldn't bring about radical change. Changes started to come about when we organized separately. For example, if a man comrade goes and raises his voice to a woman comrade, we intervene directly. How do we do that? All the women together will say that the men comrade's attitude is wrong. We see that insult as an act directed at all of us women. At the same time, we'll decide that the man comrade must explain himself by making a written report. He must present his own 'self-criticism' to the woman comrade. The subsequent process depends on his report. He is obliged to write the report. He can't refuse. That is our current internal process. It is established now, and it works fine. (Interview with Bermal, 21 March 2018)

The PKK refers to such an ad hoc, internal process as a 'platform'. It entails a session of criticism and self-criticism, where party members have to stand up in front of a group of comrades to reflect on their own practice. Normally, the leadership will initiate such a session, but it can also happen at the person's own request or following episodes where something needs to be clarified. Everyone is duty-bound to explain himself or herself, and one cannot refuse. Platforms can also be held if a complaint is made against someone or if doubt has arisen about someone's intentions. As well as acting as a clarification session, the platform implies that people are questioned. Subsequently, the comrades and leaders decide whether the member's explanation is sufficient and reasonable. In certain cases, platforms can lead to punishment that may vary from undergoing another training programme to a demotion in rank; at worst, it may involve expulsion from the PKK. A platform can last from several hours to several days. For example, Sakine Cansız writes in her book that she once ended up in a platform where she was questioned for eight hours, during which she had to stand humbly and take all the harsh and partly unjust criticisms that were put forward by different comrades.[16]

Once during my fieldwork, I witnessed a platform that was planned for a man cadre at the request of a woman cadre. The platform lasted two hours and was more a matter of interrogating him than an opportunity for him to adjust his way of 'cadre life' by facilitating his self-criticism. Instead, the cadre was exposed to harsh criticism and accused of having a way of life that did not fit into the PKK's ideology. Especially, his attitude towards the women fighters was criticized. By the end of the platform, he admitted to everything that he was accused of and promised to improve his way of life. It was not apparent to me if he sincerely agreed with the thirty people who assailed him by their criticism, or if he knew that he would not stand a chance of explaining himself and therefore might as well submit to party rules to finish the platform as quickly as possible in order to remain in the PKK.[17]

During my conversations with men cadres, they told me that they often regarded the women's criticism of them as unjust and based on what the men described as 'reflex-based criticism'. They did not mind being criticized for being men, but they found many of the concrete assailments, for example during platforms, unjustified and clichéd. The woman fighter Cane, who was responsible among other things for teaching, could certainly recognize the pattern. She said that the men often held back to avoid conflicts with the women, because the women always kept them under supervision and problematized their actions at every opportunity. Although Cane saw this as wrong, she thought that it was nevertheless necessary as a way of signalling to the men that these were new times, as the women were now an organized force who would not put up with everything and that the men were therefore obliged to change. According to Cane, the women's actions helped the men to problematize their own way of being in the world and their own masculinity to avoid being oppressive towards the women (Interview with Cane, 25 March 2018). Cane went on to say that this was necessary because the men did not even realize that they sometimes offended and harassed women merely by their body language and the way they spoke to them. According to Cane, the women's criticism thus forced Kurdish men for the first time in history to pay attention to their own actions, because until then they had spent their time 'keeping an eye on the women's actions'. Finally, Cane explained that reflex-based reactions would eventually become more natural to both women and men as they became better at giving each other feedback. In my judgement, though, Cane did not take into account the fact that the physical separation of women and men also makes it possible for the men to keep away from the women so as to avoid their control and criticism. I will elaborate on this point later in Section 5.2.

4.3. Jineoloji and the alleged natural woman of the Neolithic

This section will analyse the women fighters' narratives of how the heteronormative separation between men and women in the PKK seemingly required a form of science used by the movement to create its own collectivist, feminist figuration,[18] the 'natural woman of the Neolithic'.

With the 2005 paradigm shift towards democratic confederalism, women were allocated a central role in the new society to come. Their separate organization was successful and in the course of time, they accumulated several experiences, including the one that they needed to establish knowledge about woman as a historical phenomenon based on their lessons learnt and their perspectives through conceptualizations. This pursuit of knowledge and conceptualizations has developed into what the women themselves refer to in Kurdish as 'jineoloji'. 'Jin' means 'woman' in Kurdish and '-loji' ('ology') means science, so 'jineoloji' denotes the science of women. 'Jin' in Kurdish also means 'life', so jineoloji can also be understood as the science of women and life, and hence as something that touches on the whole of society.

According to Gulesor, who teaches jineoloji, the discipline was developed in light of the PKK's critique of existing sciences, capitalist society and feminism. The critique argued that existing sciences and capitalist society gave women no place in society. Existing sciences were too androcentric and patriarchal and were therefore not contributing to women's liberation. In this context, jineoloji advocates that history should be re-examined from a woman perspective focusing on women's contribution to society and ontology (Gulesor in FGI, 25 March 2018). They argue that formats and perspectives within the established sciences, especially the positivist ones, are men-biased and must be directed by women in a new direction.[19] Cane said that the movement's critique of positivism was mainly directed at its subject-object division – partly because it enabled strategies of othering where men could position themselves as subjects and women as objects. As an alternative, jineoloji offers a form of constructive dialectics where the subject and object form a synthesis that respects people's mutual differences, which again prevents one from dominating the other. Cane also recalled that this way of considering the subject-object relationship distinguished jineoloji from feminism, which, she said, still operates with a subject-object division that contributes to the oppression of women.

Another key point in jineoloji is the claim that once human beings existed without the objectification of women as a socio-typical tendency. Cane therefore argued that past and present patriarchal conceptions, leading to the oppression and objectification of women, cannot offer an adequate understanding of woman as a phenomenon. Cane concretized this with the following example: 'If a table is made of wood, its character and strength cannot be understood from the table as a phenomenon, only by looking at the wood the table is made of' (Cane in FGI, 25 March 2018). Here, Cane was using the wood as an allegory of woman's matter and the table as the formed product.

A third point to be addressed is the strategic advantages that follow from investments in jineoloji as a science and its promotion. While the PKK clearly distinguishes itself from Western feminism, the liberal West is likely to look with sympathy at how the PKK cares about women's emancipation, which again will help the movement obtain support and recognition in the international arena, also because the ideals for women are not limited to only Kurdish women but women worldwide. I shall return to this strategic advantage in Section 6.5, but first, the women fighters narrate how and why jineoloji was developed.

When the objectification of women was identified as the central problem, the need for jineoloji became, according to Delal, clear. She recounted that jineoloji was developed from the following questions:

> First, we looked at history. Where are we in these sciences? We asked, how was science developed in the course of history, and where were women? Where has the woman lost? How and why did she lose? How can women become free? [. . .] This precept of the Leader [Abdullah Öcalan] is very important: 'The history of women's slavery was not written down, but the history of women's liberation will be.' (Interview with Delal, 15 June 2017)

According to Delal, women in the PKK have stressed that conceptions of history are not neutral and so they must be reinterpreted and rewritten. The women in the PKK therefore took inspiration from mythological and oral narratives instead of adhering to the known, official written history. Men and power holders wrote official history, and women in the PKK therefore did and do not believe that official history tells the whole truth. New information and knowledge were used to develop jineoloji, as Delal explained:

When the existing sciences explain historical periods, they have a tendency to explain them as a horizontal timeline, as though drawn with a ruler. That means they continually consider a new period as better than the preceding period. For example, the slavery period was better than the pre-communal period. And the feudal period was better than the slavery period. The capitalist period was better than the feudal period. This is a progressive, linear interpretation of history. The pre-communal period existed for millions of years. We call that period the natural society. A society without hierarchies, where women could organize themselves. Although that society lasted for millions of years, the significance of that period to humanity isn't mentioned.[20] (Interview with Delal, 15 June 2017)

Delal's conception of history rests on several propositions and claims against a chronological progression of history that are hard to substantiate. Yet, it is striking that both Delal and the other women I interviewed agree that there were no wars, subjugation or exploitation in the Neolithic period because women were centre stage. Women were productive; they were mothers and creators; and their nature prevented men from dominating women. In that period, nobody belonged to or was owned by anybody else. Delal stressed that subjugation did not begin until after this period, with the development of men dominance. Delal never substantiated her assertions or tried to explain why men came to dominate. The same deficiency can be observed when, with reference to the Neolithic period, she claimed that the establishment of a classless, non-patriarchal society was still possible: 'This was possible for millions of years in the Neolithic period. Why shouldn't it be possible now?'

The PKK calls the woman of that period 'the natural woman of the Neolithic'. The Neolithic woman is perceived in the movement as an ideological figure with an important strategic function in the fight to achieve a society where women can enjoy freedom. In this way, the nostalgic figuration of the Neolithic woman guides, inspires and directs women fighters towards a new subject position through self-decolonization.[21] The embodied image creates a visualized subject position by which new opportunities can be discerned and by which women fighters can overcome obstacles laid out by the colonizing power of the Turkish state or discourse within the PKK that constrains women's self-realization.

With the aim of creating the ideal woman, the PKK wishes to centralize women's place in society and nature. Narratives, perceptions and connotations of the Neolithic woman contribute to reconceptualize the intra-action between women and nature, materiality, animals, plants and so on. The jineological figuration thus promotes an approach to women's identity and gender from more than just a sociocultural perspective. It promotes an identificatory process that intends to re-establish and acknowledge relations between bodies, other natural and material phenomena including human beings in general and women in particular. This came out in Helin's narrative:

The Leader [Öcalan] talks about Neolithic times. About how woman was then, her capacity for work, the contribution she made. At that time, the woman led the way. In art, agriculture, healing and protection of her family, learning, knowledge, motivation and domestication of animals. But all that contribution has been forgotten for the last 500 years. Instead, women have experienced oppression, injustice, men dominance and massacres. In the party [the PKK], we've been told how we can return to history and what we need to do today. For example, the Leader says that we must look for the things we have lost where we lost them. The Leader wants us to return to our original consciousness. Through this consciousness, we will achieve our humanity, acquire a new knowledge of animals, trees, mountains. This is the way to love everything and acquire knowledge of everything. (Interview with Helin, 24 March 2018)

I consider Helin's description to be an obvious romanticization of a matriarchal society and of woman, one that describes the woman as innocent and non-violent by nature. I consider it paradoxical that the women fighters cherished the Neolithic woman's protective and healing character traits when they themselves were 'women fighters' and proud of being better fighters than men. I will expand on this point in Chapter 5, where I describe the women fighters' own combat experiences. The point I want to make here is that the 'natural but non-biological gender difference' espoused particularly by Öcalan and the women fighters is strategically generalized to the women's advantage in order to give women better opportunities for action and centralize women's place in the PKK. Jineoloji comes in useful in this context because drawing on it as a science is a way of seeking to legitimize the ideology's ideas concerning women's nature. Zelal brings this to the fore:

Women's struggle involves a mentality revolution. You're trying to find your own truth. It's about keeping on overcoming yourself. It isn't a goal you can reach. You carry on revealing something new the whole time. [. . .] We've come a long way and created freedom in many areas. Now it's about finding solutions. Jineoloji, for example. Jineoloji is the science of women. It is a tool developed to get at the truth, because we haven't finished recreating ourselves. [. . .] It's true that I also had my own, inner searchings before I joined the PKK. But it was only after I joined that my inner search became purposeful and organized, and I became aware of seeing myself as a woman. [. . .]. Noticing gender struggle, especially. I've always loved being a woman. I had a preference for my gender. I wasn't alienated from my gender, but the [capitalist] system indoctrinated me to believe that women and men were the same. But after joining the PKK, we saw that there was a difference. So I can't change men until I myself return to my original state. (Interview with Zelal, 17 September 2017)

Here, Zelal describes the change in her identity when she narrates the course of her life before and after opting to participate in the movement. Among other things, she noted that her search for alternative understandings demanded change. The key point in Zelal's narrative is that the revolution of women's mentality is important not only to their own emancipation but also to that of men and the whole of society. The women fighters have to recreate themselves and rediscover their original state. This gives them the possibility of recreating life and society. In this context, jineoloji becomes the ideological seedbed from which their recreation must grow.[22] Switching between a first and third-person narrative, Avasin recounts the following about the process and significance of her recreation:

> I used to be a passive woman, who didn't talk much, didn't take much interest in anything or have big ideals. I believed in everything without being critical. [. . .] Not a personality that fought for anything. Someone who actually wanted to overcome her limitations but couldn't manage it. But, with the movement, Avasin changed a lot. She became aware of her strength and her courage. She learnt about herself and began to love herself. She began to hate it when her father said, 'you are like a son to me'. So big changes took place. For example, I now know what I'm capable of. Am I fully emancipated now? No, it will take more. Despite the big changes. I've got the willpower now. That's the most important thing. (Interview with Avasin, 21 March 2018)

4.4. Notions of the natural and binary genders

In the PKK, women and men are perceived as two different, natural genders, with gender to be conceived of as binary. The fundamental understanding within the movement is that nature's flora and fauna exhibit the same gender binarity, which is vital to reproduction. Although gender is conceived of as a social construct, women and men are believed to have distinct natures. The women fighters I interviewed baulked at describing these natures as biological, because they did not want to be seen as inclined to positivism. They believed, however, that gender was something inherent in their character. Character here means natural properties that go to define femininity and masculinity. While Western constructionism rejects the notion of natural gender, the PKK neither hesitates to speak of woman's nature nor to identify women with nature. The following comments on this were made by the two men cadres Mordem and Firat, and the woman cadre Dersim:

> Woman is a wonderful creature. She is fantastic. All the mysterious things about her haven't been solved yet. [. . .] life began with the mother. The mother created life. Of course, the man has a contribution to make here, too. But it is the woman who creates a new life out of nothing by giving everything she has. The woman's aesthetic beauty is also a plus. The woman is therefore a creature one can be fascinated by and in love with. (Interview with Mordem, 19 January 2018)

> When we say 'woman's nature', we mean woman's original state and the woman's truth. The man's truth is a symbol of how life has been destroyed, oppressed and how society has moved away from its original state [. . .] The man's history is the history of destruction and the fight to establish hegemony. The man's history is the warrior's history. (Interview with Firat, 26 March 2018).

A man is coarse because of his character. He lacks aesthetics, courtesy, elegance, kindness and so on because of his mentality. For example, there was a period in the mountains when the men's unit was very untidy. They had no discipline, things were all over the place and filthy. At the women's, everything was tidy, clean, greenery and flowers everywhere. When we visited them, we told them they should pull themselves together. We told them they should grow flowers, something green and clean up. Everything's a struggle, you see. It took some time. But afterwards we found that their unit became a lot better than ours. So they started to tease us. (Interview with Dersim, 27 March 2018)

These statements are stereotypical. Mordem and Firat's statements do not diverge much from those of a patriarch when woman is allotted an innocent role in which, as a creature, she is praised and almost deified. Dersim's statement is also stereotypical, reflecting naturalized conceptions of men as some who would not know how to keep the domicile clean because any domicile would be the domain of a woman.

Gulesor, who taught jineoloji in the women fighters' camp, approached gender in a more theoretical way. She mentioned that the concepts 'life', 'nature' and 'freedom', like the concept 'woman', were etymologically feminine. She meant that it was woman who first tilled the land, tamed the wild beasts and tried to create a balance between human beings and nature, including the animals. Woman is also described as part of the land. Here, Gulesor refers both to the fertile soil and to the land of the Kurds, where the nation is to be built. A symbolic analogy is drawn between the soil of the homeland and the woman body. As land or soil and as part of nature, the woman also becomes a symbol of peace and order, as Gulesor believes that 'woman's nature' does not include the inclination to yearn for dominance as is the case with men. According to Gulesor, woman's nature consists of five components:

A woman's nature has five basic properties [. . .] One of them is energy. A woman's energy is very fluid. The second is emotional intelligence and behaviour in life. Emotional intelligence is a result of her contact with nature. The third is the sixth sense, which is strong in women. And the fourth is delivery, namely the ability to give birth. Productivity. We do not consider production only as biological. We also believe that it has a sociological dimension. The fifth is menstruation, which is the most natural link between woman and nature. It is linked to periods. It makes the link between woman, nature and life stronger. (Gulesor in FGI, 25 March 2018).

Although the PKK claims not to be biologically deterministic, a number of the women I interviewed explained that they, like Gulesor, were of the opinion that a particular biological sex implies a particular sociocultural gender identity. Distinguishing between biological and sociocultural gender makes it possible to find qualities in which women are stronger than men. These are cultivated so that women can participate in the struggle on an equal footing with men. Women are thus seen as connected with the energy of nature and as emotionally stronger than men. This relationship between women and nature appears to be an attempt to compensate for women's lesser physical strength, as experienced by the women in the mountains. Women must break with all the mental, bodily and emotional patriarchal norms in order to connect to nature and reconstruct a new balance between women's and men's strengths. This is to take place through naturalization of different discursively and materially assigned gender properties. This naturalization presupposes both strict discipline and ideological instruction and induction into the movement's iterative acts such as training, the appropriation of a new discourse and methods for personality development such as self-criticism, abstinence or moderating one's needs. In addition, the naturalization process in creating this new self-understanding implies conscious intra-action not only with other people and discourses but also with non-human, organic and inorganic phenomena. Sensing the biological body, plant and animal life in the mountains and the special physical living conditions is crucial in this process. Berivan recounted that at home, she always used to have pain before her menstruation but not now in the mountains. That she used to have pain when living with her family was consistent with the fact that women's monthly periods were regarded in that setting as an illness and generally spoken of negatively in Kurdish society:

> Think how much menstruation affects a woman's psyche. Especially when it's late. Especially when you're stressed, it comes a couple of months late. I've had that happen in city life. A good example of how our psyche and body are connected. But I really find relief in the mountains. I've now found that it depends on how you look at things. Illness! If you look at it that way, of course you will feel pain. It'll affect me. It is psychological. I feel no pain when I have my period. On the contrary, I love it. (Interview with Berivan, 21 March 2018)

To her surprise, Berivan had found that despite or precisely because of the more physically demanding living conditions, she no longer had menstrual pain when in the mountains. On the contrary, she was downright happy when her period was starting, because it reminded her that she was a woman. With Barad's theory[23] in mind, it makes sense to interpret this form of gender-connoted pain as intra-actionally constituted. The pain is both culturally and materially conditioned, in that traditional Kurdish culture, the PKK's ideology and the physical surroundings and activities have an obvious effect on the experience of pain.

From the cadres' perspective, the intra-active effects and interplay are not necessarily noticeable. They are stabilized and naturalized through various processes. Gulesor said with a reference to Simone de Beauvoir that she agreed with the PKK that gender was a social construct. Society produced gender through socialization of the child. At the same time, however, Gulesor stressed that women, as well as being socialized from infancy by society, also had a nature that was not necessarily biological. This nature was a central element of her character (Interview with Gulesor, 25 March 2018). I received no concrete explanation from Gulesor as to what a woman's nature was or where it came from. However, Gulesor said that the basis of a woman's existence, including the way she defined her being, did not rest solely on her sexual organs. According to her, gender was constituted by both one's biological sex and social gender. Although the PKK aims to reinterpret and redefine femininity and masculinity, here they do not follow, for example, Beauvoir's dictum 'One is not born, but rather becomes, a woman'.[24] Rather, the fundamental conviction seems to be something along the lines of 'one is born, but also becomes, a woman'. This is apparent, for example, in statements by the women cadres Zin and Berivan:

> Either I'm ashamed of being a woman, or else I show off about it [. . .] Not to be a better gender, but it's better to be a woman than a man [laughs]. At least, we are emotionally stronger. (Interview with Zin, 23 March 2018)

> I have three identities now: I'm young, I'm a woman, I'm a Kurd. But first and foremost, I'm a woman. My womanhood is more important than my youth or my Kurdishness [. . .] Being a woman means being able to create life [. . .] For example, women have something called menstruation. Women's inner world is different. Even the spring affects women differently. Our emotions are different [. . .] Women and men are born biologically different. That affects their mentality, too. (Interview with Berivan, 21 March 2018)

Zin's and Berivan's statements show that they are blind to their own discursively influenced processes of becoming where they have become proud of their personal, embodied experiences and perceptions of being a woman. Berivan also recalled that when a woman comrade had her period, the others would say 'congratulations' to her, because menstruation reminded them of being a woman, which made them happy and proud.[25] It looks as though physical separation from men in the mountains, including living far from patriarchal social norms, gives women fighters the opportunity to form new perceptions of their body together. Similar to the *différance* feminists' understanding of the body, the women fighters recognize and insist on cultivating the bodily differences between the sexes to everyone's advantage while simultaneously fighting for gender equality.

4.5. Views on homosexuality

As previously mentioned, women and men in the PKK are considered to constitute the two fundamental, natural genders. By reference to animals and plants in nature, the PKK argues for binarity as an essential element in relation to reproduction. Consequently, the PKK emphasizes that living species exist only as woman or man. Other appearances of gender and sexuality exist, but they are not regarded as natural, rather as deviations. The man cadre Mordem explained his reservations towards homosexuality with reference not to the same-sex object of desire but to an excessive focus on embodied sexuality:

> I don't reject their [homosexuals'] condition entirely, and in fact I see it as a form
> of resistance. But the thing is, they choose to focus on their bodies rather than a
> social struggle [. . .] When they choose to focus on their sexuality, they quickly
> become marginalized. They are people who have transformed themselves into
> a sexual quest. Their quest is only limited by their sexuality. [. . .] When their
> endeavors don't include a form of social struggle, they end up being regarded as
> deviant. (Interview with Mordem, 19 January 2018)

Other cadres spoke more directly about homosexuality as a deviation; yet, their
understandings of how homosexuality arises varied. In fact, this is one of the few
topics on which the cadres did not hold a common view. Those cadres who had
been part of the struggle for a long time, or who were in charge of education and
the movement's political representation, said that everyone was free to pursue his
or her sexual identity. Those who were new to the movement did not immediately
exhibit the same need for political correctness and were very dismissive of this.
Instead, they said that in their view, homosexuals had a problem with their natural
gender identity. Some of the new cadres regarded it in this connection as a disease
or disorder that homosexuals could grow out of or for which they could get
help. Others accused capitalist modernity of encouraging people to destroy their
heterosexual human nature and conceptions of their own gendered bodies.

Among the men cadres whom I interviewed, I never heard anyone with the
experience of being in direct contact with a homosexual man in the PKK. Mordem
said that the PKK was a Kurdish movement, and it was therefore inevitable that it
would be influenced by old-fashioned patriarchal norms, including homophobic
ones. For this reason, some PKK members regarded homosexuals as amoral or
indecent, despite the fact that the PKK does not consider homosexuality a taboo.
In Kurdish patriarchal society, homosexuality is seen as morally reprehensible.
According to Mordem, this too affects the cadres' interpretations of homosexuality
and their attitudes to it:

> Some of us are very dismissive. It's also hard for these people to be together with
> us, as they are very marked by their sexual identity and want to live it out. But
> when that isn't possible for them among us, it also becomes hard for them to be
> together with us. (Interview with Mordem, 19 January 2018)

The woman cadre Berfin echoed Mordem in saying that there had been individual
women in the PKK who had turned out to be homosexual and who had not been
treated harshly or dismissively by the movement. The movement wanted them to
remain members, but they would have to stop focusing on their sexual identity, as
it was not possible for them to cultivate it while waging war. She added that they
had no special rules in the movement for homosexuals and therefore dealt with
them according to the same rules as applied to a relationship between a woman
and a man (Interview with Berfin, 22 March 2018). In a similar vein, Cane noted
that the oppression and power dominance inherent in the heterosexual woman-
man relationship could also be seen in homosexual relationships. Oppression

thus occurred not only in a relationship between a woman and a man but also in a homosexual relationship between two men or two women (Cane, in FGI, 25 March 2018).

Despite their negatively connoted perception of homosexual men, the women cadres found it easier to be together with homosexual men than with heterosexual men. During a field trip in Europe where I interviewed the woman cadre Ronahi, she soon entrusted me with her family and life story. She later told me:

> It's strange that I can just be myself with you. And tell you a whole lot of things about my life without holding back, even though it's the first time we've met. We women only tell such things to each other or Cihan [not his real navn]. (fieldnote, 26 April 2019)

Cihan is a man activist singer who has been in the mountains to make music. He is the only homosexual man to have become both well-known and accepted in the PKK.[26] Ronahi's comment makes me think that she is making a certain link between homosexuality and femininity.

4.6. Clothing, grief and beauty

As Chapter 3 has already outlined, the PKK wishes to abolish femininity and masculinity while at the same time cultivating a relatively heteronormative understanding of bodily difference as a form of natural gender. The term 'natural gender' is complex, even bordering on something self-contradictory. On the one hand, the PKK wants to transform common gender conceptions; on the other hand, the PKK intends to base this transformation on a confirmation of a gender binarity that has long been contentious in gender studies. On yet another hand, the PKK encourages an erasure of embodied expressions, connoting femininity, but also sexualizations of the woman body. Women's bodies must be de-sexualized to erase those features in women that are traditionally regarded as arousing men's desire. Steps towards de-sexualization are taken, for example, with the cadres' clothing. Both women and men guerrillas wear the same military uniform patterned after traditional Kurdish men's clothing. It is cut to fit the typical men body shape, and the uniform thus exemplifies how men norms become universalized, even though it is intended to create equality. One cannot deny, however, that the uniform makes men and women's bodies look identical, with no visual access to a person's sexual characteristics. Nevertheless, it is paradoxical that the uniform with its de-sexualizing function, supposed to place men and women on par, at the same time deprives the cadres, in their intra-actions with each other, of the body as a reference point for their new self-understanding, which jineoloji found so important. My interviews showed, though, that the women seemed happy with their new clothes, saying that the uniform allowed for their greater agility.

It seems that the de-sexualizing uniform trumps jineoloji. Cane explained that the movement was primarily a military undertaking, which necessitated wearing a uniform that was practical in the mountains as well as down in the cities (Cane in FGI, 25 March 2018). Here, I should like to add that the cadres wore their uniform all the time, because it was their only set of clothes. They slept in the same clothes to be ready for a possible attack, which could come at any moment.

Membership of the PKK seems to preclude wearing make-up. None of the women fighters I interviewed or observed wore it. This was true of both the women guerrillas and the women who served in the cities wearing ordinary civilian clothes. Only on national holidays would women members, operating in the cities, make exceptions and put on a dress or skirt. Generally, all women PKK members tried in their behaviour, speech and movement to avoid signalling anything feminine that could be misunderstood as sexual. All the women cadres whom I observed distinguished clearly the ideal of being well groomed and being vain. The only thing that stood out as a contrast to the men's appearance was the women's hair, which could be put up in a way that might connote traditional femininity. I believe that although the women expressed that they avoided being feminine in their attitude, they still allowed themselves to have long hair. It might be that the long hair functioned as a jineolojical anchor point, like their menstruation, contributing to them feeling special.

With regard to dresses and skirts, Cane said that at first she perceived it as an attack when the leadership opposed her wish to wear a skirt, but in time she understood the reason. She also said that cadres could certainly wear a skirt or dress if they were not on military service. If they nevertheless chose not to, it was because it had become a matter of course. She was one of those who sometimes missed wearing dresses and skirts. Even so, she chose not to wear them on days when she was perfectly entitled to. She justified this choice by reference to Kurdish culture as the most important reason, rather than citing the movement's attitude. Cane said:

> We are a people in pain. There is always oppression. Under these circumstances, you don't feel any desire to do anything [i.e. wear make-up] individually. [. . .] It's not that the leadership forbids it. When our lives are so politically important, I can't waste time on my hair in front of the mirror for several hours a day. It becomes superfluous. This isn't just something we do in the mountains. Our people do it, too. It is cultural [. . .] There are mothers who always wear dark clothes. (Cane in FGI, 25 March 2018)

With this statement, Cane showed that grief loomed large in their everyday life, where comrades were falling in battle and people were suffering. As Cane explained, the absence of comrades, specific bodies with whom one identified, affected the women's incentive to spend time on their appearances. Families in grief would typically wear clothes that covered the whole body. They would avoid wearing make-up or making themselves look nice. They refrained from adorning themselves as an expression of respect and to avoid appearing self-centred. By referring to the Kurdish women's mourning, Cane tried to legitimize and naturalize the women fighters' rejection of particular kinds of clothing and make-up. Here, it is worth mentioning that mourning in Kurdish culture is a very long process. For a grieving mother, the conditions are particularly onerous, as the society around her expects her to express the grief and anchor it in her own body. The longer and more harshly the woman demonstrates the grief through her own body, the more respect she will gain from the society around her. Grief as a connotation in the choice of clothing, however, contradicts the movement's unwritten rule not to mourn dead comrades, not even if he or she is a friend or relative. The man cadre Hüseyin told me that he was watching the news on television in the mountains with his comrades, when incidentally he gained the knowledge that his wife, who was also a cadre in the PKK, had died in battle by the hand of Turkish soldiers. As he received this news, he neither reacted nor showed his emotions over the loss of her. Afterwards, when he was alone, however, he cried a lot. He explained to me that his holding back of his emotions was not because he was afraid of the present comrades' reaction. He held back because he would not 'give preference' to his wife compared to the other numerous martyrs (fieldnote, 24 March 2018). In other words, embodiment of feelings as well as clothing is subject to disciplining like so much else when one enjoins the status of a cadre.

With regard to the disciplining and uniformization of appearance, the women cadres insisted that it did not affect their femininity. In fact, Delal made it a point that in contrast to Western feminism, clothing was not subjected to some official PKK policy on whether women were allowed to show or hide their gender by means of clothing (Interview with Delal, 15 June 2017). Despite their general praise of the uniform, they claim that women fighters' femininity does not hang on their clothes, bodily appearances or behaviors. Instead, their femininity is anchored in their emotions and natural bodies. In that perspective, the 'neutral' guerrilla outfit and the absence of women's typical clothes and make-up help them make their new identity visible to themselves. The citational praxis of donning the uniform and behaving in specific ways is considered central in establishing these women fighters' new, different and gendered identity.[27]

There are limits, however, to the inclusion of natural bodies. During my fieldwork, I found that cadres of the same sex did not change their outer clothing in front of each other. When I had to change my clothes, my escort Zagros always went outside. Nor did he change his clothes in my presence. This is intriguing, as this behaviour signals, on the one hand, that they take the body for granted and have a natural attitude towards it; yet, on the other hand, they hide it away and make this natural body something private.

In general, I hesitate to take their claims about the neutrality of the uniform and the elevation of the natural body at face value. I found that all the men and women cadres, whom I observed, made an effort to dress in clean clothes and 'discipline' their hair and beard style. When the cadres were about to take part in military actions, they put on their clean clothes and got their hair or beard under control. The point of this was that the enemy should not think of them as a dirty people if they were captured or killed in action. Cadres' clothing is definitely an anchor point for discourse. Certainly, it is not a Western feminist or Kurdish patriarchal discourse, but clothing is an anchor point for many PKK discourses, even contesting ones.

Summary

This chapter has shown that there are no grounds whatsoever to maintain that the PKK will encourage women to abandon their gender in order to take part on an equal footing with men. On the contrary, gender *différance* is cultivated. At this point, my book represents a rejection of Çağlayan's hypothesis that women fighters are forced to renounce their gender.[28] The assertion of gender difference led the women fighters to establish their own party, their own military units and women quotas in the leadership, and even to develop their own ideology, jineoloji, in which they draft ideals for the future on the basis of reconstructions of matriarchal societies in Neolithic times. However mythical and romanticizing the women fighters' description of the Neolithic period and Kurdish history may be, this sort of female configuration seems to help the women fighters reinterpret, redefine and recreate a new understanding of themselves and their bodies. It is, however, important to understand that the PKK, especially its women fighters, do not conceive the physiological bodily difference between men and women as something oppositional as in the alterity thinking of Western feminism but as differentiation, variation and connectedness in a network that extends to the PKK, Kurdish nature, all Kurds and the national struggle. In this context, the women fighters have a tendency to portray the gender difference to their own advantage, probably because it fuels their pursuit of new opportunities for action and strengthens their position in the PKK.

A long history of clashes with Kurdish men has led Öcalan and the women fighters to insist on a separation between men and women with women fighters having their own training camps with nothing to disturb them from engaging in acts of understanding themselves also as the future 'saviours' of society. Salvation depends on their ability to connect to their 'natural gender' and 'body', and to strengthen their 'will' with its roots in their natural inner qualities. It looks as though the women fighters have accepted this view of gender and the role that goes with it. They are committed to carrying out a total transformation of their identity and outlook. Like earlier nationalist movements, the PKK seems to have succeeded in giving women the classic role of society's saviour, as the women regard themselves as real actors and as founders of the society to come. However, the women fighters are also fighting an internal battle within the PKK, one whose conditions are good because of their contribution to the anti-colonial struggle. The women fighters have already had success in combatting tendencies towards men dominance inside the movement, and they see themselves as the true, militant ideological representatives of the movement. Furthermore, it seems that not only the women but also the men of the PKK accept that women use gender difference to women's advantage and that they insist on the role of being the true, militant and ideological representatives of the PKK.

Chapter 5

INTRA-ACTIONS BETWEEN COMBAT EXPERIENCES
AND PERCEPTIONS OF THE BODY

The chapter will analyse how the women fighters perceive the body in the midst of combat, its meaning and effect in acts of war and in their own liberation process. The purpose of the chapter is to provide an insight into how agency in combat has affected the women fighters' gender and overall identity formation.

5.1. Ambushed by nature and the self

Most of the women I interviewed indicated that they had not understood beforehand what life in the mountains would involve. They were primarily just concerned with fulfilling their long-awaited dream of becoming a guerrilla fighter, whatever it might demand of them. In this context, Arya considered her presumptions of what combat experiences would be like romantic in nature (Interview with Arya, 25 March 2018). Similarly, Bese recalled how journeying to the mountains was permeated by multiple feelings, as when setting off to a new world:

> In a way, I was proud of myself, but I was also afraid. There was also joy and love, I mean, a mixture of all the things that make you travel to some new place or other. It was like crossing from one world to another. In your head, the difference between the two worlds was like a chaos where your emotions are also interwoven with it all. So I felt a great relief when I reached the comrades. I was finally free of society, so I was relieved. (Interview with Bese, 22 March 2018)

Bese associated her journey 'from one world to another' with a bombardment of different emotions. She mentions two kinds of joy: the joy of breaking free of society and the joy of finally reaching the mountains. In the very transition between the two worlds, a chaos raged that was fuelled by the surprise of being met with physical challenges, obligations, war practices and demands to adapt to nature. For Zeri, it took time to get used to:

> The first three years in the mountains were very hard, [. . .] as regards nature, but also as regards the way of life. My integration took three years, both my

adaptation to nature and the process of making my inner search meaningful. You sleep on the ground without any kind of mat. There are times when you go hungry. We sometimes don't even have drinking water. And the same goes for sleep. The worst is the long marches and military operations. We coped with it all, of course. It doesn't mean we gave up. But not everything made sense to us at first. [. . .] It was like a transition. Coming from a dream world into reality. Then you learn what you're capable of. As the Leader [Öcalan] says, 'Knowing yourself is the greatest knowledge.' (Interview with Zeri, 26 March 2018)

Zeri recalls the first years as a process of intense adaptation. The more one adapts, the more the chaos abates. Thus, when Zeri mentions that the women fighters managed to cope with it all, she explains this with reference to their gradual insights into their own capabilities – of what they were capable of. The processes of self-overcoming the challenges enabled the recognition of their own resources and thereby their own selves. Zeri found herself able to cope with more than she expected and this self-knowledge won made her think more about her own potential. Thus, joining the PKK as cadres in the mountains not only entailed combatting the Turkish state; it also required the women fighters to combat inner obstacles in their new lives. Ronya talked about fights on many fronts:

We experienced the joy and the challenges at the same time. But we were happy, even though life was very demanding and tough. You break away from society, from the city, from civilian life, from your home. It's demanding at embarking on a new life under new conditions. Adaptation is also a problem. [. . .] It wasn't all that easy to transition from a life without systematization, discipline and planning to a life that is systematized, disciplined and planned according to fixed rules. We'd brought our petit-bourgeois mentality. We were a long way from submitting to a military life. [. . .] We were fighting on many fronts at the same time: a personal struggle, a mentality struggle, a class struggle and a struggle against men. All this is going on while we have an enemy we're fighting against. (Interview with Ronya, 27 March 2018)

As described in the 'Introduction', the Kurds are an internally divided population group. As well as being split between different nation states, the Kurds are divided by a number of other factors such as different dialects, religious convictions, adherence to different branches of Islam and clans. The clans are highly dominant within their own provinces and are often in conflict with each other.[1] There are also class differences within the movement, with some members coming from rich families while most come from poor circumstances and rural areas.[2] Some members come from Europe and cannot speak Kurdish. At the same time, there are clashes between those who come from the villages and those described as 'the intellectuals', typically students from the city. Finally, gender is a dividing factor. The chaos that emerged from this complexity only abated when Ronya and her comrades realized that they had to invest in and learn to coexist in the mountains. Combatting demographic complexity was thus yet another battle that newcomers had to engage in and even overcome before they could engage in the fight against the common enemy. Ronya recounted with a smile that had she known she would have to go through so many struggles and challenges in the course of the process, she would probably have decided not to join the movement. Ronya had a background as a student in a city. Joining the PKK as a cadre in the mountains entailed for her many conflicts with her comrades that had to be dealt with, even though she had 'only' come to the mountains to become a revolutionary (Interview with Ronya, 27 March 2018). The women fighters' internal battles explain why Dersim describes the women's struggle as a 'multiple struggle'. By this, she alludes to the fact that it was a matter of not just resisting the enemy in order to achieve national liberation but also resolving the intra-party conflicts related to the aforementioned differences (Interview with Dersim, 27 March 2018).

Although it was not said directly, women interviewees with student backgrounds indicated that they had had more difficulty adapting to life as fighters in the mountains than those of their comrades who came from villages or rural districts. The difference is not only one of class but also of physical prowess. The women from the villages were used to physical challenges from life close to nature, which gave them an advantage once they joined PKK's armed units. In addition, those who joined the movement from the villages did not have all that much to give up in their former lives before going to the mountains, having generally led a simpler life in the villages. In contrast, women fighters from the cities had a lot to give up: their education and career prospects, city life, hobbies, leisure activities, boyfriends and much more that they had to forego before setting off.

The mental process that follows from devoting one's life to the revolution and accepting the PKK's ideology is known in the movement as 'clarification'. The women who had undergone this clarification process said that they did not miss their former lives in any way nor did they oppose the movement's guidelines. Avasin, for example, said:

> We learnt that we had to go into battle with ourselves before we could fight the enemy. It's about clarifying yourself. When you are clarified inside, there's nothing you can't overcome. (Interview with Avasin, 21 March 2018)

If a fighter finds it difficult and expresses frustration at the living conditions and expectations associated with the struggle and life in the mountains, this is regarded in the movement as a sign that the fighter has not mentally clarified things with himself or herself. Fighters who have clarified things with themselves and who dedicate themselves completely to the revolution are described in the movement as having been 'PKKcized'. If members fail to PKKcize themselves, they risk being sent to retraining or having somebody from the leadership foisted on them for a while as an escort, the idea being that the escort can inspire the members to work on their motivation and clarification.

Those women fighters who had poor physical prowess upon arrival or lacked insights into their bodies' potential reflected on how these deficiencies related to the fact that they had had no access to sport or fitness activities before joining. Bermal narrativizes it in this way:

> I was used to walking on surfaced roads in Europe, of course. So walking in the mountains was hard. I fell down every other step I took. Every other step! I couldn't do it. I was afraid. Physically, the mountains were demanding. I couldn't come down from the mountains. When I looked at the high mountains, I said to myself, 'How am I to climb in them?'. I did it, but I cried and cried. (Interview with Bermal, 21 March 2018)

Not all women fighters, though, were challenged to the same extent as Bermal. Ronya's feeling that women from rural districts had an advantage in adapting to life in the mountains was corroborated by Helin, who was born and raised in a village:

> When I was at home, I used to work in the fields with my family. Doing farm work. So I'm used to doing heavy work. It didn't take me long to adapt to mountain life and military actions. (Interview with Helin, 24 March 2018)

All interviewees indicated that their experience was that being able to withstand the physical challenges and pain had a positive effect on the development of their personality and their self-confidence and on the increased respect and appreciation earned from other women fighters. Because of that perception, pain is regarded as a sort of investment in one's own future and status in the movement. Expressing oneself openly about one's pain was not considered appropriate. For example, none of the people I interviewed spoke about their bodily or psychological pain, be it stories of being fed up, in a bad mood or unhappy. Not even the women who suffered serious illnesses requiring treatment or those who had sustained injuries in combat spoke to their comrades about their condition or expressed a wish to speak about it to them. For example, Arya said that she did not tell her comrades that she had been wounded in a military operation (Interview with Arya, 25 March 2018). In my judgement, this is because, as fighters, they are trained and disciplined to think that a true militant and revolutionary must not be sorry for herself. If a fighter is sorry for herself, not only can it affect the fighter's own motivation, it can also affect the other comrades' motivation in the fight against the enemy. According to Bese, this attitude benefited how life was experienced. Life without articulations of pain seemed more meaningful after a long, hard day:

> They are only small challenges, but it still takes a while to get used to them. For example, getting up early, getting tired quickly or not being able to walk faster. You get used to it in time. When you can withstand the challenges, the comrades show you more respect. When you get tired after a long day, you also appreciate life more. A new bond is formed between you and your comrades. Your self-confidence grows, too. It's a transition that everyone has to live through. (Interview with Bese, 22 March 2018)

Other women fighters described how they had converted their pain into strength and self-respect by hiding their illnesses and injuries from each other or making light of their significance. The new, the sick, the weak, the injured and the wounded are not fit to take part in military actions or take on demanding tasks. For this reason, the cadres conceal their mental and physical challenges from each other so as to be allowed to take part in the struggle and thereby fulfil their dreams.

What is desirable in this context is that the person believes in himself or herself and is strong-willed. This can be exemplified with Berivan. When I came to interview Berivan, I was informed that she had recently been detained by the movement for three nights for attempting to cross the border into Rojava without the leadership's permission. The reason she gave for doing this was that she wanted to take part in the battles in the Afrin Province between Kurdish forces and the Turkish military. Berivan later told me that she had left the camp in Iraq alone and managed to travel over 200 km before being stopped by her comrades. She did this despite knowing it was against the PKK's orders to take part in the battles in the Afrin Province. Her reason for doing so anyway was, Berivan told me, that she could no longer bear to wait and look on as the Turkish military killed innocent Kurds. In a way, she was proud of having been detained by the movement, as it was not something that happened all that often. It thereby made her unique. Although I could see that her comrades were critical of her for her disobedience, I also sensed that several of them admired her for her stubbornness and willpower. One reason for this was that being strong-willed is the ultimate and greatest demand made of all by the movement. All the great martyrs of the movement are admired for their strong will and stubbornness, which have resulted in what would otherwise have been very difficult actions ending well. The basic understanding is that willpower creates scope for action by overcoming the body's sociocultural limitations and creating new possibilities of self-realization. With regard to this, Arya explained:

> It's actually about getting to know your own strength and your potential. Before, we couldn't lift a watering can, but now we lift 100-kilo sacks. That's more than some of the men can manage. Before, when my mother wanted me to help her, I often said I couldn't. Here, I've discovered my physique. My previous physique was a disaster. Before, I couldn't walk as fast as my men comrades or lift as much as them, but now everyone looks up to me. You change and are changed in every way. Life produces this development itself, and you learn to be patient. I was so impatient before, but now you sit in the sun and wait for the enemy for weeks, so your lips get dry and your skin gets burnt, while your hair is such a mess. (Interview with Arya, 25 March 2018)

Arya's narrative exemplifies that subjectivity must be understood as an embodied phenomenon. Indeed, in our conversation, she expressed the conviction that she was creating herself by realizing her potential and becoming conscious of the strength of her own body and will. Arya also explained that she saw herself as a creator because she had the ability to meet her own needs and create her own identity on the basis of intra-actions with the body, the PKK camp and its mountainous environment. Arya's experience is about having the opportunity to explore her body and thereby maximize her actions. Arya also said that it was her experience that a natural process of becoming takes place in intra-actions between her and her human and non-human environment. Life in the mountains enabled Arya to take an active part in creating a future that stands in opposition to her previous life. For her, life in the mountains implied new activities, interests, perspectives and frameworks hitherto unexplored. The iterative acts that Arya had to engage in not only increased her chances of survival but also gave her the opportunity to explore her own body, its ability to carry much more than expected and to find peace in waiting patiently under the burning sun.

5.2. Combatting the 'man mentality'

This section focuses on another front, on which the women fighters have had to fight – that is, against the 'man mentality'. Especially first- and second-generation women fighters recall having had major challenges collaborating with their men comrades. At the beginning of PKK's armed resistance, the leadership consisted of men who did not think there was any need for women in the war or any room for them. Accordingly, they sent the many women who came to the mountains back home shortly after their arrival. Tragically, the Turkish military forces lay in wait and killed or captured and imprisoned some of these spurned women on their way back from the mountains, which is a story that feeds the women fighters' notion of a man mentality within the PKK.[3]

The term 'man mentality' denotes what they perceive as a patriarchal, masculinist and primitive conviction found in some men that women cannot wage war on an equal footing with men. According to the women fighters, such men have a tendency to make life difficult for the women in the PKK. The 'man mentality' was particularly dominant from PKK's beginning until the conspiracy of 2004.[4] Today, the 'man mentality' is no longer as prevalent, but the women fighters still meet and fight attitudes associated with this mentality.

Throughout PKK's history, men have had various assertions as to why women should not be fighters. One assertion was that women are not physically strong enough to wage war. Another was that women could be taken prisoners or killed by the enemy and that there was an impending risk of abuse, either of them while alive or of their dead bodies. On this basis, the men argued that it would be better if the women kept away from combat zones and let the men protect them. The men wanted the women to settle instead for taking on logistical duties that generally did not require direct confrontation with the enemy. This might mean working in the PKK's political offices, the press units and the kitchens. Based on the suitability of such logistical responsibilities, some men fighters had treated the women like their sisters or mothers, even expecting them to cook for them and wait for them while they were out on military operations.

Another example of men's resistance to women in combat is reflected in men fighters blaming the women when the men's own operations failed or in hesitating to issuing weapons to the women to prevent them from taking part in military operations, because the men thought the women would be a burden to them in combat. Berfin, who is from the second generation of women in the PKK, narrativized past prejudices in this way:

> The men said, 'How can a woman join in a military action? What if she falls as a martyr? Who will protect her?'. They didn't believe in women at all. They didn't think women had the physique to wage war. I remember clearly that when we were to stand guard, they didn't trust us. They kept an eye on us from a distance and watched us to make sure we were doing it properly. They didn't believe that the unit's fate could be entrusted to women at all. It was pointless us fighting against the men, because they had the authority. In time, we realized that they were judging us solely on the basis of our gender. Their treatment was just unbearable. For example, they called everyone together before the military operation started. We [women] were there too. We were excited. Then they chose some people and then said that the rest could return to their posts. They didn't choose a single woman. We pretty much went crazy. Although all the women volunteered time and time again, none of them were chosen. (Interview with Berfin, 22 March 2018)

The women interviewed, including Berfin, said that the men's attitudes and discrimination against women actually contributed to the women becoming more aware of the effects that gender perceptions had. At the beginning, women were far from being organized within the PKK, which prevented them from fighting against the men's deplorable treatment of them. At the same time, the women were loyal to the leadership, accepted the men's conditions and complied with the prevailing culture, dominated by the man mentality, without putting up any noteworthy resistance. Ronya described it as follows:

> Men tried to treat us similar to how they treated us at home. It was imperative for us never to experience it in the PKK, which we'd joined to gain our freedom. We couldn't tolerate that kind of treatment. [. . .] yes, we rejected that treatment, but didn't have the strength to fight against it. We were against it, but at the same time, we accepted it, because we thought it was him that was the leader and had the authority. Also, there's a mechanism in the military that you can't get around. It's a chain of command that you have to comply with. But we had thoughts, reflections, considerations [. . .] They simply didn't want us to take part in military actions. We asked why, and then they explained that it was to protect us, so we wouldn't fall into enemy hands. They saw us as their honour. They said: 'A woman comrade can be taken prisoner by the enemy. We would rather sacrifice ten men martyrs to avoid that. That's why you mustn't take part in military actions.' (Interview with Ronya, 27 March 2018)

Starting from a military mindset in which orders are obeyed, Ronya explained that power mechanisms in the PKK and the women themselves contributed to the suppression of the women fighters' ambitions. The men in the PKK opposed women's participation in military actions. Based on the ideology of honour, they regarded the women as their property and did not want 'their women' to risk ending up in enemy hands, just as they did not expect much of women's bodily physique and strength. The women fighters would not deny their lesser physique. However, when explaining men fighters' reluctance to include women in military actions, the women fighters point to the sociocultural conditions out of which Kurdish masculinity is constructed. Sociocultural norms create more advantages for men than biology does. They have access to everything from childhood onwards, said Dersim. A Kurdish man encounters the state and society earlier than a woman. He also has compulsory military service in the Turkish army, work experience and so forth. All that contributes to the formation of a masculinity that connotes many competences relevant in war. When men will not share their privileged access to military engagements, it becomes very difficult for women to increase their agency. According to Dersim, the men were of the opinion that it was the men's war and that men therefore should decide who was to take part in it and to what extent (Interview with Dersim, 27 March 2018).

The women fighters associated these patriarchal attitudes with the mountainous context prior to the coup of 2004. The mountains were a long way from the Beqaa Valley, where the PKK had its main base under Öcalan's leadership. Öcalan was fighting for the men to regard women as equal comrades, but he was not always successful, especially not when he was not in the mountains himself, recalled Helin:

> There [in the Beqaa Valley], the men didn't dare show their reactions. They kept them to themselves. For example, they said to us: 'Do you think you can stay here forever? Wait and see till we get to the mountains, then you can see who has the strength to be in charge' [laughs]. Because they couldn't stand the Leader [Öcalan] showing special interest and protecting us from them. They didn't dare show their true face because of the Leader. [. . .] The Leader also told us [women] that we should intervene if we saw something that wasn't working in accordance with the movement's precepts. We were very critical of their attitudes and decisions from the start. There were only three of us women in the unit. Afterwards, the men always gave the toughest assignments to us, because we criticized them. They wanted to punish us that way, but we didn't give up and carried on criticizing them. (Interview with Helin, 24 March 2018)

The women fighters who had received ideological instruction and military training from Öcalan in the Beqaa Valley said that they saw themselves as lucky. It was a great honour for them to meet Öcalan and be inspired by his ideas. These women, who had all met Öcalan in person, also stated that they felt themselves to be his followers and that they felt stronger than the women who had not had the honour of meeting him. These women also said that they saw it as their ideological duty to ensure that life in the party operated according to the ideological precepts set out by Öcalan.

The women fighters I interviewed cited innumerable episodes that they felt exemplified their struggle against the 'man mentality'. At the same time, they explained to me that men can be strategically skilful at concealing their underlying opinions about women. The women fighters call this strategy 'man cunning'. Bese also narrated that the men from the training camps often did not show their real attitudes to women because the team's women and the leadership would clamp down quickly on their disparagement of women. Only in military actions outside the training camps did the women first experience the 'men's true selves':

> In the training camps, the men are very careful, because life is disciplined and controlled there. There's a collective life there. There were some men, and women too, who hadn't met the Leader [Öcalan]. There were some people who didn't really invest in their self-development and sometimes acted in ways that weren't compatible with our values. The way these men talked to us, as if they were talking to their little sister or the girl next door. They expected the same of us. They said to us, 'You can't be like men. So you can't always take part in military actions. If you get captured by the enemy or killed, then what?' They had a feudalist mindset. (Interview with Bese, 22 March 2018)

Some of the women fighters reported that man cunning still existed in the PKK. According to Zeri, man cunning had reshaped itself, as the women grew stronger after the paradigm shift in 2005. Some men adapt strategically so that they can engage in interaction with women. They say one thing when they are with the women, but say or do something quite different when they are together with other men without women being present.

Not that it is indicative of any man cunning, I still recognized a change in the men fighters' behaviour if women were present. During my fieldwork, I observed that the men cadres spoke and moved in a very relaxed way when they were alone without women being present. If a woman was present, the character of the men's conversation changed immediately and was obviously designed to fit in with the ideological and moral values of the movement. One day, when I was with Zagros, my escort, in our hut, a man leader and four men fighters from his unit visited us. The leader spoke on the phone to his woman co-leader. I sensed some kind of disagreement between them, but he said nothing condescending to her on the phone and ended the conversation politely. After ringing off, he surlily handed back the phone saying: 'These women interfere in everything and understand sod all!' There was no reaction from the men present. I got the impression that they agreed with him and that they therefore thought there was no reason to say more. Especially not when I was present among the men as an observer. They had no wish at all to come into conflict with the women, regardless of the nature of the conflict, because they knew that their attitudes, because they were men, could always be problematized with reference to their gender. Zagros said to me: 'A man must be really stupid if he comes into conflict with the women in the PKK' (fieldnote, 22 March 2018).

Avasin of the third generation of women in the PKK interpreted the contemporary conditions in this way. If the man mentality as a subculture still played its part in the movement despite official statements and if the male mentality still sometimes limited women's agency, it was not only because of men's conviction that they owned the world but also because the women looked up to those men. Avasin reported feeling annoyed that after all the years of women's struggle and ideological instruction, there were still women in the PKK who were dependent on the men (Interview with Avasin, 21 March 2018).

5.3. *The significance of the body and bodily difference in combat*

This section goes into detail with the women fighters' combat experiences of how their bodies matter and how they differ from the bodies of their men comrades.

The women fighters reported that the first women in the PKK tried to be as masculine as men. They tried to prove that they too were physically strong and even competed with the men. Some women paid a high price physically in terms of injuries such as back trouble. Dersim of the second generation of women in the PKK cites her own injured back in corroboration of this. In her case, it was not just the men who forced her and other women to do more physically. To ensure that women could also join in warfare, she and the other women also wanted to prove that their bodies were just as strong as the men's. The women fighters built what has been referred to as a form of 'masculine militant femininities'.[5] These women strove to be like men and to be respected like them. They walked, acted and talked just like men. A number of women admired those physically strong women who distinguished themselves in battle against the enemy. Dersim said:

> We alone have sacrificed thousands of martyrs in the war just to prove our worth as women. Not to prove it to the enemy, but to our men comrades. The men comrades believe the world belongs to them. They see the army as their own, too. After all, a man already sees himself as the power. The Leader [Öcalan] often said he realized that the men fighters were angry with him for taking from them the power they had possessed for 2,000 years. The Leader shared that power between women and men. There have been many platforms, hearings, and investigations in the history of the movement to combat the old mentality in the men. Women who tried to be like men were also questioned. Even though it was unavoidable for those women to imitate men. When he carried a sack, you wanted to carry a sack, too. When he defended a hill, you wanted to defend one, too. A competition. An imitation. (Interview with Dersim, 27 March 2018)

Dersim said that it was Öcalan in particular who was against women imitating men. Öcalan did not believe that imitation of men would equip women for war. Women had to find their own way of waging war without disowning their nature. Öcalan wants women to make peace with their own bodies and have faith in the bodies in all their distinctiveness. He also believes that it is possible for a woman to be a better fighter than a man despite their bodily differences.[6]

The women fighters said that many eventually realized that men and women are different and that their bodily constituency has a direct effect on their physical possibilities of self-realization, just as it indirectly forces the women to reconceptualize their role in the PKK. In this connection, the first generation of women fighters with many years of combat experience said that physical and mental separation from their men comrades helped them to find the right way of fighting and to find a new way of thinking of themselves. This reconceptualization implied an appreciation of the separate training camps for men and women in the mountains to provide the women fighters with a place where they could see themselves reflected in each other's bodily, morphological specificity. The separation has contributed to women and how they frame the bodily difference between men and women as something positive, just as intra-actions and interrelations between human and non-human agents have been cultivated as a kind of liberation that follows from being a woman fighter within the PKK. The women interviewed stated that it was only in the mountains that they first acquired a new relationship with their bodies. There, they became able to notice what their bodies could do and how to understand them. Ronya made the following comment on the women's contribution to the war based on the reconceptualization:

> A woman's will in war is stronger than a man's, because women are the strong-willed gender. The will of the oppressed grows stronger. Women's tactical manoeuvres are also better than men's. At the same time, women's adaptability to nature and the way of life is stronger, which gives her an advantage. (Interview with Ronya, 27 March 2018)

Ronya's narrative indicates that there is a conscious strategy on the part of the PKK to make women active in the war. To do this, women's strength is framed through internalized discursive imprints and instruction/training mechanisms that have a performative effect on the waging of the war. Men's physical superiority is not denied, but strength of will is placed above physical strength to give the woman a sense that she possesses some special inner powers that she can be allowed to develop by strengthening her will. Historical narratives are also framed so as to generate conviction, and these help to indicate that the Kurdish woman through the ages has always been a better fighter than the Kurdish man. For example, Bermal said:

> When we look at the history of Kurdistan, we can clearly see that women have always been a part of the resistance struggle. The woman has always had a belief that she has always been the bravest and most dedicated. In Kurdish history, you can see that the woman has always been the one who never accepted surrender. She will even throw herself down from the mountains to avoid surrendering. What does all this show? That the woman's will is stronger and that she is braver than men. (Interview with Bermal, 21 March 2018)

Bermal's account is an example of the way the PKK systematically attempts to create a historical, geographical and cultural context for the women fighters. A context in which, like the historical heroines of the Kurdish past, they take part in the battle for the homeland and are better fighters than men. This is mainly in order to give the category 'the Kurdish woman' a special and meaningful role in the anti-colonial struggle, but also to give the women fighters the feeling that they are fully capable of representing themselves and contributing to the collective objectives within the PKK. The women fighters' own interlinked experiences also go towards strengthening the mentality in which the women play down the significance of the body's physical strength. Instead, the women fighters highlight other factors, such as balance, speed, skill, perspective, courage, strategy, mental attitude and flexibility, that frame as equally important in the conduct of the war. Zeri recalled:

> We were on a military action. Our load was far too heavy. When we had to withdraw, there were me and a couple of other comrades left. We had very heavy ammunition with us. We had to either take it with us or leave it for the enemy. I put my headscarf down and lifted all of it onto my shoulders. Then I set off down. The mountainside was steep, and our route was full of big stones. It was really hard to walk down with the heavy load on my shoulders. But I wouldn't leave it for the enemy. In these moments, you feel there's a determination and conviction growing inside you. When I got down the mountain, a man comrade came and offered his help. I said okay. He tried several times to lift the load, but he couldn't. He asked: 'What's in it?'. I answered: 'Cut the chat. Take it or don't take it. We've got to hurry. There's a Cobra [a type of military helicopter] coming.' He couldn't do it. I felt sorry for him, so I said to him: 'OK comrade, you must go. I'll take it.' I lifted it again. So we continued on our way. In that moment it occurred to me that it [the body] isn't everything. (Interview with Zeri, 26 March 2018)

Zeri's story is an example of a progressive narrative in which she developed into something better.[7] Not only did Zeri describe herself as someone who increased her strength; she also positioned herself ideologically as more faithful to the movement's standards. She did this when she said that it was she who took responsibility for the load. When Zeri recounted how she felt a determination and conviction growing inside her, she realized that her body had changed. It thereby occurred to Zeri that the body did not necessarily have an essence that was given and permanent. It changed with the tasks and the materiality around her. She experienced the change gradually. Still, to Zeri the point was not that she could lift more than a man, but that she had a stronger strength of will than the man comrade. At least, this explains why Zeri asserted that women can be stronger in war processes than men.

5.4. *Women's contribution to the development of the war*

As described in the foregoing sections, the women are fighting many different battles: against their own patriarchal mentality and body perception, against nature in the mountains, the internal battle within the PKK against the man mentality and finally an anti-colonial struggle. The interviewees' narratives show that these battles, combined with Öcalan's support, have contributed to women in the PKK now feeling that they are fighters at least as good as their men comrades. It is for this reason that men no longer perceive women fighters in the movement as 'corrupting women', which was the case in the earlier years of the movement. The idea of the corrupting woman is that women are the weak and vulnerable sex and that it is therefore not possible for them to live up to the movement's standards for militants of the revolution.[8] In addition, the corrupting women are held responsible for tempting some men into intimate relationships, which again led the men either to leave the movement or being unable to commit themselves completely to the national struggle as they were expected to. The point worth noting here is that it is a woman's fault that a relationship has arisen. The woman is perceived as weak and incapable of coping without being in a romantic relationship with a man. With her body, her emotions, her attraction and her sexuality, the woman is believed to be responsible for leading the man astray from the revolution. According to the women interviewees, men therefore used to regard women and femininity in general as potentially dangerous and as something that could be exploited by the enemy and the capitalist system to damage the PKK. Mordem, however, proudly reported that this primitive conception of women no longer existed in the PKK as women had demonstrated on all fronts that they were to be trusted (Interview with Mordem, 19 January 2019).

In the earlier years of the PKK, Öcalan too had a tendency to use similar patriarchal attitudes in his analyses of women members. Today, his attitude has changed as well. He now argues for the importance of women in the PKK. He explains that women's devotion inspires confidence. Accordingly, there is no longer any reason for considering women potentially dangerous.[9] This change of attitude in Öcalan was possible only by virtue of the women's struggle of several years to prove that they are indispensable to the PKK in the war. It is not just any form of femininity that Öcalan praises and confides in. For Öcalan, the feminine ideal mirrors the personality of 'the martyr Zilan' (see below) who was ready to sacrifice herself for the national struggle.

The women fighters explain the PKK's improved results on the battlefield within recent years with reference to their own participation. In particular, these results hinge on the heroic actions of women martyrs, Öcalan's current positive analysis of women and women's ideological loyalty to Öcalan and the PKK's standards and values. In this way, the women are praised because they have expanded, redefined and redeveloped ways of waging war. Helin reported:

When we were on a military action in the mountains and had wounded comrades, the men comrades didn't take care of them. It was mostly women comrades who took care of them. When a woman comrade was wounded, we women would naturally take care of her. We had the spirit of comradeship, after all. You could never leave your comrade behind. It was often the women comrades who took care of the wounded that the men comrades had left behind [. . .] That's just one of many examples. Women are much better and more disciplined than men when it comes to going on actions in accordance with the movement's military guidelines. (Interview with Helin, 24 March 2018)

In Helin's narrative, she distinguished between women and men fighters as regards their standards and moral values. She related that men could be unreliable, whereas women were disciplined, loyal, caring and ready to save their wounded comrades whatever the cost. Helin thereby indicated that men were unreliable in battle, while women were 'saviours', as women's nature did not allow them to act unconscionably. According to Helin, these traits turned women into heroes who now defined the ideal. When asked, Bese explained why women are more capable in war processes:

For one thing, women are more disciplined. For another, women take things seriously which war demands. Thirdly, women are good at following guidelines. In war, you can't leave things to chance. At the same time, women's determination is stronger. If a woman has a goal, she reaches it! No doubt about it. (Interview with Bese, 22 March 2018)

These positive, articulated ideas about women's combat skills enable the women fighters to compensate for the men fighters' stronger physique in war processes. The areas in which men are superior to women are spoken of, but their significance is undermined in the women's narratives. Bese's narrative is paradoxical, however. On the one hand, she stated that, ideologically, the PKK spoke of abolishing the distinction between masculinity and femininity; on the other, femininity was set against masculinity.

Avasin represents a different approach to gender diversity. According to her, men and women contribute differently in war:

We have found on countless occasions that actions carried out by men and women together are more successful. There are two kinds of reasoning. And two kinds of body. When those potentials are woven together, it ends up with a new kind of success. (Interview with Avasin, 21 March 2018)

When Avasin said that men and women together carried out more successful actions, she was saying that this physiological difference between men and women need not be oppositional. She refuses to measure men up against women. Instead, she appreciates the differences as complementary. Avasin did not want to focus on the limitations of men and women respectively or engage in otherings of the opposite gender. For her, it was important that men and women retain bodily difference, variation and differentiation.

In sum, the women held different views with regard to men and women's capabilities. Some women fighters said in their narratives that the task for both sexes was to take the focus away from sociocultural gender and to express bodiliness, gender difference and the specificities of bodies in alternative ways.

However, there was also a tendency to portray gender diversity to women's advantage. For example, Berfin stated that the military units containing both men and women were stronger and braver (Interview with Berfin, 22 March 2018). Zeri added that it was not a matter of physique or how skilled you were at using your weapon; it was important to devote yourself to the struggle and overcome all your limitations, fears and concerns, and be strong-willed, as women always were (Interview with Zeri, 26 March 2018). Arya said that women were better at planning and at reading enemy actions. As leader of a mixed unit containing both men and women, Arya added that she nowadays found that men fighters hesitated to set off on military actions if no women fighters were involved. The men felt more courageous when women were also involved (Interview with Arya, 25 March 2018). Zelal reported that just a single woman fighter's participation in a military action involving several men helped to increase the action's chances of success (Interview with Zelal, 17 September 2017).

In conversations with men fighters, I was not able to confirm these claims made by the women fighters about their contributions to the way that the PKK now waged war. The men fighters never mentioned hesitation to go on military operations alone or of feeling stronger when women fighters were with them. Nor, however, were the men fighters dismissive. I judge that their attitude was strategic. Men leaders, especially, did not want to take the women fighters' pride away as long as they were contributing to the struggle. According to the foreign fighter Nick, who came from the West to take part in the YPG's struggle, it is a matter of giving the women more space:

> [...] the men who are leaders try to put a bit of a damper on themselves. So as not to kind of come across as too domineering. It's a masculine trait of course, but you have to be careful about coming across to your colleague as domineering, because then you're kind of challenging feminism [...] But externally at least, it seemed as though they were just taking a step back. And making room for the woman. (Interview with Nick, 12 July 2017)

The gender difference asserted by the women fighters in relation to men and the women's combat skills is also evident in the way the women describe the difference between men and women unit leaders. The women fighters said that men leadership is based on masculine values such as strength, body attitude, muscles and authority, while women's leadership supports being feminine, empathetic, thoughtful, friendly and humane. Arya noted that empathy and understanding were particularly characteristic of women. Nick, who had done military service in his own country before joining the YPG, demonstrated agreement with the women fighters in his interview with me:

> I mean, just from meeting them [women leaders], they radiate such authority – they don't need to give orders or act tough as people did in the Western military, so they had authority, but at the same time they were totally down to earth. As I said, there was one of them – I can't remember her name – she was

this high-ranking woman leader [. . .] I would gladly follow her to the death if it came to it. (Interview with Nick, 12 July 2017)

Like Nick, other men cadres said that women brought something more humane to the war. For example, the cadre Drej told me at a workshop in Europe on democratic confederalism:

Women's participation in the PKK has altered men's way of waging war. As men, we were used to fighting the war pitilessly and barbarically, but the women have taught us to wage war with empathy and to avoid resembling the enemy, who is inhumane. We have learnt from women to combine emotional reason and rationalism. Emotional reason, especially, is strong in women. (fieldnote, 26–28 March 2017)

When Drej said that the women had taught the men to fight with empathy, I suspected that he was influenced by the patriarchal view that women represent all the soft values and so he defined women as sweet, kind and non-violent.[10] It would furthermore substantiate the PKK's objective of producing a new conceptualization of womanhood that would motivate women's engagement in the PKK. Yet, not all men fighters agree with Drej, when he suggests that women fighters have brought the war to a higher moral and ethical stage. Brusk told me that women at war can certainly be coarser than men. He described a military operation where his unit, comprising both men and women, had had nothing to eat for several days. The women fighters caught some frogs and threw them alive onto the fire. The frogs burned and then almost exploded around them. The women fighters collected the pieces and ate them. Brusk himself did not eat, as Kurds do not normally eat frogs, but he also thought it was unacceptable and brutal to throw them alive onto the fire (Brusk in FGI, 24 March 2018). Brusk's narrative is a subtle, yet audible, protest against the stereotyping claim that women's participation in political violence can be trusted as just, while men's engagements will be interpreted as radical and brutal.[11]

Even among the women fighters themselves, some disagree with Drej's perception that women tend to wage war with empathy. Berfin recounted that on several occasions the fighters had known the Turkish military forces to abuse the bodies of their dead comrades, for example by cutting off heads, noses or ears. One woman fighter therefore wanted to take revenge on the dismembered dead comrades and began collecting the ears of the dead enemies. When the leadership learned about this, she was questioned and brought before the 'platform' where she had to explain herself to her comrades and the leadership. The platform took several days, because her act gave rise to a discussion of how to wage war according to morals rather than emotions and how to avoid hurting one's enemy more than necessary. Berfin recalled that this women fighter was punished after the platform, as it was decided that her actions were unacceptable. Berfin noted that both men and women were influenced by the brutality of war (Interview with Berfin, 22 March 2018).

While the women fighters narrativized their bravery and skills in battle, they said at the same time how sensitive and vulnerable they were. They did not describe themselves as violent prior to joining the PKK. They reported that participation in war gave them the opportunity to practice their ideological and personal calling, but that their aim had never been to mete out violence and achieve a result by so doing. They tend to associate the use of violence with an anti-colonial act but not as a tool to attain more power.[12] As an example, the women reported that none of them had found it easy to hurt the enemy. It took them a long time before they learnt to shoot at the enemy in order to kill. Most had to see those closest to them killed first before they experienced a drive for revenge. It should here be noted that revenge in this context has a double function. It is not only about legitimizing the use of violence against the enemy but also about the inner struggle to find the courage to distance oneself from one's old way of life. In my judgement, when they call themselves 'fighters', this does not necessarily mean that they associate war with violence and weapons. Rather, it is about being part of a people who fights for something, where the interim use of weapons is seen as necessary. Under no circumstances, therefore, do they want to be described as people who inflict violence and kill senselessly. For example, during my fieldwork there was nobody who spoke about how many soldiers they had killed or how skilled they were at using weapons, or who exhibited any kind of close attachment to their weapon. They spoke of seeing the weapon as a temporary and necessary tool to enable them to carry out the revolution and prevent the enemy from hurting them. Berfin said:

> Killing another person affected me badly. It was never my choice. I'm a very emotional person, so it affects me badly when somebody dies in action. It is against my principles to kill another person. But the circumstances we live under, the violent, technically advanced military operations against us and our people, create the desire for revenge inside you, consciously or unconsciously. This desire for revenge makes it possible for you to kill. Even after several years of combat, I'm badly affected when I see a dead body. If we hadn't experienced all that oppression, I don't believe I could kill anybody. But oppression produces a reaction, a desire for revenge. (Interview with Berfin, 22 March 2018)

According to Berfin's account, the Turkish oppression and attack against the Kurds justified her in permitting herself to kill another person. She also stated that this did not happen by her own choice. It was a slow process, a becoming that developed over time into a feeling of revenge. Sarya also said that killing another person was never easy:

> When you saw the fear in the Turkish soldier's eyes, you actually felt sorry. I sat down and wept after every single soldier I killed. [. . .] Unlike the soldiers, we had a gleam in our eyes when we went on military actions. We weren't afraid of death. [. . .] When I shot at the soldiers, I tried to avoid killing them. Just wound them. At the same time, we knew that the soldiers who were put in front in military operations were of Kurdish origin. We didn't want to kill them. They

sang in Kurdish when they came near us, so we could recognize them and avoid killing them. (Interview with Sarya, 29 December 2019)

It should also be mentioned that the interviewees said that despite the violent consequences of the war, their participation in it had helped them as women to overcome their own limitations and build self-confidence. Taking part in the war was therefore more a question of overcoming one's own lack of self-confidence than of killing as many Turkish soldiers as possible, said Bese. Participation in the war was necessary for women to develop a status in society and demonstrate their worth. The women had a perception that the men had not had the same need to take part in the war in order to demonstrate their worth, because they had had high social status beforehand, ever since they were born (Interview with Bese, 22 March 2018). In my opinion, what the women were not taking into account here was the upbringing and socialization that they, in contrast to the men, had had and its influence on their attitude to the use of violence, including war. Men are often brought up to take an 'aggressive role' as fighters, while women are assigned a passive role involving reserve and pacifism. I found that the women were inclined to explain their own lesser interest in the use of violence by the previously mentioned point about 'woman's nature' rather than pointing to socialization through patriarchal upbringing.

5.5. The women fighters' categorization of 'attack'

The women fighters' narratives on how they contribute to warfare centre on two important categories: 'attack' and 'defence'. While attack and defence are central in any kind of hostile confrontation, the women fighters have invested in claiming and redefining these categories as feminine.

Among women fighters, the category of 'attack' has been greatly influenced by the suicide mission carried out by the 'martyr Zilan', when she found it 'necessary' to use her own body as a weapon in order to eliminate the enemy and sap the enemy's fighting spirit. Within the PKK, actions like that of Zilan and similar martyrs are not described as suicide acts but as *fedai* actions. *Fedai* signifies a person who sacrifices his or her own body, not merely to kill the enemy out of desperation but for a higher purpose out of an ideological conviction with the strategic objective to improve results in the struggle. When Zilan sacrificed herself in 1996, the higher purpose was to signal to the enemy that they could not be safe and secure in their own base. At the same time, by her action, Zilan sent a message to her own comrades that they had to develop their way of waging war if they were to have a chance of victory over the enemy.[13] The significance of Zilan's action for women fighters and the development of a new discourse of martyrdom are defined by academician Düzel as follows:

> With Zilan, this nexus was amplified: the difference she made, killing others alongside herself, created tight constructions of female militancy in terms of

sacrifice and devotion expressed in mythical idioms, that is, goddessness, fire and rebirth, and culmination in death (Düzel 2018: 138–9).

Although the women fighters whom I interviewed historically regard war as men's doing, they also said that they, as women, were better fighters than men. This view is almost always exemplified by Zilan's action, because she was not only the PKK's first woman *fedai* but the first militant at all to attack the enemy in 'his own cave' and 'paralyse his ability to fight'. Her act had the enemy in shock at the courage of Kurdish women. In citing Zilan, the interviewees were indicating that they themselves were ready to carry out a *fedai* action should they or the movement find it necessary during the ongoing national struggle. Bese said:

> Being a woman means being in battle twenty-four hours a day. In a mentality battle. In organizational battle. In a military battle. . . . Being a woman means living like Zilan. Feeling like Zilan. Thinking like Zilan. That's how we [women] are. (Interview with Bese, 22 March 2018)

According to Bese, Zilan is more than a *fedai*. Zilan is also a role model for later women fighters. Asked why women should be better equipped for *fedai* actions than men, Bese replied:

> Because the woman's [inner] world is purer, she has more chance of attaining her goal. The man tends to be cunning. The man always is self-promoting. But the woman isn't like that. When the woman believes in something, she is ready to sacrifice herself to achieve it. So she is more determined. (Interview with Bese, 22 March 2018)

In the women fighters' narratives in the previous section, they similarly portrayed the men as sly, thinking in advance, before setting out on operations, about how they could return unharmed to the camp. Men were cunning and thought more about their own safety rather than considering the purpose of a military operation, and they therefore did not always follow the movement's guidelines. In contrast, the women fighters looked at Zilan as someone who had kept the objective in mind and not looked for an excuse to opt out of a military operation. Certainly, it would be detrimental to the PKK's objectives if they launched an attack well knowing that they themselves would be killed. However, war requires demanding and hazardous missions, and here the women fighters claim that they, like Zilan, have more strength of will than men. For example, the women fighters said that they always picked themselves to be first to the front in combat, although they knew that it increased the risk of being killed. They had found that some women fighters even became emotional and wept if they were not allowed to take part in a frontal attack. Ultimately, though, it was the leadership who assigned missions to the fighters depending on their experiences and combat skills.

None of the interviewees wanted to undergo what they themselves called a 'cheap death'. Here, a cheap death means a senseless death. It is death resulting from disease, accident or an enemy attack in which the fighter had no opportunity to realize his or her potential and maximize his or her combat skills. The women fighters would therefore rather die like Zilan in a military offensive against the enemy. Death cannot just be about a physical separation from the world. To be meaningful, death must produce military and/or ideological results in the form of loss and fear among the enemy and positive reports among one's own comrades. A meaningful death furthermore includes acts of saving one's comrades in battle. Avasin said:

> Men are physically stronger. But when it comes to strength of will, it is often women who come first. For example, the first *fedai* action in Afrin was carried out by comrade Avesta. (Interview with Avasin, 21 March 2018).

Avesta Xabur (Zelûh Hemo) was a member of the YPJ in Rojava who died in the fight against the Turkish invasion in Afrin. Avesta's *fedai* action took place on 27 January 2018 when she blew herself up to damage the Turkish tanks and thus save her comrades. She subsequently became a symbol of the resistance to the Turkish offensive. Avasin recognizes that Avesta's *fedai* as the first in this particular battle also made it prestigious.

When women become symbols of the uprising or the resistance struggle against the colonial power, it creates advantages for the PKK's propaganda. As discussed previously in Chapter 1, the rhetoric of martyrdom is often used in the PKK's propaganda to influence the Kurds and arouse their sympathy for the national struggle, but women martyrs have even more effect on both the public and the PKK's membership. There is a tendency, for example, for more members of the public to attend the funerals of women fighters than those of men fighters.[14] In some cases, it is mothers and sisters who carry the woman martyr's coffin to the grave, although this is not common in relation to Muslim rules and traditions.[15] There are some differences between an Islamic and a PKK-motivated martyr death. In Islam, a martyr's death is about sacrificing oneself in a holy struggle, while the PKK's struggle is secular, not sanctioned by some absolute, transcendent authority. In the Islamic conception of Paradise in the next world, a martyr is believed to have an immortal soul with which he or she can access it while leaving the body behind in this world. As the PKK is a secular movement with a socialist ideology, the martyr's self-sacrifice in battle does not carry the expectation of going to Paradise, where 'divine reward and riches', among other things, are expected.[16] When the PKK says, as it often does, that martyrs are immortal, it means that their contribution or death as martyrs is invaluable and will never be forgotten.[17] One therefore need not actually die in active combat to be regarded by the PKK as a martyr: a member can also be awarded this status if he or she died from injury, disease, a road accident or something similar. This will happen when the member has made a lifelong contribution to the struggle and shown loyalty to the movement's values until death. The movement therefore often holds cultural and political activities to commemorate the martyrs and signal to the Kurdish people that the martyrs' contributions will not be forgotten. The Kurdish academic and politician Hisyar Özsoy reflected on Kurdish martyr culture in his PhD thesis:

> [. . .] the semantic and symbolic significance of dead Kurdish bodies in the struggle between the Kurds and the Turkish state focusing on the last three decades (1984–). On the one hand, I trace funeral ceremonies of Kurdish fighters as a key site for the production of the mythology of Kurdish national martyrdom. I argue that this mythology is structured by a moral and symbolic economy of 'gift' which creates moral, symbolic and political exchanges between the Kurds and their dead and promotes the sense of a Kurdish nation identity as a sacred communion of the dead and the living. (Özsoy 2010: 22)

As Özsoy points out, when the PKK bestows the gift and title of 'martyr' on someone, it is part of a moral and symbolic economy that 'resurrects' the dead members, because death does not exist; there is only martyrdom. This explains why a PKK member would never say that a martyr has died.[18] In this way, the PKK justifies in front of the Kurdish population the human losses that the PKK has caused. In addition, the celebration of martyrs is also a motivating factor that generates a capacity for action. Potential martyrs will enjoy narrative and symbolic immortality after death. New PKK fighters adopt the names of martyrs, which is one way of resurrecting the martyrs.

Another effect of women's martyrdom is that funerals of women martyrs increase the pressure on men fighters, as it signals that the men are weak since they do not exhibit the same kind of devotion as the women fighters do. In Rojava, I met the man leader Huseyin, who had previously been the aforementioned Avesta's leader. He showed me some pictures and videos of their training, with Avesta taking part. I could tell by looking at him that in a way he was proud of her, because he had been her leader and she had carried out a 'successful action'. But he was also filled with a feeling of shame, telling me that she had been braver and more courageous than himself (fieldnote, 29 March 2018). Similarly, Nick described how men fighters were particularly affected when women fighters fell in the struggle:

> Perhaps we overdo the special treatment of women a bit. For example, when it was someone from the YPG [the men's unit] who was wounded or died, of course it was sad. Especially for those who knew him. But if someone from the YPJ died, it was clear that it affected people a lot more. You could also see that the comrades were extra affected. And that's interesting, you know, because if you want to have equality, but still feel you have to protect – or that it's extra bad if it's a woman who dies – then there really isn't full equality. (Interview with Nick, 12 July 2017)

It needs to be stressed that the rhetoric of martyrdom is so strong in the movement that the PKK as a whole is often described as a martyr movement. Almost all day-to-day activities, stories of heroes/heroines from earlier battles, jokes and so on are framed with reference to the martyrs. Heroic songs are written about the *fedai*. Geographical locations, institutions, training camps and new units are also named after martyrs such as Zilan and Avesta. This is one reason for the interviewees not wishing to undergo a cheap death. Their willingness to initiate attack and embrace martyrdom reflects the hope of increased dignity in their names and stories continuing to be spoken and remembered even after their deaths, given that dead bodies also have a high political value.[19]

5.6. *The women fighters' categorization of 'defence'*

The women fighters have also claimed and redefined the concept of 'defence'. They do so with reference to assertions about 'women's nature', as defined in Chapter 4. It would be contrary to this 'nature' if women engaged in yearnings for dominance or ownership, which are yearnings associated with 'men's nature'. A woman therefore wages war only when forced to defend herself. The aforementioned co-founder of the PKK Sakine Cansız is categorized as true to her feminine nature when she defended her people against the ideological threats of colonial dominance. In contrast to Zilan, who 'courageously' paralysed the enemy by her attack, a picture is painted of Sakine Cansız as the fully free woman who ideologically organized her body and mentality in such a way that the enemy's way of life and his attacks no longer had any effect on her personality. She led a revolutionary life according to the PKK's ideology and guidelines until she was assassinated in Paris in 2013. She is the symbol of the free and autonomous Kurdish woman who does not attack the enemy but is nevertheless a threat to them as she offers a new alternative way of life.

Another significant woman who exemplifies woman defence is the martyr Beritan (Gülnaz Karataş). She died when she threw herself from the cliffs during fighting to avoid being captured by the Kurdish Peshmerga forces[20] in Iraq who collaborated with Turkish military forces in the campaign against the PKK in 1992. The women fighters say that many of the Peshmerga forces subsequently laid down their arms and no longer wished to be part of the internal conflict among Kurds,[21] because they were shocked by Beritan's act as a woman. Although the women fighters frame Beritan's act more in terms of its later political and military effects, it was also an act carried out by Beritan out of necessity in order to defend her own honour. As a woman, she risked abuse in the form of rape or similar violations if she was taken prisoner. In the PKK's propaganda, there are several similar narratives of women fighters who killed themselves with their last bullet or bomb to avoid being taken prisoner. While one would expect the PKK to emphasize that the women's bodies belong to the women themselves, women choosing death to avoid rape and similar violations indicates a discursive pressure within the PKK upon the women fighters to make it their responsibility to protect and defend their own bodies, according to the honour ideology described in Chapter 1. In paying tribute to women fighters such as Beritan, the movement sends a signal to other women fighters that they too must act as Beritan did if it becomes necessary for them to defend their honour.

Defence of embodied honour is a strategy that pertains to psychological warfare that may help demoralize the enemy, said Arya (Interview with Arya, 25 March 2018). While Zilan paralysed the enemy's combat abilities through her attack, Beritan chose to defend her honour by choosing death. Accordingly, her act is regarded not as a suicide operation but as a *fedai* action – an ideological protest against the enemy's imagined intentions of rape and thus a refusal to allow men to control her or her body. According to Zelal:

> Woman has proved herself. Beritan did that with her personality. Zilan did it, too. They drew a line for us regarding how the free woman should be. They didn't only influence us, but men, too. The men have since changed and evolved a lot. They [Zilan and Beritan] created a new ideological and military warrior spirit for us. A '*fedai* spirit'. Zilan and Beritan woke everybody from death. Woman is no longer just a mother. Or someone who cooks food. Or a sister. Woman is the colour of life. Woman's will is strong now. Woman is now a 'guide'. Heval Beritan's action was against traitors and collaborators. Therefore, it influenced everybody. Including comrades and the leadership, who were obliged to be self-critical. We [women] have since changed everything. [. . .] Beritan's action helped us women to become a separate military force, while Zilan's made it possible for us to create the women's liberation ideology in our political party, the PAJK. They each contributed to a new transition. (Interview with Zelal, 17 September 2017)

Zelal's reflections indicate that women's defensive *fedai* actions in addition to guarding their honour also produce ideological advantages for the PKK that contribute on more levels. First, it mobilizes more young Kurds to join. Second, it increases backing of the Kurdish population. Third, it brings the movement to reflect on and evaluate its ongoing conduct of the war, which are necessary steps to bring about a transition to a new phase in the movement's military organization and strategy. Fourth, it motivates those already engaged in the movement, which again generates cohesion, belief in the ideology and revolution. Fifth, it signals to the enemy how strong the movement has become. To understand the advantages of women fighters' defensive ways of waging war, it should be mentioned that Beritan's *fedai* action took place just at a time when the women fighters were having difficulty living and fighting in the mountains together with men, and when the women fighters considered their separate organization. Beritan's *fedai* action became the catalyst that accelerated the process towards separate organization. This is what Zelal means when she says that Beritan united the women into an independent army.

The women's tendency to frame the war as a defence is referred to by them as the 'legitimate right of defence'. This means waging war only when necessary, but at the same time reserving the right to defend oneself if attacked or threatened by the enemy. However, this is a matter not just of reacting if the enemy attacks but rather of organizing oneself so strongly that the enemy is deterred from attacking.

Through this kind of defence, the Turkish military forces have to undergo a change of mentality and consider if they seriously want to wage war against Kurdish women who will never allow themselves to accept any form of subjugation. Avasin said:

> The man only thinks logically. If we look at the man and his history, we can actually see that he has always striven for power. [. . .] But when woman got involved in the war, then emotions came out. In woman's nature, there is no question of eradication. The aim is to change and convert the enemy. When it's necessary, of course you eradicate them, but the intention is change and conversion first and foremost. (Interview with Avasin, 21 March 2018)

Avasin's narrative draws on assumptions, analysed in Chapter 4, on the difference between men and women's natural gender. Women are assumed to be more inclined to wage war humanely and with empathy with the purpose of protecting what is already hers. If an enemy backs away from threatening and taking what is not his or her, a woman, so Avasin claims, would have no need to hurt the enemy. Accordingly, women are inclined to keep warfare at the defensive level, as they are not interested in having power over others or taking over their territory. It is thus a matter of conducting war carefully and conscientiously in line with women's natural inclinations. Cane said:

> If you've used more violence than necessary, acting only according to a mechanical military mentality to take revenge, it may well be that you'll assume the military operation has been carried out successfully. But it is not ideologically successful. Unfortunately, such military operations happen at times, but we do not approve of them. Regardless of who has carried out the operation, the person will be punished, because it is ideologically wrong. If you've liberated a village by inflicting more violence than necessary, we won't just accept it because the village is now liberated. We will say that the way the village was liberated is wrong, to prevent the same unnecessary use of violence happening again. And women play a vital role here, ensuring that the guidelines are observed. (Interview with Cane, 25 March 2018)

Cane's narrative is just one of many examples of women fighters claiming to be better than men at observing the humanitarian and moral rules applicable in war and the PKK's own ideological and moral guidelines. From narratives like Cane's, it looks as though, out of their essentialist conception of men's and women's qualities, the women fighters are waging an internal war in the form of a battle of the sexes by stressing how the character of their warfare against the Turkish state differs from that of their men comrades. Cane indicates that women fighters guarantee that all ideological guidelines are observed and that men's lust and striving for more power will be curbed, thanks to them. Especially since Öcalan was imprisoned in Turkey, internecine conflicts have characterized the PKK and the women fighters feel an obligation to secure the ideology and guidelines of Öcalan. It is for this reason that most women fighters claim that the PKK as a political movement could never have become as big or as strong without the participation of women (Interview with Avasin, 21 March 2018).

Apparently, the women fighters have been successful in instilling the general perception among Kurds that women have superior morality. Many men fighters agree that women's way of waging war is better than men's. This view is cultivated in various iterative acts within the PKK such as training, instruction and other forms of activity aimed at creating the new human. Once, I was permitted to observe one of the movement's public education meetings in Europe, at which ordinary people sympathetic to the movement were introduced to the movement's ideology. When I happened to ask a critical question as to why the movement's pronouncements always presented matriarchal society as better than patriarchal society, I was attacked more by the men present than by the women. The men clearly thought that women had superior morality and that women's character traits were better in every way than their own (fieldnote, 26–27 August 2017).

Another way in which particularly women fighters use their bodies as a battlefield and a means of protest is by starving themselves to death on hunger strikes or by other ways of self-immolation. Both strategies add to the arsenal of defence methods based on their immediate access to harm one's own body with fatal consequences and thereby spread a political message. The PKK is well aware that such defence strategies can have a bigger impact than killing a couple of enemy soldiers. In Chapter 1, I mentioned how fatal acts of hunger strikes and self-immolations among PKK inmates took place at the Diyarbakir Military Prison to protest against the rough treatment at the hands of the prison authorities. At that time, these actions were carried out mainly by men PKK members, but the number involving women has since grown. Zekiye Alkan, who died on 21 March 1990, is thought to be the first Kurdish woman to have set herself alight in the city of Diyarbakir, where she was a medical student. She was not a PKK member but was sympathetic to the movement. Since then, there have been numerous women, not only women fighters in Turkey and Europe, who have carried out similar acts of protest against the Turkish state's treatment of the Kurds and in particular against the isolation of Öcalan, who is serving a jail sentence. One thing that these women have in common is that they all stated that their acts had a higher purpose. For example, Sema Yüce (d. 17 June 1998) set herself alight on Newroz Day, 21 March 1998. She left behind a letter stating that the purpose of her act was to take the Kurdish women's struggle to a higher level. She wanted to regenerate life from her ashes, describing women as sparks from the Kurdish fire.[22]

The last major act of defence to be mentioned here is the hunger strike initiated on 8 November 2019 by imprisoned Kurdish parliamentarian Leyla Güven of the pro-Kurdish HDP party. She demanded an end to the isolation of the imprisoned Öcalan so that he could meet his lawyer and family. Thousands of people from all over the world took part in her protest, which lasted for 200 days. Four Kurdish women and four Kurdish men joined the hunger strike and eventually died from starvation. Like earlier protests, this action was only called off at Öcalan's urging. Although Öcalan has previously stated that he does not find such protests, in which Kurds damage their bodies, acceptable, neither he nor the PKK can prevent such actions from occurring. More women than men seem to engage in this type of defence act against colonial rule.

Summary

The chapter demonstrates that there have been difficult times and major challenges for the women fighters over the years, especially when life in the mountains was being established in the 1990s and before they were permitted to take part in the war on an equal footing with their men comrades. The women have fought a battle on more fronts: a battle with their own patriarchal and liberal mentality, a physical battle to adapt to life in the mountains and nature, a battle with their men comrades who did not want to accept or value their engagement in armed combat and finally an armed struggle against the colonizing powers. However, the struggle to liberate themselves from the passivity assigned to them, including their bodies, due to patriarchal values has not been an easy one. Initially, women fighters found it necessary to prove that they were stronger in battle than men. Yet, Öcalan backed various initiatives, mechanisms and methods within the PKK to encourage women to break free from the men of the PKK in order to take control of their own lives and way of resisting. Subsequently, the women fighters as a group have undergone a change of mentality, gained a new conception of their bodily potential and hence found new ways of waging war that did not depend on physical strength alone. It is a central argument in this book that the women fighters' engagement in the PKK is not only about decolonizing Kurdistan but also about them achieving a status within Kurdish society where they can prove their worth as women. Due to this double objective, the women fighters are characterized by a willingness to contribute maximally and sacrifice themselves if need be. This willingness to sacrifice, once it is embraced, changes both the women fighters' self-perception and the way in which the struggle is conducted and how the women fighters are perceived by other PKK members. Today, the overall Kurdish population, including men fighters, consider the death of women fighters – that is, their martyrdom – more worthy than men's. When women's liberation is regarded by all as the road to the nation's liberation, the women fighters feel that their participation in the national struggle is significant and obligatory because of their responsibility for the nation and humanity. Women fighters' acts in the form of *fedai* can therefore be seen not merely as the PKK's instrumentalization and disciplining of them but also as the women fighters' own desire to be presented as fighters and revolutionaries, as the women fighters seem to have more reasons than men do to carry out such *fedai* actions.

Especially when women fighters talk about their combat experiences, they emphasize that their contribution to the development of the war and warfare is more important than that of men. They claim that they are stronger-willed, more ideologically aware, more empathetic and better able to wage war, including a readiness to die as a *fedai* if necessary. Today, the concept of *fedai* connotes something feminine rather than masculine, probably because of women's greater will to self-sacrifice. This entails that the martyr culture, which has always been a defining feature of the PKK, experiences a feminine transformation, since it ascribes more importance and prestige to the women martyrs compared to the men martyrs. In addition, the correct way to die and sacrifice oneself is defined from women martyrs' way to wage war. Here, the women fighters have seemingly succeeded in transforming to their own advantage the heteronormative gender understanding cultivated in the PKK, where femininity is almost always praised above masculinity. One consequence of this is that the women regard themselves as guarantors of the PKK's struggle and ideological agenda, and this seems also to be accepted by the men and the leadership of the movement due to its many advantageous effects.

Chapter 6

THE WOMEN FIGHTERS' DREAMS OF A NEW SOCIETY

This last chapter of the analysis will focus on the interviewed women fighters' orientation towards the future with regard to their personal and ideological expectations, when they must one day break away from life in the mountains and encounter the society in which they seek to implement their new gender ideals. The chapter analyses in combination interviews with women fighters of the PKK – associated with the Turkish-dominated part of Kurdistan – and with women fighters of the YPJ – a Kurdish military unit associated with Rojava, the de facto autonomous area controlled by the Kurds in the north-eastern part of Syria. This combination allows insights into how the women fighters of both movements mutually inspire each other and share a similar socialist ideology, which have enabled Kurdish women across official borders to form an anti-colonial coalition. Because Kurds have dominated Rojava since 2013, the analyses of this chapter provide a unique insight into how Kurdish women, with the opportunity, implement their gender ideals in Rojava as a real-life experiment.

6.1. Future expectations

Throughout my interviews, I found that the women fighters from the PKK had difficulty addressing the question of their personal wishes and expectations for the future. For them, it seemed difficult to imagine a life outside the PKK as their values and ideology required them to devote the rest of their lives to the struggle. In addition, they had also grown accustomed to a life of community and solidarity, thereby forming for themselves a kind of collective identity, where individual dreams would seem off course. This collectivist thinking became apparent, for example, when they unanimously stated that their greatest dream was that they would one day meet their leader, Öcalan, and have a conversation with him. For example, when I asked Farasin, 'Where do you see yourself when you're no longer fit for fighting or you're getting on in years?', there was a long pause before she answered: 'I would like to meet the Leader [Öcalan].' Her reply met ideological, collectivist expectations, but is also better understood when one knows that Farasin had previously been in an arranged marriage. Shortly after her divorce, she chose to join the PKK. She stated that she would never marry again (Interview with Farasin, 30 March 2018). Here, Farasin's pause before responding indicated that thoughts of returning to civilian life arouse unwelcomed memories of the past.

The uncertainty regarding a personal future is no doubt also due to the interviewed women fighters having nothing to return to or to re-establish if they should one day break away from life in the PKK. When women travel to the mountains, they say goodbye to their families well aware that they might never return and thus not enjoy the prospect of re-establishing their old lives within their families. Life in the PKK therefore becomes not just their present but also their future. For example, Bese said that the character of her relationship with her family had changed after she joined the PKK. She no longer saw her biological family. Instead, she turned towards her comrades, with whom she shared moral values (Interview with Bese, 22 March 2018). The women fighters described their new family, referred to as the 'party family', as their be-all and end-all. They also emphasized to me that their greatest fear was not dying in battle or being unable to be reunited with their biological family but leaving their party comrades, who were now their nearest and dearest. Zeri said:

> I came close to death several times. I've never been afraid to die as a martyr, but I was afraid of losing my comrades. Since being wounded, I've had the feeling that it seems as though I'll never get to see my comrades again if I close my eyes. It's probably that feeling that keeps me alive, to be close to the comrades. (Interview with Zeri, 26 March 2018)

The women fighters also indicated that they would always be part of the struggle and contribute to it in one way or another, even when old age caught up with them. Yet, old age seemed to be a theme that they did not talk about or value, probably due to the martyr culture of the PKK mentioned earlier. When so many people are falling in battle at a young age, dreams of a long life are seen as both unrealistic and insensitive to those who will never experience it. Many of their comrades had died in combat at a young age, so the women fighters did not necessarily expect to grow old. There were hardly any old comrades around them, in whom they could see themselves reflected. With the strong martyr culture, a long life would, furthermore, be seen as a failure to make sufficient sacrifices or indicate that a long-living person had been too 'cunning' in his or her way of fighting, verging on cowardice. As recounted in Chapter 5, such cunning was an accusation directed at some of their men comrades who had survived many battles and grown older. In other words, the interviewed women fighters did not necessarily think of life as divided into such stages as youth, adulthood and old age.

The women fighters said that it was difficult for them to talk about a day-to-day life outside the national liberation struggle, in which they now took part. They did not dream of a future life with marriage, children, work or home. For them, the life of a woman revolutionary means taking part in a never-ending struggle as fighters who seek an all-encompassing liberation. On this point, Berivan said:

For example, we've now had the revolution in Rojava, right? Imagine it's happened in all four parts of Kurdistan. So the revolution has happened and we have control of all four parts of Kurdistan, where our people have gained their freedom. So I've become a free woman. Is that good enough? Is the freedom struggle over? I don't think so. Freedom is unattainable. (Interview with Berivan, 21 March 2018)

If the struggle is never-ending for the women fighters, and there is nothing called 'after the revolution', then the future becomes a mental abstraction, something unattainable for them. Life and time happen only in the present, while questions about future plans and activities are often answered with: 'The party knows', that is, it is up to the PKK and its leadership to judge where members are to serve and what missions they are to perform in the future. The women's hesitance in answering questions of their own personal future is presumably also due to the women's perception that they are no longer in control of their lives. When they joined, they signed over their lives to the party. As Avasin of the PKK said: 'You don't belong to yourself any more once you've joined the party' (Interview with Avasin, 21 March 2018).

It is customary for the PKK to receive a personal report from all once a year. In the report, members must reflect critically on their practice to date, focusing mainly on their personal development. They also have to make suggestions, based on their personal wishes, for future tasks and assignments. With the report as a starting point and in dialogue with the member concerned, the leadership makes a decision. There seems to be an expectation among the members that everyone will write in their reports that they want to be in the mountains to engage in active combat. When a member expresses a wish to be in the mountains, they signal to the leadership that they do not shrink from tough, demanding duties.

All those I interviewed stated that whether fit for fight, wounded or injured, they all wanted to be in the mountains to contribute to the struggle. To serve in big Turkish cities or in Europe would be an unbidden assignment. The leadership has had to pressure or even force members to serve in Europe. With regard to the women fighters' plans for the future, should they no longer be able to engage in the armed struggle from the mountains, an assignment in the big Turkish cities or Europe would definitely not be attractive. First, they do not want to go far from 'Kurdistan' because the capitalist way of life in such areas was much more demanding than the simple life in the mountains. Second, the interviewed women fighters of the PKK did have one dream, after all, of the future – that is, to arrange their lives according to their own ideological norms and values, as they have done more or less in the mountains.

A significant source of inspiration for the PKK women fighters is the YPJ women fighters' influence on the implementation of a new societal model in Rojava. Since 2013, the region of Rojava has enjoyed de facto autonomy due to the Kurds' successful resistance to Syrian military forces as well as their ability to push back the Islamic State from the Kurdish territory in Syria. For Kurdish women across official borders, Rojava is thus not just a region where Kurds can lead an ordinary life without being persecuted by colonial powers. It is also a place where women fighters can influence the establishment of a society based on the ideals and ideologies that are current in the mountains. Some PKK women fighters told me that if they were someday to withdraw from the struggle in the mountains to lead an ordinary civilian life, it would be in Rojava, where the first women's revolution is in the midst of being implemented.

6.2. Breaking with the PKK: Women who have left the struggle

Despite the dominant view that enrolment in the PKK was a lifelong commitment, some women fighters have left the movement. Other women fighters did not reveal to me any purely negative conceptions of such women. Still, their choice was not considered ideal. Berfin from the PKK recounted:

> It's not so easy to leave the liberation movement [the PKK] and start a new life. You've got used to life here, so you have to go back to life in the system, which is full of difficulties. Personally, I don't approve of their decision to leave us. But we are also a humane movement, so we can't force people to be with us. We can't hold onto people by force. It'll be better if they carry on being patriots in their new life. They can get involved in some political and humanitarian work in their new life, for example. (Interview with Berfin, 23 March 2018)

Like Berfin, most interviewees indicated that they could certainly understand those who left the movement as long as they did not change sides in the struggle or become 'traitors'. However, although their choice was accepted based on everyone's right to determine his or her own life, the interviewees still did not consider leaving the movement to be the right choice. The interviewees unanimously stated that as fighters, they themselves had a hard life in the liberation struggle, which challenged them both physically and mentally, but that like anything else, the liberation struggle came at a price that had to be paid. During my interviews pertaining to the subject of leaving the PKK, I sensed a fear that cadres who had left the movement might signal a rejection of or discredit the movement's national struggle and call for a 'new free life'. It may deter young Kurds to enrol in the movement as well as inspire members who are considering leaving the movement to make the leap or even give the Turkish state an opportunity to substantiate a counter-propaganda against the PKK. The movement has therefore taken several measures to prevent 'weak personalities' from leaving the movement.

Berfin said that the PKK's countermeasures to prevent discontinuation of membership include sending a member who expresses a wish to leave the movement back for ideological instruction in a unit where his or her motivation will be intensively worked on. The cadre with doubts might also be assigned to accompany one of the movement's leading figures for a while to find inspiration. If the movement still does not succeed in holding onto the cadre after such steps, the cadre may be allowed to leave with the offer that he or she will always be welcome to come back. If the cadre is determined to leave the movement, he or she will be presented with the option of continuing as a patriot, carrying on with political activity in civilian society on behalf of the national struggle. This applies, of course, to those cadres who have not acted traitorously against the movement. Loyal cadres who wish to leave should be kept continuously close to the movement for it to be able to draw on the member's resources in legal work and still influence his or her life processes. At the same time, such an arrangement will enable the member to avoid a limbo of confusion and uncertainty in the transition to civilian life, where the member may well have a sense of failure because he or she chose to opt out of a supposedly lifelong commitment to the movement. The interviewees noted, as Berfin said, that life in the movement and life in civilian society are very different, and there is no easy life waiting for those who choose to leave the movement (Interview with Berfin, 23 March 2018).

It was not easy for me to find women fighters who were no longer active in the movement and yet willing to talk to me about their experiences of life before and after the movement. With the movement's help, a woman who now lives in Europe was willing to give me an interview. Unfortunately, her husband intervened and cancelled the appointment the day before, so it never took place. I find it highly intriguing that it was her husband, with whom I had had no previous contact, and not she, who cancelled the interview. The PKK members in Europe tried to set up other interviews between me and their ex-members but for a long time with no success. Everything indicated that it was difficult for the women ex-members to meet somebody and talk about what they themselves perhaps understood as a 'failed life' or a 'hard life' of a traumatic nature.[1] Finally, I managed to get in touch with one woman ex-member of the PKK, Sarya.

Sarya now lives in Europe with her children and husband. She came to Europe from Turkey at the age of twelve and decided to join the PKK on her eighteenth birthday. She recounted with a smile that she was only eighteen years old and weighed 47 kilos when she set off, but that she had the courage to change the world.

Sarya cried several times during the interview with me. She told me that she had not cried in the mountains, not even when she had to bury her dead comrades. She would typically cry when she had to talk about her comrades, whom she referred to as martyrs. Sarya said that she could never look at the palms of her hands because they reminded her of her comrades' blood that had once filled her hands while she tried to help them. During military operations in the mountains, there had been no time to cry for dead comrades, said Sarya. She very much resented not having been able to bid farewell to her dead comrades as they deserved. Many of the dead did not get a proper burial or ceremony that could have facilitated such farewell.

Sarya narrated about some clashes between her and the PKK that fuelled her wish to stop being on active service for the movement. The first clash happened when she was not allowed to carry out her planned *fedai* action as a 'self-sacrifice action'. It was cancelled by the movement the day before. She was one of the first candidates for the *fedai* action. After the cancellation of the action, life simply lost its meaning for her. She explained that by cancelling her *fedai* action, the movement forced her to live a life that she no longer valued. The second clash was the continuation of an internal power struggle in the movement. The third clash was connected with her being sent to Europe in 2006 to do service there. When she found that the movement's representatives in Europe were far removed from the movement's ideology and were, in her words, 'corrupt', she chose to become a passive member in protest, although she has since regretted this. By 'passive member', she meant that she was always loyal to the movement's norms and ideology, just as she patriotically participated in all national events arranged by the movement. However, she had stopped carrying out anything concrete on behalf of the movement. When she chose a passive life in the absence of better and available alternatives, she had to live with her family for a time. This was awful, according to Sarya. Although her family supported her and showed understanding, life in 'the system' was a long way from her ideals. Sarya recounted:

> When I came to Europe, I thought the society was awful. The more I listened to acquaintances, the more I isolated myself. Imagine, you've been away from these people's reality for so many years. You expect everyone to deal with each other without expecting anything selfish from each other. That's how our life was in the mountains. We believed we'd also changed society to some extent. [. . .] My elder siblings talked about nothing but jewellery, perfume, clothes, their hairdresser. I thought, how was I to live with them. (Interview with Sarya, 19 December 2019)

Here, Sarya indicates that in civil society, she felt that everything was meaningless. It was neither possible to adjust to society nor to establish meaningful relationships. It hurt Sarya to find that her family had also grown used to a life without her. Sarya indicated in the interview that her life had changed drastically, from planning to end as a meaningful *fedai* to instead experiencing a deep meaninglessness. At this state, she even considered suicide.

In my view, Sarya's narrative about her life both inside and outside the PKK is full of traumatic experiences, and it is most likely that her post-combat state of desolation is related to some kind of post-traumatic stress disorder. For example, she recalled sleeping only three hours a day, eating very little, often dreaming of life in the mountains, often crying, being aware of people feeling sorry for her, having difficulty accepting that she was now a wife and mother and having difficulty telling others about her life and her experiences in the mountains. Sarya said with a smile that her husband occasionally reminded her that she was their children's mother, not their commander. Nevertheless, and to some surprise in the midst of these challenges and rather dark recollections, Sarya considered herself lucky. She had gained access to a life and a supportive family in Europe. She had established for herself a new platform for life. She had enrolled in further education and was now a certified teacher. When explaining her relative acceptance of her current life and how she was now functioning as a person, wife and mother, Sarya pointed to the importance of being given the chance, a couple of years ago, to do political work for the Kurdish women's movement. While unfortunately I cannot compare her appreciation of a post-combat connection to the PKK with other women ex-members' accounts, I can – especially from my conversation with Mordem, who is responsible for the training of members – point out, it corroborates the PKK's claim that their strategy for ex-members is of mutual benefit (Interview with Mordem, 19 January 2018). What Sarya was doing was nothing much, but it gave her a feeling of being part of the PKK and the collectivist world. She is in touch with a number of her comrades who have also chosen to leave the PKK. They have it worse than she does, said Sarya:

> We have a problem with being part of society. We carry things we've experienced in the past on our backs, like a burden. I mean, not everyone can justify to themselves the decision to leave the PKK. Life is lonely for those who've left. We feel that we are guilty. Our conscience isn't good. Every day, we see that the comrades we used to fight with are falling in battle as martyrs. Although I cook ten dishes, I'll only eat one of them. I can't stop thinking of our sparse table in the mountains. Our biggest challenge here is becoming part of society. I have it a bit better than most, because I am partly in the PKK. Those who come to Europe get no help. They are completely alone. They don't know anyone. They experience loneliness. It's unfair to experience that, considering how much we've sacrificed. So most comrades don't have it so good mentally. Their souls are wounded. (Interview with Sarya, 19 December 2019)

Sarya's accounts address how the transition from a full-time military life to a civilian life entails multiple difficulties and challenges for returnees and their families. No matter what her civilian surroundings made think of her, she herself belittles her experiences and challenges in comparison with those of martyrs and heroes/heroines. She narrates how she and her comrades, who have also left, feel weak and guilty for having chosen to leave the struggle. They even feel disloyal to their martyr comrades.[2] The noteworthy thing about Sarya's narrative is that she felt like an 'other', at least until she returned to a peripheral position with a civilian function for the PKK. She blames, however, only herself for everything that had happened. I consider that her feeling of guilt comes from the strict ideological disciplining that she received in the PKK. In the mountains, if anything went wrong or a task was not carried out satisfactorily, one was expected to reflect self-critically on one's own deficiencies. I cannot generalize on the basis of one interview, but Sarya's loyalty to the PKK despite the clashes mentioned earlier indicates that women ex-members react much differently from men ex-members, which calls for further exploration.

6.3. The Rojava experiment: The Kurdish women movement's village of Jinwar

This section will focus on how the meeting of ideology and sociocultural reality is experienced and realized at a concrete, local level in the Kurdish women movement's village of Jinwar in Rojava. With the PKK's ideology of democratic confederalism as a starting point, the section will provide an insight into the PKK's ideals of direct democracy and its visions for women, as well as into the concrete challenges that women fighters face in the transition from service in the mountains to service in civilian life.

I visited Jinwar on 29 March 2018, accompanied by two YPJ women fighters. We arrived in the afternoon and were eventually given permission to spend the night in the village. Ruken from the Kongra Star,[3] who was primarily responsible for the construction of the village, said that I was the first man to be allowed to spend the night there. Many men had wanted to do the same but had not been allowed to. 'Men are extra interested in everything women do alone', said Ruken critically, yet with a smile.

The name 'Jinwar' is composed of the words 'jin', Kurdish for 'woman', and 'war', which means area or land. The two words together make up the word 'woman's village'. According to Ruken, the village was founded under inspiration from Öcalan's ideas about how harmful city life has become to people and about the need, especially for women, for a free territory in which to recreate themselves and be themselves. Women need shelters, workshops, villages and institutions where they can cultivate their nature and be free of men dominance. The idea of Jinwar was developed in the mountains between eleven and twelve years ago, said Ruken. Due to Turkish military interventions, an experiment like Jinwar had not been possible in territories officially claimed by the Turkish state. However, Kurds in the north-eastern part of Syria had the opportunity and seized it. They initiated the process towards the establishment of a village on 25 November 2016 and inaugurated it on 25 November 2018, associated with the 'International Day for the Elimination of Violence against Women', proclaimed by the United Nations. Women affected by violence constitute one of the village's target groups. For example, Ruken spoke about Dicle who came to live in the village soon after its establishment. Dicle had been forced as a thirteen-year-old to enter a marriage with a violent husband, and her own family had done nothing to stop his wife battering. Dicle had managed to move away from him, but also away from her family, yet at the heavy price of living without her three children. They had to remain with their father in Iraq. Ruken explained that Dicle, on top of this traumatic experience and break, was quite unable to live a city life with all its obligations. She needed peace in order to recover. Jinwar housed another woman who had escaped her violent husband. She could no longer stand him and his violence, especially not after he had married a second, younger wife. She, however, had managed to hold on to her three children, so they lived with her now in Jinwar.

'Where are all the women victims of violence to seek refuge?', asked Ruken while stressing that the purpose of Jinwar was not to detach women from society, but rather to give them the opportunity to re-establish their relationship with society and their trust in it. The idea of welcoming women, whether victims of violence or not, corresponds with Öcalan's claim that city life is especially harmful to 'women's nature'. Öcalan associates cities as units of capitalist modernity with the exploitation of women as sexual objects in the pursuit of reproducing men power.[4] While Ruken did not mention Öcalan in her presentation of Jinwar to me, the correspondence between his ideals and their practice of welcoming women on the run from such a city life was striking to me.

Ruken went on and explained that Jinwar also prioritized housing the wives and children of martyrs. In the region where Jinwar is situated, around 3,000 families have lost a member who died in the fight against the Turkish state, the Syrian state or the Islamic State. These families are referred to as martyr families, and many of them have nowhere to live and no form of financial security. When Ruken spoke of her commitment to taking care of martyr families, the reason is that the Kongra Star sees the care of martyr families as a duty of honour. These families are considered the 'relics' of martyrs.

In Jinwar, a school is being built to attend to the education of the children who have followed their mothers to the village. Other projects involve the establishment of a library, a cafe, women's workshops and a jineological institute to educate the residents according to the ideals of jineoloji. Women can carry on living in Jinwar as long as they want, but men cannot live there. If a woman of Jinwar and a man want to get married, she would have to move out of the village, said Ruken. She added proudly that the presence of Jinwar had already begun to influence the surrounding area. Men from neighbouring villages had told her that their wives had started threatening to leave them and go to Jinwar if a disagreement occurred.

During my seven-day visit to Rojava, a number of women claimed that there were fewer violent attacks on women in Rojava than elsewhere in Syria. Their explanation for this is that the people in Rojava understand that the newly implemented system of confederalism protects women and that the Kongra Star is strongly organized. At the same time, the local population is beginning to embrace the new norms and values, associated with the PKK, even though there is still a long way to go. Canan, the woman co-mayor of a town, said that conditions for women have probably improved significantly since 'the revolution of establishment of Rojava', but there are still many attacks on women that go under the radar and that the local authorities do not know about. The interesting thing about her account is that she said from her own experience that while men posed challenges and carried out attacks on women because of their patriarchal values, many women were complicit in contributing to patriarchal values by maintaining traditions and norms. In this way, some women as well as men were guilty of exerting social control over other women. She said that it would be difficult for her to last out her term as co-mayor, because everyone was against her – women especially – as local women were not used to seeing women in positions of leadership in society. When people were unable to break her will, they tried to split her family by putting pressure on her husband and in-laws. For instance, numerous rumors were put about, with some people encouraging her husband to marry again on the basis that Canan was almost never at home. Others suggested to her that she should resign and stay at home to save her marriage and family (Interview with Canan, 28 March 2018).

Canan's narrative reveals a noteworthy discrepancy between, on the one hand, the way women fighters picture society in accordance with jineoloji and confederalism, and, on the other hand, the resistance they encounter in society. The interviewed women fighters of the PKK often claimed that women in civil society would accept their ideology and values without resistance because of women's natural sympathy with each other and because they were ready to be 'saved'. Yet, the evidence of local resistance, even among women, to other women's political influence indicates that many challenges lie ahead if the project of the overall Kongra Star is to be realized.

Jinwar was built on a vacant site that was allocated to the Kongra Star by the local Kurdish municipality. As befits a democratic project, women from neighbouring villages were included in the decision-making processes. The men's ideas were 'weeded out' to rid the project of men influence. Jinwar will not be the only women's village in the district, said Ruken. The idea is that every town will have its own women's quarter, where women can seek refuge when they need it. This will allow them to get their breath back when they are faring badly in the cities and/or in patriarchal society. In this way, Jinwar is merely a restructuring, in a societal context, of the training camps or mountain districts where the women fighters live, said Ruken. She added that Jinwar can be a place where Kongra Star can cultivate and practice its ideology with a view to influencing the surrounding communities.

In Jinwar, the Kongra Star is in charge of educating the local population and supporting them in saying no to forced marriage, child marriage and polygamy. I could already witness how young local women who had come into contact with the Kongra Star had become active in the struggle against patriarchal values. The local districts are organized into council assemblies on which all individuals and groups of different ethnic, religious, linguistic, gender and intellectual orientations are represented as far as possible. Below the level of the council assembly, the women organize in a separate political organ where matters pertaining to women are discussed and problem-solving attempted before unsolvable and major issues are referred to the supreme people's council, where men and women sit together. In all political organs in Rojava, the Kongra Star has succeeded in claiming a women's quota stipulating that women must have at least 50 per cent representation on the boards. A system of men/women co-chairs has also been introduced, so that men and women share power. The Kongra Star assumes that this division will decentralize power, reinforce consensus and signal a more ideal, harmonious relationship between women and men in public offices.

Ruken related with pride that Jinwar was being built primarily through the voluntary efforts of women. In a few cases, it was not possible to find women to carry out a task, such as when electrical power was to be installed; men were then brought in to tackle these specific tasks. Thirty houses were to be built, but the plan was to expand the village to fifty houses. However, this did not mean that all women or families would get their own house. Farasin, the other woman behind the Jinwar initiative, said that some women might well choose to live together if it suited them better.

The construction of houses in Jinwar is inspired by old, local traditions of using mud-bricks. Visually, the new houses stand in contrast to city buildings of metal and concrete. Jinwar's construction work furthermore ascribes to ideals of ecological and climate-friendly solutions. For example, electricity and heating are provided by solar power to avoid exhausting natural resources. Financially, women and their children do not have to pay to live in Jinwar. In return, however, they must contribute to the shared economy by being active in one of the women's workshops, where they may engage in needlework, till the village land and/or look after the animals. The sharing economy requires that Jinwar aims at being self-sufficient. With regard to local decision-making, there is to be a women's council, which will act as a kind of board, said Ruken. All decisions are to be taken jointly on democratic principles based on democratic confederalism. For example, Ruken said that in the initial phase, it had been a joint decision to let the wild rue serve as the symbol of Jinwar. The wild rue is used by local people as a healing herb for its alleged ability to stop negative thoughts and to cure more than 200 different diseases.

Ruken explained that the decentralized organization of the towns into autonomous districts with everyone's contributory influence is a conscious strategy to avoid alienation and loneliness associated with industrialized city life. People are not meant to isolate themselves in big, tall buildings with no contact with each other. Accordingly, there is no fence around Jinwar. Jinwar comprises single-storey houses with big courtyards that turn in towards each other to increase visibility and human interaction. 'We prioritized settlement models that would facilitate a collective life where mothers can bring up their children comfortably and where life in general is accessible and functional', said Ruken. Finally, Jinwar is to be multi-ethnic and multi-religious. All women should be able to live in Jinwar, according to Ruken, provided they comply with Jinwar's social contract

When asked, Ruken said that she did not want to stay in Jinwar when the town was fully built. She has been active in the women's struggle for twenty-six years, with assignments in various parts of Kurdistan. She cannot see herself with a permanent home and a set job. She would therefore like to move on to new, more active assignments in the Kongra Star. However, she did not rule out the possibility of one day returning to Jinwar. Like Ruken, Farasin too had no intentions of settling down permanently and breaking off contact with life in the mountains. Both Ruken and Farasin were former YPJ women fighters. For them, leaving the mountains and getting used to life in civil society was not a pleasant experience, even though they continued to work for the revolution. Farasin had temporarily accepted service in Jinwar because she was under medical treatment. She expected to return to active service as a woman fighter when she was fully fit again. As previously mentioned, several interviewees said that service in civil society was more demanding than when they were with their comrades in the mountains, where everyone more or less agreed on everything and led a standardized, collective life. The mountains figure as a place of refuge that the women can always go back to when they find things difficult in civil society. Dersim of the PKK similarly related that life in the mountains was very different to life in civil society. I see this perception as reflecting the fact that the women fighters of the PKK in general were out of touch with developments in civil society and that its revolution still seemed beyond reach. It is most likely therefore that Dersim looked at the Rojava experiment and felt hope for the revolution, hope that it will be possible to implement a new system despite the fact that it is also very difficult to overturn the whole of society (Interview with Dersim, 27 March 2018). Arya, who had previously served the PKK in a big city, said that she felt that civil society had become worse since she had joined the PKK. Her perception was that the individual-focused capitalist consumer mentality had taken over further. She could not help thinking that they were sacrificing their lives for the people, but that the people did not really appreciate their fighting for them (Interview with Arya, 25 March 2018).

6.4. Orientations among women fighters of the YPJ

This section takes its point of departure in my four interviews with women Kurdish YPJ fighters Soze, Hebun, Roza and Ruber (29 March 2018). While they joined the YPJ for more or less the same reasons that motivated the women fighters of the PKK, the YPJ women fighters operate on different premises, since their task is to protect the population of Rojava only. Accordingly, the enemies of the YPJ will be those who threaten the existence of Rojava and its inhabitants, which in this case means Assad's forces and the Islamic State. In contrast, the PKK wages a struggle on behalf of all Kurds across official borders of the region. Another difference is that the PKK's struggle takes place mostly in the mountains, whereas the YPJ's military struggle takes place in the cities, where the YPJ's members are also part of civil society.

When it comes to military organization, the Kurdish YPJ and its men Kurdish counterpart, the YPG, both contribute to the coalition of ethnic militias and rebel groups in north-eastern Syria, known as the Syrian Democratic Forces (SDF), that serves as the semi-official army of Rojava. The SDF is a recognized alliance partner of the international coalition against IS, led by the United States. The purpose of devoting a section to the YPJ is to illustrate how the women fighters of the PKK have inspired ideals and coalitions across official borders that work for new gender positions.

The relationship between the PKK and its Kurdish north-east Syrian counterparts, the YPJ and the YPG, is complex. Officially, all parties deny any form of organizational collaboration. As mentioned previously, the PKK has attracted many members from among Syrian Kurds in Rojava. The PKK had its training camps in the Beqaa Valley, which was under Syrian control until the Turkish state forced Öcalan to leave Syria in 1998. However, after the outbreak of the civil war in Syria in 2011 and when Kurds from Rojava began to experience the war in their own local area, young Syrian Kurdish women began to join the YPJ instead of the PKK. Some Syrian Kurdish PKK members also left the PKK. It is unknown whether this was by agreement with the PKK leadership, but they did it to take part in the war taking place in their home region against the Assad forces and the Islamic State. Several ex-PKK members have been directly involved in founding the YPJ movement in 2013 in Rojava. For example, all four women fighters interviewed had several family members who were in the PKK and who had died in combat against Turkish military forces. Accordingly, Rojava is therefore a region where the PKK and the YPJ/YPG are entangled on multiple levels, especially with regard to ideology.

The YPJ was originally an offshoot of the Syrian Kurdish military protection unit comprising both women and men. This military protection unit was established in 2012 under the name of 'People's Youth Units' (*Yekitiya Xwendekaren Gel*, YXG), yet renamed the same year as the YPG. On Öcalan's birthday, 4 April 2013, the YPJ was founded as a women's branch of the YPG. All women fighters who had previously been in the YPG automatically became members of the YPJ. YPJ spokeswoman Nesrin Abdullah told me in conversation that the YPJ today has over 20,000 members, who constitute almost a fifth of the combatants within the overall coalition of the SDF. This makes the YPJ the world's largest women's military unit (fieldnote, 19 December 2019).

The woman fighter Soze, who is now twenty-two years old, was seventeen when she attended the founding congress of the YPJ in 2013. She is one of the YPJ's most senior leaders, responsible primarily for the education of women fighters with an Arab background. She told me that she also did research on great female Arab figures in history. This research was important, according to Soze, because there was a lack of knowledge of Arab women's contribution to their own national struggle. Soze added that this knowledge would make it easier for Arab women to identify with their heroines and the YPJ to mobilize Arab women, make the YPJ's women's struggle transnational and hence not restricted to a Kurdish focus. It seems from Soze's narrative and research interests that the YPJ wants to create a sort of ideal image of the Arab woman analogous to the PKK's aforementioned jineolojical efforts to construct meaningful configurations of the Kurdish woman.

The women fighters said that they took part in the YPJ with their parents' approval, as their parents regarded enrolment in the YPJ as a kind of military service. The inclusion of parents is understandable given the significantly younger age of women fighters in the YPJ than those in the PKK. Most women join the YPJ as teenagers to engage in military combat. Not only have they discussed this decision with their parents, the YPJ leadership also had their doubts as to accept them this young. Soze, who has been a YPJ member since the age of seventeen – that is, for five years, described herself in the interview with me as an 'old member' of the YPJ. Not many teenagers live to see life in the twenties, because many will die before that 'high' age due to armed confrontation with the Assad regime, the Turkish state and the Islamic State.[5]

All four interviewees described themselves as cadres. This means that like the women fighters of the PKK, they have dedicated the rest of their lives to the struggle for the permanent revolution, but – unlike the PKK women fighters – YPJ members need not all be cadres. Roza noted that when somebody joins the YPJ, for the first three months they have to follow a basic training programme. After that, they are allowed to visit their family for a couple of weeks in order to decide whether they want to join as a lifelong cadre or sign a time-limited contract with the YPJ instead. Under this contract, the woman is in the YPJ for a period of two years. After two years, the contract can be renewed, but they can always choose to leave the YPJ. Although Roza said that one can always choose to leave the YPJ or settle for a time-limited contract, it was clear in my conversations with the interviewees that the YPJ's objective is for all participants to join as cadres. Cadres would be more stable, loyal members, more detached from civil society and more likely to accept conversion into the revolution's new humans. Iterative acts of instruction, training, discipline and so on contribute to making newcomers sign up as cadres, similar to the disciplining that PKK members undergo to become new humans (see Chapter 3). When the YPJ offers the possibility of taking part in the form of a time-limited military service, this is due to the YPJ's temporary need to arm everybody and utilize everybody's resources in order to resist attacks.

As the YPJ's conflict with Assad's forces and the Islamic State takes place mainly in the cities, YPJ members are in constant touch with their families and can visit them and stay the night with them with their leaders' permission. This arrangement seems to give them a number of advantages compared to the women fighters of the PKK, who have only limited contact with their families and the society they come from. While the YPJ women fighters' bond with their families constitutes a source of influence, it is, however, also a channel to be used in the opposite direction. YPJ women have direct opportunity to influence their families, their local communities and society. For example, Roza recounted that her family was proud of her and that her mother often boasted of having a daughter who was in the YPJ. Roza's enrolment even increased the prestige that Roza's mother enjoyed in her civil context.[6]

In contrast to PKK members' remote fight in the mountains, YPJ members enjoy visibility when stationed in cities or nearby. Roza says, for example, that 'We are never detached from society, and we live together with them'. At the same time, when young women of the YPJ ride around the streets in their big, new pickups, they advertise the attractiveness of being a woman fighter and thus contribute to more women joining the YPJ. I have also seen that the way women fighters ride around the urban landscape in their big cars, with their weapons and military outfits, influences not only women but also men in the local community. When the YPJ also allows anyone, regardless of affiliation and faith, to be a member of the movement, this too makes room for a diversity that is advantageous in multi-ethnic, multi-religious Rojava. Ruber of the YPJ, for example, wears a hijab, and she reported that being a practising Muslim in the YPJ had never been a problem for her.

I also saw for myself that young women were much more visible in Rojava than men were. This is true not just of women fighters driving back and forth in their big pickups but also of civilian women who were active and did a variety of political and humanitarian jobs in various organizations. Being in Rojava as an outsider, it seemed to me that the local population comprised significantly more women than men. Despite women's increased contribution to the fighting in recent years, I wonder if there are nevertheless more men dying in combat. Men fighters seem exclusively involved in military work, while women fighters engage in more diverse tasks, of which not all involve high-risky military operations. Next to their contributions in combat, the women fighters invest a lot to transplant their ideology and ideals of liberation into a society model like the experiment in Jinwar. As Ruber puts it, women in Rojava are trying to implement their own revolution in the midst of the fight against Syrian forces and the Islamic State.

As a consequence of ongoing attacks against Rojava since 2013, Rojavan society has become partially militarized, and everyone must be prepared at all times to engage in war at some level when necessary. During my fieldwork in Rojava, I visited several families. All had weapons in their homes, whose walls were decorated with pictures of deceased family members, now martyrs, Öcalan, Kurdish flags, as well as YPG and YPJ-symbols. I observed that several people from the same family were active in the revolution. While the young people became members of the YPG and YPJ, the fathers might be in the *Asayish*, which is Rojava's internal security forces. The mothers were often members of either the women's council or the martyrs' council. Similar to the women fighters of the PKK, the YPJ women fighters narrated with pride that their mothers, who had been oppressed in Kurdish patriarchal society, had become more politically active after their daughters had chosen to join the struggle.

The Kongra Star invests a lot in and appeals to women's active participation in both the armed and the political struggle. The call for such participation seems discursively anchored in portrayals of women as central agents in the defence of the Kurdish nation and the founding of a new society. A hitherto understudied trait is the cultivation of the woman fighter as a heroine. Women in anti-colonial struggles, be it in the Kurdish region or other parts of the world, are encouraged to take control of their lives and break free of patriarchal values through processes where the temporary use of weapons and violence is regarded as necessary to achieve freedom and implement new gender roles. Temporality is plastic, and the practice of violence and its consequences are slowly becoming part of everyday life.[7] The Rojavan population is aware of this habituation, and accordingly, it was intensely debated how Rojavan society is to demilitarize itself in a post-conflict period. Yet, the debate and the planning of first steps towards demilitarization are challenged, even inhibited, by rushed political and geosocial developments in the region that threaten the continued autonomy of Rojava and its experiments. Since 2013, the region has developed from a society where women had no voice or rights in public life to a society where women are visible, perhaps more than men, in the streets and the political organs. What course of developments will take place in Rojava is uncertain but calls for continued attention. In addition, years of militarization as well as ideological experiments have most likely affected men and masculinity, even though this effect has not yet been studied. In general, a closer examination of changes in and challenges to masculinity during societal upheavals of a revolutionary nature like Rojava's deserves its own study.

6.5. Women fighters' coalitions across ethnic and religious boundaries

This section examines coalitions between women from other ethnic and religious groups in Rojava and Kurdish women fighters. The transnational character of the Kurdish women's movement has seemingly inspired the cooperation of non-Kurdish women in Rojava in their anti-colonial struggle despite ethnic and religious differences between them. The transnationality and the inter-ethnic and religious coalition making may be indicative of future anti-colonial groupings of relevance beyond the Kurdish region. The section is based on an interview with an Arab woman (Leyla) enrolled in the YPJ, and a focus group interview with two Christian women fighters of Assyrian origin (Maria and Nisa) and a Christian woman fighter of Armenian background (Melissa). All three are members of the Bethnahrain Women's Protection Forces (HSNB), a Christian military movement, also operating in Rojava.

It was the YPJ spokeswoman Nesrin Abdullah who welcomed me and introduced me to the Arab woman fighter Leyla. Nesrin Abdullah proudly told me that Leyla was their unit leader in the Deir ez-Zor region in southern Syria, an Arab-dominated region but part of the Rojava autonomy. The pre-meeting with Nesrin Abdullah, Leyla and another Kurdish woman fighter of the YPJ named Asya took place in Nesrin Abdullah's office, which resembled an ordinary military office. As I do not speak Arabic, Asya acted as interpreter for the conversation between Leyla and me. Leyla was twenty-four years old and had joined the YPJ four years earlier. When studying agriculture at university, Leyla came into contact with some Kurdish women. Through their friendship and her dialogue with them, she became interested in the Kongra Star. Kurdish women's ideals of women's emancipation and visions for women's positions in a future society had particularly caught Leyla's interest. Leyla related that she had chosen to join the YPJ to avoid leading a meaningless life of routine as in patriarchal Arab society – a realistic prospect despite the planned university education and the ensuing opportunities. When Leyla said she had been born into a conservative Muslim family, Asya added that it was very common for Arab families to be conservative. I have found that Kurdish women from the YPJ are generally of the opinion that Arab society is more conservative and religious than Kurdish society is. For example, Roza of the YPJ said that Arab women were more oppressed than Kurdish women were, and that child marriage and polygamy were common phenomena in Arab society.

Leyla said that she chose to join the YPJ together with some of her classmates before completing her first year at university. At first, Leyla's family did not understand her decision. At the beginning of the civil war, it was unusual for Arab women to join the YPJ. However, Leyla recounted with pride that following her enlistment, all the young people from her network and family, including all her siblings, chose to join the YPJ or YPG. Leyla wore the hijab at that time and did so during her first year in the YPJ, too. She later chose to take it off. Leyla said that taking off the hijab was her own choice, but that her family was against it. They thought it was immoral and against their faith. Leyla disagreed and said that she was still a practising Muslim who fulfilled her obligations of fasting and prayer.

A noteworthy aspect of Leyla's circumstances is that unlike the Kurdish women fighters, she was and still is married. Her husband is also a YPG member. They got married when she was twenty, and two years into their marriage, they decided together to join the protection units. They have no children yet. Leyla said:

When Syria is a free country again, with safety in society, perhaps I can consider having children. When peace has come. I realize it may take several years. But my first priority is my country, my society and defending my people. My partner agrees with me, too. (Interview with Leyla, 19 December 2019)

Leyla insisted that her enrolment in the YPJ was not a provisional decision: she has joined as a cadre, which means that she has dedicated the rest of her life to the revolution. Leyla and her husband were in touch on a daily basis and could also see each other when off duty. However, Leyla had difficulty saying what their relationship was like now. She said, 'sometimes we're like a married couple, sometimes we're like comrades' (Interview with Leyla, 19 December 2019). It clearly caused difficulty for Asya, our interpreter, when I enquired about Leyla's marriage. At one point, Asya interrupted my series of questions and said that we should not focus on the subject any more: 'Let's move on from that topic, heval. It's a bit complicated. They are Arabs and not like us.' As the interpreter's role of translator, Asya was not solely the passive one. She chose to block the conversation when I asked for more information about Leyla's marriage. On the other hand, Asya's essentializing remark about Arabs made me think that different standards and expectations are applied in the YPJ to those of non-Kurdish background. The YPJ appears unprejudiced and tolerant towards the norms, values and lifestyle of non-Kurds so as to make it easier for non-Kurds to join the YPJ and to signal that everyone, regardless of ethnic and religious background, is welcome to participate in the YPJ on an equal footing with Kurdish women. Yet, different standards seem to apply. This can also be seen in Asya's account of how the YPJ teaches Arab participants about religion:

If there is a new Kurdish participant, we can certainly talk about everything to do with religion with that person. But we're a bit careful when it comes to Arabs. With them, you can't put religion on the agenda. It's not something you discuss. You can't have a dialogue with them about whether God exists or not. Or whether it's important to be a practising Muslim. We keep away from discussions like that. [. . .] All new participants get two days' teaching on the history of religion. But we don't do that with the Arab participants. We don't want them to think we're forcing them into anything. We just leave them be. (Interview with Asya, 19 December 2019)

It seems that as the Syrian Defence Forces primarily recruits from among young Arabs, the YPJ is obliged for strategic reasons to take a pragmatic approach to young Arabs' interests so as to avoid conflicts with Arab members of the local community. Remarkably, Asya said that the YPJ expected the young Arabs on their own initiative to renounce their religious views in time and adopt the Kurds' secular, socialist values. In accordance with Foucault's understanding of power and his analysis of the emergence of normativity, the power mechanisms in the YPJ will give the impression that the member is accorded a certain autonomy and scope for action where a notion of individual free will is maintained, but the power mechanisms have already chosen which actions are normal and which abnormal.

It is therefore expected that the regulation of the embedded culture of the YPJ, combined with the member's repression of earlier normativity, will contribute to the member eventually becoming critical of his or her own background and therefore moving towards YPJ's normative standards. In line with this, Asya expected that Leyla's marriage would break up of its own accord when both spouses were lifelong members of the protection units and became accustomed to life as a cadre.

My interview with Leyla took place in December 2019. This was about eighteen months after my first fieldwork in Rojava. On my first visit to Rojava, I found in my conversations with Kurdish civilians and political/military representatives that they seemed sceptical as to whether their collaboration with the Arab population could endure if they were one day to come under attack from the Turkish or Syrian state. 'Could the Arabs decide to change sides?' This was a big question for most and a worrying one. On my second trip to Rojava, I found a sense of relief in everyone, as they had seen the Arab population fight valiantly alongside them against the latest Turkish invasion.[8] Leyla saw this as meaning that the Arab population welcomed the Kurdish-led autonomy and that Kurdish values, including democratic confederalism, had been well received. Kurds and Arabs, who make up the largest population groups in the region, no longer resemble two different populations. Rather, they seem to belong to the same stateless, yet democratic, nation that does not problematize ethnic differences. It was evident during my second trip that the collaboration with the Arab population as well as with other ethnic groups had boosted the Kurds' confidence in the future of democratic confederalism.

The 'successful' collaboration also extends to the Christian population that makes up the third-largest population group in Rojava. In conversations with me, Christian political representatives, who play an active part in the autonomy, indicated that they welcomed the collaboration with the Kurds and being part of the self-governing administration. However, this does not mean that there is complete agreement among the Christians regarding the Kurds' project of democratic confederalism. What matters most to the Christians, given the attacks on them from all sides, is survival. At the beginning of the Syrian civil war, the vehemence of attacks, carried out by the Islamic State in Iraq, especially against non-Sunni minorities, especially the Yezidis in Sinjar,[9] made them consider establishing their own defence units in order to protect themselves. The Syrian Military Council (*Mawtbo Fulhoyo Suryoyo*, MFS) was therefore created in 2013, followed in 2015 by the women's brigade, the Bethnahrain Women's Protection Forces (HSNB). The leader of the HSNB, Maria, recounted:

> Christian women were being raped, killed, sold and enslaved as property. All this was happening in Iraq before our eyes, so we in Syria decided we had to set up our own protection forces before it was too late. Another reason to set up our own units was to make our women powerful. Help them reject the patriarchal mentality they had been dominated by for thousands of years in the Middle East. Men want us women to just be their wives, housekeepers and mothers who produce children for them without the right to be part of political, social and military life. (Interview with Maria, 19 December 2019)

The HSNB now consists of over 100 women, while the men's unit, the MFS, has a couple of thousand members. Asked whether the women could not just settle for being part of the MFS (as a mixed unit), Maria replied that it was impossible. Maria argued that the Christian people were more conservative in many ways than the Muslim community was. Young Christian women and men ought not mix with each other, and women have very limited rights in the public sphere. Accordingly, it took a long time for their families and community to accept that they joined a military organization. In line with the narratives of the PKK women fighters, Maria said that the fact that women organized separately from men has made it easier for their patriarchal families to accept their daughters as part of the military. In addition, Maria added that this separate organization enabled women to arrange their own campaign as they saw fit. In her interview with me, she also mentioned Ishtar, the goddess of war and love in Babylonian/Assyrian mythology when she explained that like Ishtar, women should be strong and free of men dominance. Next to the HSNB, they had therefore established a women's academy with the purpose of teaching women's history, women's rights and so on to all women in the region. Maria made no secret of the fact that the Kurdish women fighters were a source of inspiration both because they had introduced the phenomenon of women fighters in the region and because of their experience in organization, mobilization of the people and waging war.

The young Christian women fighters addressed a generational issue in their narratives. According to them, the older generations among the Christians in Rojava were inclined to travel to the West to seek asylum, whereas the younger generations wanted to stay in the region and defend it. The Christian women fighters explained that Christians could easily obtain asylum in the West because of their shared religious affiliation, but the young people did not believe that fleeing was the solution. Maria emphasized that the Christians wanted recognition as both a religious and an ethnic minority. For ages, they have enjoyed minority rights in Syria as a religious minority group, even under the Assad regime, but not as an ethnic group. Mohanty claims that people who are stateless are also not represented in the world as historical and political actors.[10] In corroboration of this, Maria's struggle is not just about survival but also about the right to be represented in one's local society with one's own cultural and national values.

The other Syrian Christian woman fighter Nisa, who was twenty-six years old, said that it was hard for her family to accept her enlistment in the HSNB because she was married and had a seven-year-old son. Her husband and son had moved in with his parents after Nisa joined the HSNB. When I said that this was the reverse of the traditional gender roles in patriarchal society, where men usually went into the army while women stayed at home and looked after the children, she said with a smile that 'these were new times'. Nisa normally has a week off each month with the right to be with her family, and she could take time off at any time, by permission, to go home. She did so occasionally if her son indicated that he was missing her, but generally, neither Nisa nor her son found it difficult to be separated. Like the Kurdish women fighters, Nisa enlisted as a lifelong cadre with no plans of having more children. Asked whether she had any plans for the future, she said 'none' with a smile. She did not even know whether she would survive the next morning, but she wanted her son to grow up in a society where there was peace and security.

Like Nisa, Melissa said that she did not dream of a future with a husband and children. Her parents were of Armenian Christian background. She said that she might as well have chosen to join the YPJ, but she happened to enlist in the HSNB. Women could choose to join either unit because, ideologically, they were based on the same values. She too described herself as a cadre. In line with many of the PKK women fighters, Melissa talked a lot about the 'importance of strength of will in the struggle'. She suggested that women's struggle, especially against the Turkish invasion, was a fight between the highly developed technology of the Turkish forces and the women fighters' strength of will. The women fighters had nothing to put their faith in but their strong will.

Both Maria and Melissa considered women's strength of will a powerful tool also against their men comrades. Like their Kurdish counterparts, the women fighters of the HSNB assessed that their motivation to engage in military action and to develop combat skills was much stronger than men's. Maria said:

> Men are physically stronger than us, but our motivation is stronger than theirs. Men feel stronger when they go on military operations with us. They have to man up. We are psychologically stronger. We train ourselves to be. We know that, if we are captured by the enemy, we will find worse things happening to us than can happen to men. We need to defend ourselves in a better way. Either we fight, or we will be slaves. (Interview with Maria, 19 December 2019)

It is highly characteristic of women in Rojava, whether of Kurdish or non-Kurdish background, that the fear of the Islamic State accelerates their decision to join the women's protection units. Most wanted to join the struggle from as early as their teenage years in order to strengthen their own positions or to avenge the atrocities committed in the region by the Islamic State. The women talked about a desire to liberate themselves from all forms of men dominance, also from men in their own society. In line with this, Maria insisted that their struggle was more than just a military one. Their primary aim was to reform their society, to rid it of its patriarchal norms and values and thereby bring about women's liberation. She said, 'We want to have a continuation, after the revolution as well'. The women fighters' consciousness about why they participate in the struggle for liberation and revolution is a counterargument against Yuval-Davis's already-mentioned claim that women's participation in similar struggles would not necessarily constitute a conscious act but arise randomly as an adaptation to new conditions.[11] My interviews clearly demonstrate that the women choose, after lengthy and thorough deliberations, to join the struggle with a definite agenda and an expectation of a lifelong commitment to the struggle. War has become a zone for both men's and women's engagement with gender as one among many intra-active identificatory factors.

Summary

Women fighters' reflections on the future have been analysed in this chapter. To most women fighters of the PKK, it is difficult to think of a life outside the movement, to which they contribute so actively. It seems that the collective lifestyle and ideology of the PKK entail a lifelong commitment to the struggle. Yet, expectancy of a long life as a woman fighter is unrealistic, which makes it hard for them to relate to questions about their personal wishes and expectations regarding the future. Those women who have left the movement, and thus in principle have more realistic chances of enjoying a future, suffer on more levels. They experience that society has changed a lot since they left for the mountains, and accordingly, they have difficulties adapting to regular life in civil society. They suffer from a bad conscience, blaming themselves for being disloyal towards the martyrs they knew and their comrades who are still fighting in the struggle. They live a life marred with frustrations and feelings of guilt, shame, betrayal and probably also suffer, at least to some extent, from post-traumatic stress disorder. Furthermore, they feel let down by family and friends in civil society who seem ignorant of how much they have sacrificed for the national struggle by fighting in the mountains.

One prospect of hope for the future, given the current support and backing of men in the PKK of all ranks, is that it will be possible to maintain and cultivate the values and norms current in the anti-colonial struggle and even enable a subversion of Kurdish civil society as far as gender roles are concerned. The women fighters seem very determined to implement their 'women's revolution' while the anti-colonial struggle is ongoing, as they believe that, if this is not done now, they will have difficulty carrying it out once the anti-colonial struggle is over.

The women fighters of the PKK do attach general hope for the future based on experiments in the north-east Syrian region of Rojava. Certainly, the Rojavan women's movement, Kongra Star, meets local opposition to their relatively radical ideals of women's liberation. However, women's projects, especially the experimental village of Jinwar, hold so much promise for the future in that they have already succeeded in implementing many ideals in this concrete society. The inspiration found in Jinwar thus enables the PKK women fighters to imagine an alternative to constant fighting in the mountains and some even embrace the idea of returning to an experimental, eventually civilized life like the one in Jinwar.

The inspiration goes both ways. The PKK's women fighters have inspired non-Kurdish women in the Middle East to adopt a cadre lifestyle where they are willing to devote the rest of their lives to women's struggle to prevent attacks like the ones that they and their loved ones were subjected to by the Islamic State, Assad's forces and Turkish military forces. Via the YPJ in Rojava, the Kurdish women's movement has become a heterogeneous, transnational movement for all Kurds in a region across Turkish, Iranian, Iraqi and Syrian borders that mobilizes women of differing backgrounds in a complex struggle to improve the future circumstances of all women. This multi-ethnic and multi-religious coalition even enjoys domestic as well as international support. The ability of women fighters to play a significant role in the movements' abilities to achieve political and military objectives should not be underestimated.[12]

CONCLUSION

At the beginning of the book, I presented its guiding research questions, namely: how Kurdish women fighters explain their decision to join the PKK; how women's political and militant involvement in the PKK affects, perhaps even subverts, local gender norms; and how various aspects of materiality matter to how the women fighters 'do' their gender. By asking these questions, the book's overriding purpose has been to create a broader understanding of women's choice to participate in political militant combat. Even though a substantial number of women, especially since the late nineteenth century, have chosen to enter ethnic and national movements, research on how women's participation in such movements has affected local gender positions is very limited. The research that exists, after all, is mostly occupied with wider sociological lines that often draw generalized images of women and their choices; furthermore, it suffers from poor empirical and one-sided local insight in its attempt to explain why women would choose to engage in militant combat. The motivation of this book has therefore been to supplement the existing research with more complex answers. The vantage point for such a supplement has been practice-oriented with a focus on how identificatory, sociocultural and material factors intra-act according to the interviewed women's narratives. To curb any scholar's almost inescapable tendency to homogenize, I have looked for differences with regard to geographical and educational backgrounds, age, ethnicity and religion to further a recognition of diversity and variation within the interviewed and observed group of women fighters.

The book's contextual and situated enquiries have been aimed at registering the significance of everyday and lifelong experiences for the interviewed women fighters. This called for a project design that could set up democratic conditions for interviewing and observing them in ways that would allow for their nuanced responses as well as a critique of the questions. Trust had to be established; I had to reflect on how not to endanger anybody's life with my presence; and I had to be attentive to the nuances of their narrativizations without ignoring possible romanticizings and ideological correctness. Transcriptions of thirty-six interviews with and fieldnotes of observations and informal comments of mostly Kurdish women fighters, but also a few Kurdish men fighters as well as non-Kurdish women fighters, make up the book's empirical material. It has been submitted to analysis and running discussions from a composite theoretical perspective. The perspective has been influenced by a processual understanding of identity, associated with Gilles Deleuze and Félix Guattari, Michel Foucault, Judith Butler,

Donna Haraway and Karen Barad. Especially, Haraway and Barad's writings have been inspirational with respect to recognizing the diffractive effects – that is, new identificatory becomings on the basis of intra-action that follow when many – material and immaterial – factors intra-act.

The analyses show that the women fighters' life stories point to the importance of various clashes with material and more abstract cultural conditions in their Kurdish patriarchal contexts that affected their initial decision to join the PKK. All the interviewed women fighters mentioned how prospects of contributing to the national fight as Kurds as well as improving their conditions as women mattered. The women fighters have touched upon emotional and physical experiences from their time at school, such as bullying, discrimination and violations. They have mentioned the Turkish state's homogenizing project and assimilation policies. They have narrated about their first contacts with members of the PKK and how they introduced and exemplified the ongoing national fight and its consequences. These and many other experiences created a sense of 'awakening' in the women fighters to be. In the women fighters' narratives, gender-specific experiences from the childhood stand out. Kurdish patriarchal norms forced the young girls, at that time, to accept a gender-specific upbringing, where an honor ideology has and still plays a decisive role in the understanding of women's sexual bodies and women's possibilities in life. Inspired by Gayatri C. Spivak's concept of 'subalterity', I found that the women fighters had been exposed to processes of double othering where they were oppressed both as Kurds and as women.

The effects of colonization, with clashes and confrontations as a result, were increasingly prevalent in the women's youth, which is also the period of their life where they ascribe increased value to the PKK's fight for liberation and the guerrilla life. A life in the mountains as fighters becomes more and more attractive because it promises both access to self-representation and the ability to act. The generational differences among the women fighters indicate that gender as a category (from the launch of the PKK's fight until today) has grown into a primary motivational factor in the women's choice to enter the fight. The youngest generation of women in the PKK is the most gender-conscious. They join the anti-colonial fight as women fighters while striving for new understandings and perspectives that can counter the patriarchal Kurdish and Turkish liberal values, as well as Western feminism.

Once the women enlisted as cadres in the mountains, it seems that the PKK with its bases and training camps created a room for subversion, which entailed radical changes in their practical way of life and in their identity, particularly with regard to gender. In PKK's pursuit of a new collective Kurdish identity, women newcomers must undergo an intensive ideological and gender-specific training based on ideological instruction and various new embodied acts and practices based on the assumption of sexual difference, including women's unique, and essential, character traits and nature. The all-women training camps in the mountains offer the women a recreation of their selves in a special intra-action with nature. By means of ideological instruction and bodily practices, the PKK wishes to remove the distinction between culture and nature, which includes substantial changes in the women fighters' self-understanding. Such changes are considered pivotal for the women fighters' self-development and their ability to survive in the mountains with all the warfare that this situatedness entails. Their subsequent success in combat is explained with reference to this respectful approach to nature and its multiple effects on their identity as women and fighters.

The road to being recognized as combatants on an equal footing with men has been long. Challenges and overt resistance from men members of the PKK have been significant. Still, the emancipatory fight, in parallel with the anti-colonial struggle, has contributed to the creation of all-women parties and military units as well as to the women fighters' greater visibility and influence on the overall PKK's agenda which they see themselves as pivotal. Today, most men fighters and their leaders seem to accept the women's perception of being real participants and founders of the forthcoming society. In the course of this struggle and with combat experiences, the women have reached a new perception of their bodily potential. The majority now defines the physical differences between men and women not as a hierarchy but as two resourceful, complimentary sets of gender-specific skills. The women fighters seemingly accept this heteronormative understanding of gender, especially because they enjoy how both men and women now consider the differences in skills an asset to be used for securing women's inclusion in the military and high expectations of them in all positions, also in combat. Many women even insist that they are more important and better than the men are.

Based on the analysis of the first chapters, I found that the women fighters' initial choice to join the PKK happened after long and thorough deliberations, and that the decision was in no way coincidental. The PKK's conceptions of women and the ensuing jineoloji present women with prospects of self-development and for improving their conditions of life. The PKK's wish to use the women's resources in the fight feeds back into women's inclusion and possibility of influencing the national fight and its agenda. The women see themselves as both the nation's saviours and those responsible and capable of founding a new society. In this process, they have taken the lead in defining the PKK's policies on gender and dissociating Kurdish culture from the traditional, patriarchal as well as colonial norms, values and roles.

Based on these findings, I can answer the first research question of why Kurdish women fighters decide to join the PKK based on their own narratives. My answer is simultaneously a counterargument to Yuval-Davis's claim that women choose to engage in political/militant struggle in an ill-considered and/or random way or as a form of adaptation to new conditions.[1] The women fighters' choice of the PKK is not random, nor does it reflect a dream of travelling to no matter which militant organization in search of adventure. The women were aware from before their entry that the PKK held a promise of self-realization and thus increased chances of improving their living conditions. My corrective to Yuval-Davis also prompts us henceforth, rather than casting doubt on women's choices and motives, to keep an open focus on what women see in these movements and how their choices create meaning for them, so that their narratives will be respected as a source of information. Based on this argument, my analysis points at four gendered factors in a colonial as well as patriarchal context that add to our understanding of why the interviewed women fighters chose to join the PKK to become women fighters:

1. The ability to recreate themselves as women so that life would become meaningful in the light of new understandings.
2. Individual motivations such as prospects of altering or bettering living conditions for oneself or for others, vengeance or political conviction. Such differences help explain the variety of profiles among the women fighters.
3. Survival as a person and as a woman entangled with specific ethnic and religious affiliations.
4. The need for freedom to represent themselves both as Kurds and as women.

In general, the interviewed women fighters justified their participation in the armed conflict as a necessity to be able to cope in a men-dominated world. That being said, I am not blind to the possibility that the women are unconsciously reconstructing the past and their motives in a way that fits in with their current situation, nor do I claim that women's participation in war is positive, since war will always be about killing and destruction regardless of its feminist agenda.[2] From an academic point of view, however, the point is to attain a better understanding of these women's actions, choices, becomings and hence their subjectivity, as well as to remain open to the possibility that their motivations may have changed over time. For example, some women fighters stated that they originally joined in the struggle in order to liberate Kurdistan, but that later it occurred to them that they must first liberate themselves and become true to their feminine nature.

This leads to the answer to the second question of whether women's political and militant involvement in the PKK affects, perhaps even subverts, gender norms in the PKK and the Kurdish contexts in general. The answer implies an important finding in this book that counters the position of Sancar 2001a, Çağlayan 2007, Düzel 2018 and Käser 2021. It makes no sense to discuss whether women's decision to join in the struggle is or is not symbolic. As mentioned in the 'Introduction', such a debate only contributes to fixing women firmly between objectification and subjectification. In line with this, I demur from scholars who have questioned the way the PKK has defined Kurdish women fighters as both symbols and actors.[3] Even if the women fighters exert symbolic power, being symbols does not necessarily mean that the women fighters are exploited as passive instruments. For one thing, the women fighters themselves utilize their symbolic connotations and contribute to shaping them. The women fighters themselves define the PKK's gender policy and the way in which their involvement in the PKK is to be framed. For another, for Kurdish women, being an actor is a matter of not just choosing to take part in the war and thereby accepting assigned roles but also taking and developing the opportunities to represent themselves. Today, the women fighters have acted and negotiated their way to a position where they can change the PKK's political agenda, in which the subversion of gender norms and the prioritization of gender difference, especially women's distinctiveness, have become key issues. The PKK's identity has been renewed, with gender – especially feminine – ideals becoming an indispensable part of the PKK's political and ideological objectives. It thus seems that not only does women's participation in political and militant movements contribute to fulfilling women's expectations of joining the movement but that a form of mutual influence arises between the women's gender positions and the movement, with the movement's strategies and norms also being redefined. Yes, the women fighters' engagement in the PKK has changed the movement's conceptions of gender, and from the increased importance of gender behind young women's decision to join the movement, one can also drive home the finding that the women fighters' gender ideals have spread and exerted influence in local Kurdish communities.

Finally, in answering the third question whether and how various aspects of materiality matter to how the women fighters 'do' their gender, I have shown how the effects of life in, and dependence on, the mountains influence the women fighters' ways of 'doing' gender in war. Furthermore, the cadres' eating and sleeping habits, their attachment to each other's bodies, their emotionally and culturally distinctive attachment to Kurdish nature, clothing and biological body processes such as menstruation intra-act with discursively marked conceptions of gender and identity and leave their imprint on the women fighters' self-understanding and ability to succeed in combat and in their organizational strivings. These findings provide insights that I would have been unable to capture had I drawn on purely constructionist theories of gender.

Behind my three overarching research questions lay a motivation to achieve an understanding of what the phenomenon 'women fighters in politically militant struggles' does to women, rather than showing what the phenomenon 'women fighters' covers. Here, I can conclude, as I hypothesized early on, that the conception of the phenomenon 'women fighters' is mutable and context-dependent. Women's participation in the PKK has changed shape and character over time, with the women having different expectations of their participation. It would therefore be an oversimplification to put all Kurdish women together under the category 'Kurdish women' or all women fighters under the category 'women fighters'. In other words, I have tried to pursue an understanding of dynamic processes and consequences of becoming in connection with being a woman fighter, rather than finding a segmenting answer to the question of what a woman fighter is. But, irrespective of the women fighters' religious conviction, ethnicity and sociocultural background, common to the women fighters in this study's agential cuts is that they all feel that the double identity of both woman and fighter provides prospects of freedom.

One spin-off insight of this book pertains to the fact that it allows reflections on the success of the women fighters to cause changes for themselves and the region in accordance with the ideology that fuels the armed resistance. Based on the women's strong organization in the PKK, support from the PKK leaders, especially that of Öcalan's, and the men members, it seems that the women fighters' struggle for change has resulted in a good foundation for women's future agency and recognition within the PKK and eventually for spreading to the Kurdish population in general. Popular acceptance is, however, not a matter of course yet. Based on the book's brief inclusion of findings in Rojava, the north-east Syrian Kurdish population is split between reluctance to accept women holding public offices and its gratitude to Rojavan women fighters for protecting it against attacks and atrocities of war. Nevertheless, the women-led experiments in Rojava, such as the women's village of Jinwar, hold much promise, even for Kurdish women fighters in the Turkish-dominated areas. PKK-inspired ideals of transnational cooperation against colonial oppression, of democratic confederalism and of women's separate organization have spread to Rojava where its Kurdish women's movement has become increasingly heterogenous, transnational and even mobilizing non-Kurdish women in various coalitions to better the future conditions of life for all women. Accordingly, my analysis shows that the Kurdish women's movement with its militant, political and organizational efforts against a man-dominated world plays a decisive role in many groups' fight for survival and democracy, including better conditions for women. An important reason for the success of the Rojavan women's movements, Kongra Star, is that their purpose and efforts have not been limited to a defence against military attacks, but supplemented by organizational initiatives and countermeasures against the influence of patriarchy.

One of the reasons why the Kurdish women's movement, whether in the PKK or the YPJ, attracts attention is that hardly any political upheaval in the past centuries, where women have engaged in and contributed to whatever objectives people were fighting for, have resulted in women's conditions being improved or their efforts recognized once the upheavals had resulted in victory,[4] not even when women were seminal to the political and national revolutions ending in victory.[5] Since the Kurdish women of the PKK have been so successful not only in engaging in military combat but also in organizing women's mobilization, education and change of mindset, many people, including outsiders, are wondering if the Kurdish women's movement will be the first to succeed in implementing their ideals of women's liberation when the anti-colonial fight is over. The experiments in Rojava indicate the Kurdish women's gradual success in subverting not only gender roles but also ways of organizing society that are true to the revolutionary ideals. Their gradual success seems related to the fact that the women have not postponed or settled for change after the fight against attacks and oppression. They have insisted to start founding communities, such as the women's village in Jinwar, while the conflict is still going on, which seems an efficient strategy to establish a more radical and sustainable upheaval in society in accordance with the revolutionary ideals. The women fighters of the PKK as well as outside scholars therefore follow with great interest what characterizes the women's movement in Rojava, how it develops and how their initiatives differ from former 'failed' Kurdish[6] and non-Kurdish[7] women's militant fights in the region.

Appendix 1

INFORMANTS

Name	Movement	Age in 2020	Gender	Year of participation	Participated from	Interview place
Berfin	PKK	45	F	1991	Turkey	Iraq
Bese	PKK	41	F	1989	Turkey	Iraq
Zin	PKK	28	F	2003	Turkey	Iraq
Bermal	PKK	43	F	1997	Europe	Iraq
Helin	PKK	48	F	1993	Syria	Iraq
Zeri	PKK	35	F	2005	Turkey	Iraq
Arya	PKK	32	F	2004	Iran	Iraq
Gulesor	PKK	41	F	1997	Turkey	Iraq
Cane	PKK	36	F	2002	Turkey	Iraq
Berivan	PKK	20	F	2016	Turkey	Iraq
Avasin	PKK	24	F	2012	Turkey	Iraq
Ronya	PKK	49	F	1989	Syria	Iraq
Dersim	PKK	*	F	*	Europe	Iraq
Firat	PKK	53	M	1988	Turkey	Iraq
Andok	PKK	*	M	*	Turkey	Iraq
Cudi	PKK	50	M	1992	Turkey	Iraq
Brusk	PKK	*	M	*	Turkey	Iraq
Hüseyin	PKK	*	M	*	Turkey	Iraq
Farasin	Activist	*	F	*	Syria	Syria
Ruken	Activist	*	F	*	Turkey	Syria
Canan	Mayor	*	F	*		Syria
Hebun	YPJ	25	F	2011	Syria	Syria
Roza	YPJ	27	F	2011	Syria	Syria
Ruber	YPJ	25	F	2011	Syria	Syria
Soze	YPJ	23	F	2013	Syria	Syria
Leyla	YPJ	25	F	2015	Syria	Syria
Maria	HSBN	*	F	*	Syria	Syria
Nisa	HSBN	*	F	*	Syria	Syria
Melissa	HSBN	*	F	*	Syria	Syria
Afrin	PKK	34	F	2003	Syria	Europe
Bozo	PKK	*	M	*	Iraq	Europe
Mordem	PKK	*	M	*	Turkey	Europe
Zelal	PKK	32	F	2006	Turkey	Europe
Delal	PKK	*	F	*	Turkey	Europe
Evin	PKK	28	F	2018	Europe	Europe
Ronahi	PKK	*	F	*	Turkey	Europe
Sarya	Ex-PKK	42	F	1996	Turkey	Europe
Nick	Ex-YPG	*	M	2016	Europe	Europe

* Stands for undisclosed.

Appendix 2

INTERVIEWS

In Iraq, interviews with

- Thirteen women fighters from the PKK (one of them as ethnic Iranian)
- Three male leaders from the PKK
- One focus group interview consists of three male fighters from the PKK
- One focus group interview consists of two women fighters from the PKK

In Syria, interviews with

- Five women fighters from YPJ (one of them as ethnic Arabs)
- One focus group interview consists of three women fighters from (HSNB) (two of them as ethnic Assyrians, one as Armenian)
- One woman mayor
- Two women activists from the women's village Jinwar.

In Europe, interviews with

- Four women cadres from the PKK
- Two male cadres from the PKK
- One male ex-member of the YPG with an ethnic European origin
- One new woman participant in the PKK
- One woman ex-member from the PKK

NOTES

Preface

1 Cf. Haraway, 1991: 188.
2 Cf. Haraway, 1989: 4.
3 Cf. Fujii 2009; 2010: 237.

Introduction

1 On the movement in Latin America, see Cizre Üsür 1989; Kampwirth 2002; Viterna 2013; Chase 2015; and Nush 2005; in Northern Ireland as IRA members, see Roulston 1997; in Sri Lanka, see Ann 1993; in Syria, see Knapp et al. 2016; and in Turkey, see Westrheim 2008; Käser 2021; Dirik 2022.
2 See Yuval-Davis & Anthias 1989; Yuval-Davis 1997; West 1997.
3 Scholars such as Barth 1969; Gellner 1983; Jenkins 1990; Hobsbawn 1990; Kedourie 1993; Smith 1995, who have written on ethnicity and nationalism, have not addressed whether the activism of women fighters affected the orientation of their political and militant movements.
4 There has been some research focusing on women's motivations and roles as progressive and democratic forces in revolutionary areas, in which PKK can also be placed. These researches (e.g. Luciak 2001; Kampwirth 2002; Wood 2003; ; Weinstein 2007; Alison 2009; Parkinson 2013; Viterna 2013; Parashar 2014; Shesterinina 2016) specifically explore smaller militant conflicts in circumscribed areas. This work analyses topics such as the significance of social structure for ideology in militant organizations; their recruitment practices; their operational strategies; the nature of the violence; and women's contributions to conflicts. These conflicts typically involve armed insurgency against the state within its borders, with violence used for political ends. In many cases, these political conflicts are portrayed as terror against civilians and security forces, and indeed the PKK is regarded by various parties as a terror organization, despite defining itself as a liberation movement. I regard the PKK and comparable movements as social and political movements, taking no stand on whether they are terror organizations. This choice is important in the light of the fact that existing research on women in war mostly proceeds from women's roles in the state and in professional armies. Against that background, this book offers a nuanced conception of women in combat in non-state social and political movements.
5 See, for example, Sancar 2001a; Çağlayan 2007; Düzel 2018; Käser 2021.
6 Cf. Goldstein 2003.
7 See Dirik 2014: Geerdink 2021: 174.
8 Other scholars before me have criticized this tendency. Leila Ahmed, an Egyptian American scholar of Islam, problematizes how custom and law relating to women have often been conflated under a Muslim/Arab template despite the size, complexity

and extremely long cultural history of the Middle East, as well as the variety of regimes in the region (Ahmed 2008: 11–13). See also Darhour & Dahlerup 2020: 12.

9 Unless otherwise indicated, all translations from Turkish and Kurdish are my own.

10 Cf. Yeğen 2006: 52.

11 Cf. Karpat 1988: 45; Kirisci & Winrow 1997: 83.

12 Cf. McDowall 1996: 450.

13 Cf. Yeğen 1999: 236.

14 Cf. Kinnane 1964: 31; Beşikçi 1991: 78–84; Dersimi 1988: 287.

15 Cf. Kandiyoti 1989: 126–45; Durakbaşa 1998: 140; Arakon 2015.

16 Cf. Yüksel 2006: 784–6.

17 Cf. Mojab 2001: 21.

18 Cf. Kirisci & Winrow 1997: 103; Tezcür 2009. I regard 'Kurdistan' as an emic term, and I shall therefore refer to it when my informants use it to categorize a particular land area.

19 The PKK's first text was published in 1978: Kurdistan Devriminin Yolu: MANIFESTO [The Road to the Kurdistan Revolution: The Manifesto], 6th edition, Serxwebun Publishers.

20 Cf. Öcalan 1999b, 1999c: 32.

21 Cf. Jongerden & Akkaya 2015: 11.

22 Cf. Romano 2006: 73; Güneş 2013: 250.

23 Cf. Barkey & Fuller 1998: 24; 51.

24 Cf. McDowall 1996: 420; Barkey & Fuller 1998; Güneş 2012: 85–90.

25 Cf. Bozarslan 2008: 343–5.

26 There were also some Kurdish women fighters in the Komala Party of Iranian Kurdistan, founded in 1969, and in the Kurdish Democratic Party in Iraq, founded in 1946. However, these were only individual women or women's units and no notable social or military changes were involved. When the women's participation ended, they resumed their traditional gender roles (Al-Ali & Pratt 2009).

27 Cf. Yeğen 1999: 67.

28 See Human Rights Watch, https://www.hrw.org/tr/report/2012/09/03/256357. Retrieved 28.12.2022.

29 Cf. Üstündağ 2019: 140.

30 Cf. Güneş 2012: 3–7.

31 Cf. Öcalan 2009: 246–50.

32 Under democratic confederalism, the supreme governing body of the Kurdish national struggle is no longer the PKK but the Kurdistan Communities Union (*Koma Civakên Kurdistan*, KCK), of which the PKK is a part. Founded in 2007, the KCK is responsible for implementing democratic confederalism throughout Kurdistan. The PKK remains a movement fighting only for Kurds in Turkey, while the other Kurdish regions in Iran, Iraq and Syria have their own political and military organizations. Öcalan remains president of the KCK, which is led by a thirty-strong Central Council elected every other year. The Central Council is headed by a co-chairpersonship consisting of one man and one woman. The women's party (PAJK) and their confederative women's movement, the High Women's Council (*Koma Jinen Blind*, KJB), are also part of the KCK.

33 Cf. Jongerden & Akkaya 2012; Dirik 2018; Koefoed 2019.

34 Cf. Bookchin 1990: 13; Bookchin 2015: 147.

35 Cf. Öcalan 2008: 32. The term 'Mesopotamia' is an emic term, which I use because all my informants and PKK's material use it. The Kurds regard Mesopotamia as

their original homeland. References to it include many associations significant for Kurdish identifications. When I use the term, it enables me to refer to what the Kurds understand as their land in contrast to territories associated with four nation states that divided Kurdistan between them in 1923 and the geographically and culturally vast region of the Middle East.

36 Marx has argued that great social upheavals cannot take place without a feminist agenda (Marx & Engels 1988: 184). In Marxist-Leninist ideology, gender is understood as a historical and social construct. Feminist Marxists strive to denaturalize the categories of 'woman' and 'man', as they claim that gender and gender difference are by-products of capitalist society's organization of production, the economy and the family. They hold that it is possible to change the gender categories by organizing society and its production differently (Lykke 2010: 94).

37 Of the twenty-three people who attended the PKK's founding general assembly in 1978, two were women. In 1981, when the party set up its first training camps in Lebanon, there were twenty-five women among the party's first 180 members. I owe this information to one of my informants, Mordem, who was one of the first members of the PKK.

38 Cf. Özcan 1999; Çağlayan 2007: 18; Tezcür 2019: 723, 734.

39 Cf. Yalçın-Heckman & Van Gelder 2000: 351; Çağlayan 2007: 27; Üstündağ 2019; Açık 2013: 133.

40 https://www.tbmm.gov.tr/develop/owa/milletvekillerimiz_sd.dagilim. Accessed 29.12.2022.

41 Cf. Açık 2002: 280.

42 Cf. Çağlayan 2007: 98–101.

43 Cf. Çağlayan 2007: 18.

44 Cf. Tezcür 2019; Käser 2021; Dirik 2022.

45 Cf. Jayawardena 1986: 2–3, 259. Sceptics have retorted that women's contributions to these revolutionary efforts did not have any lasting effect on their conditions (Berger-Gluck 1997; Turshen 2002; Viterna 2013), and some even claim that women are rarely active in national and military struggles (Oldfield 1989; Cudworth 1988).

46 Cf. Enloe 1983: 4.

47 Cf. Enloe 1989: 44; 64.

48 Cf. Yuval-Davis & Anthias 1989: 7.

49 These critics include Walby 2000; West 1997; and Yalçın-Heckman & Van Gelder 2000.

50 Cf. Yuval-Davis 1997: 9–11.

51 Cf. Yuval-Davis 1985: 661; 1991: 35; 1997: 95–9. See also Enloe 1983, 1989, 1993..

52 Cf. Cohen 2016; Hill Collins & Bilge 2016: 130.

53 Cf. Yuval-Davis 1997: 101.

54 Cf. Zerai 1994.

55 Cf. Alison 2004: 448.

56 Cf. Yuval-Davis 1985; 1997: 104.

57 Cf. Yuval-Davis 1997: 106–7.

58 Cf. Gilbert 1983: 436.

59 Cf. Petersen 2001; Cederman et al. 2010: 113.

60 See, for example, Cooke 1993: 181.

61 Cf. Yuval-Davis 1997: 94–6.

62   Cf. Moghadam 1993: 249–56.
63   Cf. Goodwin 2001; Alison 2004; Humphreys & Weinstein 2008.
64   Cf. Gonzalez-Perez 2006; Wood & Thomas 2017; Wood 2019.
65   Cf. Yuval-Davis 1997: 101.
66   Cf. White 2000; Özcan 2006; Romano 2006; Marcus 2007; Güneş 2012; Aras 2013;
      Jongerden & Akkaya 2015.
67   Cf. Scalbert-Yücel & La Rey 2006.
68   See, for example, Üstündağ 2016; Dirik et al. 2016; Knapp & Jongerden 2016;
      Toivonen & Baser 2016; Dirik 2018; Dean 2019; Schmidinger 2018.
69   Cf. Çağlayan 2007: 17.
70   Cf. Çağlayan 2007: 91.
71   Cf. Gürer 2015: 258.
72   It is furthermore problematic that Çağlayan, along with several other researchers,
      uses the term 'Kurdish movement' without defining what it covers. I estimate that
      this concept has been transferred to academic studies from politics. For several
      years, it has been difficult for politicians in Turkey to say the name of the PKK in
      public, because they risk being accused of sympathizing with the PKK. To avoid this,
      the term 'Kurdish movement' was coined, and it evolved to cover both the PKK and
      the PKK's related political parties. This may explain why Çağlayan, whose research
      was conducted in Turkey, uses the 'Kurdish movement' rather than the name of the
      PKK.
73   Cf. Çağlayan 2007: 112.
74   Cf. Watts 2010.
75   Cf. Yüksel 2006; Dirik 2022.
76   Donna Haraway and Karen Barad have inspired this book's critical stance on the
      effects of the researcher on the knowledge produced. For more, see Haraway 1991:
      183–201; Barad 1998: 87–128.
77   All the interviews with informants of Kurdish origin and one Iranian were conducted
      in Kurdish. Two interviews with non-Kurdish informants were conducted in Arabic
      with an interpreter, while I also had an interview in English with an informant of
      Western origin. All interviews have been transcribed by me, and translations into
      English are mine.
78   Cf. Ann Lee Fujii's reflections on fieldwork in war zones in Fujii 2009, 2010.
79   In my MA thesis from 2008 (Topal 2008), I had interviewed twenty-six Kurdish
      women who had undergone forced or arranged marriage in Denmark and Sweden.
      Gender is always an interacting factor, but I found that women were prepared to talk
      about their private lives to me as a male stranger. It depends on the conditions for a
      trusting conversation that are set up.
80   For more on these precautions, see Fujii 2010: 237.
81   I discuss democratic confederalism later in this chapter, but, in brief, it is a form
      of government based on a shared humanity that has been liberated from capitalist
      domination and material exploitation. Its main investment is in creating space for
      human creativity, direct democracy and communal self-government as a new societal
      structure and form of government where people may live an ethical life (Bookchin
      2015: 147).
82   The YPJ and the HSNB are alliance partners and members of the Syrian Democratic
      Forces (*Hêzên Sûriya Demokratîk*, SDF), a military umbrella organization composed
      primarily of Kurdish, Arab, Armenian and Syrian militias together with some smaller
      Armenian, Turkmen and Chechen forces.

83 See Appendix 1 and 2 for an overview of all the informants that I have interviewed and facts about interviews.

84 Underlying this decision is physicist Karen Barad's ideal for science not to postulate any stable knowledge but to admit to science only being able to offer 'agential cuts' into an empirical field. For more, see Barad 1998: 104–7.

85 The book's focus on interacting factors and their effects is inspired by biologists Donna Haraway and Barad, who both apply the concept of 'diffraction' to describe the effects of multiple factors interacting. Diffraction results in constant new becomings in line with the book's understanding of identity as something not stable but dynamic and processual. For more, see Haraway 1992: 202; Barad 2003: 802–3; 2007: 94, 167.

86 The women's experience of double otherness invites the use of the concept of 'subalterity', coined by literary critic Gayatri Chakravorty Spivak (1988), associated with postcolonialism. While I agree with Spivak that colonized women fight on more fronts for liberation and while I applaud the informative value of the concept of 'subalterity', I disagree with her claim that subaltern subjects cannot affect their situation as doubly suppressed (Spivak 1988: 288). Here, I am much more in line with constructionist thinkers such as Michel Foucault, who explains processes that bring some subjects from positions of unintelligibility to positions of self-representation (Foucault 1979), and Judith Butler, who points to the subversive potential of engaging in iterative acts within a culture (1990).

87 Throughout the book, I am inspired by Gilles Deleuze and Félix Guattari (1987) as well as Elizabeth Grosz in their approach to desire. Instead of seeing desire as oriented to mend a lack (e.g. searching for a replacement for the impossible love of the parent of the opposite sex), these 'philosophers of becoming' understand desire as a driving force in a subject's strivings for self-realizations to unfold his or her potential. For more, see Deleuze 1998: 32; 2000: 109; Grosz 1993: 171; 2011: 53.

88 'Cadre' refers to a full member of the PKK who has dedicated his or her life to the struggle for shared humanity, to his or her people and to the leader, Abdullah Öcalan.

89 Inspired by Karen Barad's rehabilitation of Judith Butler's theory of performativity, it is an original contribution of this book to look for both discursive and material factors in Kurdish women fighters' motivations and orientations. Barad agrees with Butler (1990) that gender/identity is processual and constructed or subverted through our doings, but Barad insists that interactions with matter have an effect on gender/identity as well. For more, see Barad 2003, 2007.

90 Especially Chapters 3 and 4 are inspired by historian of ideas Michel Foucault's approach to disciplinary (bio)power, naturalization of discourse and subjectivization to investigate how power mechanisms operate in the PKK as an institution, in and through its members' relations, and what strategies and channels are deliberately introduced by the PKK in order to constitute the new person known as the cadre. For more, see Foucault 1979.

91 I choose to use the word *fedai* rather than *suicide*, as the PKK distinguishes between the two terms, although I would think that both concepts have the same definition and refer to a person who commits a suicide action. But *fedai* actions are not regarded in the PKK as suicide actions but as self-sacrifice actions. The PKK argues that *fedai* differs from suicide in that it means sacrificing oneself for the national struggle by carrying out an extraordinary act, and *fedai* are therefore accorded more respect and prestige than other martyrs and people who die in the struggle.

92 In Chapter 5, where various forms of chaos are often addressed, I am inspired by Gilles Deleuze and Félix Guattari and their immanentist ontology. To them, concepts like gender and other cultural constructions are produced in reaction to current entanglements, either to unfold one's potential or to ward off a very immanent chaos. I find it a refreshing alternative to constructionist conceptions of gender – to see gender not as a purely cultural construction but primarily as a very concrete attempt to navigate immanent challenges, be they cultural or natural. For more, see Deleuze and Guattari 1987: 204–5.

Chapter 1

1 As part of the previously mentioned Turkish homogenization policy, in which ethnic homogeneity is regarded as the foundation of the existence of the nation state, 'Turkish' is automatically entered as the holder's identity. No other ethnicity is officially recognized in the country. Article 3 of the Turkish Constitution of 18.10.1982 states that the Turkish state, with its territory and nation, is an indivisible entity and that its language is Turkish. Article 4 decrees that Article 3 cannot be amended nor can its amendment be proposed. This principle does not allow another ethnicity or language to be recognized as official.

2 Here, I follow Kenneth J. Gergen's understanding of identity, cf. Gergen 1997: 191–2.

3 Here, I draw on the British cultural theoretician and sociologist Stuart Hall on 'the meeting with the significant Other'. See Hall 1991: 48; 442.

4 Here, I follow Bronwyn Davies and Rom Harré on how the subject is developed and develops itself through different subject positions, cf. Davies & Harré 1990: 43–65.

5 In the *Communist Manifesto* of 1848, Karl Marx calls upon the international proletariat to rise up and take power over their lives in a revolution. The manifesto concludes with the following words of Marx: 'Let the ruling classes tremble at a Communistic revolution. The proletarians have nothing to lose but their chains' (Marx & Engels 1973: 51).

6 Gergen puts forward three kinds of variation of narrative forms relating to the individual's self-narrative and self-formation. (1) The individual uses 'the stability narrative' to talk about himself or herself in a way that conclusively describes how he or she has always been the same and will continue to be so in the future, so that the individual appears in the narrative with a constant, integrated identity. (2) In 'the progressive narrative', the individual presents himself or herself as part of a sequence in an ascending movement, where the individual develops over time into something better, aiming for a more favourable appraisal. (3) 'The regressive narrative' is the opposite of the progressive narrative: the state described is in decline. Through descriptions that sound like an apology, a disaster, a defeat or a drama, the individual can secure intimacy and concern from his or her relations (Gergen 1997: 195).

7 See Foucault 1979: 81–3 on counter-power and Butler 1990: 169 and her elaboration on Kristeva's work (1982) on abjection.

8 Cf. Foucault 1979: 30 on how discursive strategies function through institutional props and anchor points.

9 Cf. Ahmed 2004: 20–1.

10 Cf. Gergen 1997: 197.

11 Cf. Öcalan 1993.

12 Diyarbakir Military Prison lies in Diyarbakir, the largest Kurdish city. The prison is
    known for the political prisoners' lengthy hunger strike against brutal conditions in
    the jail, including forced intake of their own faeces and sexual abuse (McDowall 1996:
    420–5). The biggest act of martyrdom in Diyarbakir Military Prison is associated
    with Mazlum Dogan, a PKK Central Committee member who hanged himself in
    his cell in 1982. His example was followed by four other prisoners known as 'the
    Four' because they committed suicide by fire, hand in hand. When their comrades
    attempted to put out the flames, the Four insisted they should stop because this was
    a 'freedom fire' (Cansız 2014a: 185). Many jailed PKK members chose to commit
    suicide in the prison to protest against the conditions under which they lived. As
    martyrs and role models, they inspired new generations of PKK adherents (Romano
    2006: 72).

13 My use of the concept 'transnational social field' follows Peggy Levitt's and
    Glick-Schiller's (2004) definition: 'A set of multiple interlocking networks of
    social relationships through which ideas, practices, and resources are unequally
    exchanged, organized and transformed' (Levitt & Glick-Schiller 2004: 1009). These
    transnational social relations and practices create a bond between the individual
    and the nation that may be either social or symbolic. 'Social bonds' emerge through
    constant transactions between people in different geographical areas, including
    countries, where the transactions link interests, expectations and obligations to
    shared norms and values. These bonds can be maintained by means of technical
    aids, institutions, personal involvement, clan links and the like. 'Symbolic bonds'
    are not dependent on direct contact in the same way but emerge from presumed
    similarities such as ethnic and religious communities or nations. Like the
    transnational field, both social and symbolic bonds are fluid but always present
    (Levitt & Glick-Schiller 2004: 1009–10).

14 Cf. Spivak 1988.

15 My translation. The book's original Turkish title is *Hep Kavgaydi Yaşamim*, in three
    volumes, 2014, 2014a, 2015.

16 Cf. Hassanpour 2001; Yalçın-Heckman 2002.

17 Yalçın-Heckman 2002.

18 Cf. Foucault 1979: 128.

19 For more on family relations within patriarchal culture, see Joseph 1999a: 115–17.

20 For a similar conclusion with regard to Middle Eastern family roles in upbringing,
    see Ghanim 2009: 145–6. The collectivist identity expected of each family member is
    referred to by Joseph (1999b) as 'patriarchal connectivity'. The concept helps clarify
    how the individual, to experience success within the gender and age hierarchy, has to
    acknowledge his or her dependency on the family (Joseph 1999b: 9–14).

21 On women's symbolic link to the soil where reproduction and fertilization take place
    and man's symbolic link with the nation, see Saigol 2000. I elaborate on this point in
    Chapter 3.

22 For more on Kurdish tribes and clan systems, see Yalçın-Heckmann 2002: 217–18,
    292. Anthropologist Forouz Jowkar has carried out research in small, traditional
    rural societies in the Mediterranean region, where state institutions are non-
    existent or absent or where civil society plays no part in protecting women. He
    points out that men in these societies are more inclined to act as guardians of
    'women's protection' so that the family and traditions can survive, cf. Jowkar 1986:
    47–56.

23 Cf. Kandiyoti 1991: 430.

24　Şemdin Sakık (nicknamed 'Fingerless Zeki') is a former high-ranking PKK leader. He
　　left the movement in 1998. Shortly afterwards, he was captured and later sentenced
　　to life imprisonment in Turkey. At his trial and in subsequent statements, he was very
　　critical of the PKK and Öcalan. The PKK regards him as one of its worst traitors. In
　　the movement's rhetoric and literature, he is often mentioned as an example of the
　　classic Kurdish man with weaknesses. His approach is known in the movement as
　　'Şemdin's line'. This refers especially to the atrocities and anti-ideological acts he is
　　believed by men in the movement to have committed. This includes sexual abuse of
　　women fighters, being against women's participation in the movement, the murder
　　of guerrillas who had been critical of his line and collaborating with the Turkish
　　intelligence service. In other words, it is the exact opposite of what Öcalan stands for,
　　making Sakık the figure most hated by women fighters.

25　A woman's pre- or extramarital intercourse with a man is an absolute taboo and will
　　typically result in some kind of very violent punishment such as 'honour killing',
　　usually carried out by a man of the family – father, brothers or the woman's own
　　husband. Less 'harsh' methods include stoning the woman, severing her nose, cutting
　　off her hair or pouring acid on her face, something still carried out by extremist
　　Muslim Kurds, cf. Hassanpour 2001. Honour killings used to be more widespread
　　among Kurds. If the trend is abating, it is primarily due to the transfiguration of
　　gender roles and the transformation of the honour ideology that the PKK's later view
　　of women has helped to bring about.

Chapter 2

　1　The women fighters' narratives exhibit similarities with research on other colonized
　　indigenous people, for example in Latin America, where the indigenous people see
　　the soil as a divine source of life, cf. Özbudun 2012: 124.
　2　Cf. Öcalan 2004: 208–36.
　3　Cf. Hall 1991: 48.
　4　Cf. Flach 2007.
　5　Flach 2007. *MANIFESTO*, 38–9.
　6　Cf. Demir 2014: 16.
　7　Martyr Mizgin (original name: Gurbet Aydin), also known as Singer Mizgin because
　　she was a singer before joining the PKK, died in the mountains in 1992 in combat
　　with Turkish soldiers. She is regarded as one of the PKK's first female leaders.
　8　Cf. Levitt & Glick-Schillers 2004.
　9　http://www.yjastar.com/tr/sehitlerimiz/37-zilan-zeynep-kinaci-arkadasin-mektubu.
　　Accessed 23.08.2019.
10　Cf. Çağlayan 2007: 163.
11　Cf. Cansiz 2014a: 348.
12　Cf. Güneş 2012: 180; 2013: 254.
13　Cf. Çağlayan 2007: 114–17.
14　Cf. Sancar 2011b: 75.
15　Gürer 2015: 274; Tezcür 2019.
16　Cf. Tezcür 2019; Käser 2021.
17　Tezcür 2019; Käser 2021. *MANIFESTO*
18　Cf. Cansız 2014a: 278.
19　Cf. Cansız 2014a: 350–2.

20 Cf. Cansız 2014a: 298.
21 Cf. Haraway 1992: 295.
22 Cf. Demir 2014: 108.
23 The diary of the deceased woman fighter Gurbetelli Ersöz is filled with examples of tales of the challenges she has faced as an academic in the PKK. It focuses on the 1990s, when many women joined the PKK. For more, see Düzel's article (2018), where she analyses women fighters' diaries and shows how 'masculine militant femininities' dominated the PKK in the 1990s. Düzel's analysis highlights competing forms of femininities among PKK's women fighters with the 'idealized masculine woman' as the dominant one and in contradistinction from women with a university or city background, but also from traditional Kurdish women, whom the PKK deemed 'emotional, weak and gentle, an impediment to military success, and a sign of colonized womanhood which was at the root of the Kurdish subjugation' (Düzel 2018: 144).
24 Cf. Yuval-Davis 1997: 95.
25 Cf. Viterna 2013: 66.
26 Cf. Viterna 2013: 76.
27 Cf. Gergen 1997: 191–2.
28 Cf. Çağlayan 2007; Käser 2021: 203.
29 Cf. Öcalan 1997: 19.

Chapter 3

1 The material that guerrilla uniforms are made of.
2 Cf. Öcalan 2004: 136–8.
3 Cf. Ersöz 2015: 31.
4 Cf. Öcalan 1992: 130.
5 Cf. Käser 2019: 14; Foucault 1995: 138.
6 Cf. Westrheim, 208: 85.
7 Cf. Westrheim 2008: iv.
8 Cf. Gürer 2015: 158–9.
9 Outside the natural sciences, the concept of 'diffraction' refers to the changing effects that follow from the lens, perspective or measuring tool that is used to see and understand something, cf. Barad 2003: 803.
10 Cf. Gergen 1997: 195.
11 FGI stands for 'focus group interview'.
12 According to my own theoretical apparatus, it would be faulty to assume and speak of women's or any gender's nature or essence. A certain essentialism is, however, part of the PKK's ideology, as it can be seen in the women fighters many references to it. In rendering the women fighters narratives, it is important to stick to their terminology and conceptions.
13 Cf. Öcalan 2013: 40–51.
14 See the following studies that cover the PKK's creation of the new human from different perspectives (Romano 2006; Grojean 2008; Käser 2021; Dirik 2022).
15 Cf. Foucault 1995: 211.
16 Cf. Öcalan 1992: 130.
17 Cf. Barker 1984.

18   The concept 'real socialism' refers to the hypothesis that the economic realization of
     socialist ideology from the 1960s onwards in the Soviet Union was not true socialism
     but a bad implementation brought about by necessity.

19   Cf. Öcalan 2012: 170.

20   Cf. Öcalan 1992: 13.

21   Cf. Öcalan 1998: 249.

22   Cf. Öcalan 1999b: 116.

23   My translation. Originally in Turkish: *Kadin ve Aile Sorunu* (1992). Published in
     1992, the book consists of articles and speeches by Öcalan from the period between
     8 March 1987 and 8 March 1992.

24   Cf. Öcalan 1992: 13.

25   Cf. Öcalan 2016: 28–34. Öcalan's critique of Western feminism is ill-founded.
     He does not say whom he criticizes, nor does he provide any references. More
     importantly, Öcalan's critique lacks nuance and knowledge of Western feminism, its
     development and its variations. For example, the first charge – that feminism rests
     on an opposition between men and women – is not correct. Judith Butler (1990: 5)
     in particular has dispensed with the view of identity as disidentification, because it
     entails a maintenance of hierarchy, oppression and exclusion that, according to Butler,
     is not in women's interests, much less in those of the human race. As for the second
     assertion, in which Öcalan calls for Western feminism's historical evaluation of
     power and its significance, Öcalan overlooks that all Foucaultian-inspired feminism
     has analysed complex structures of power, particularly in the West. In respect of the
     third charge that Western feminism has been disinterested in securing women their
     economic independence, I should claim, with regard to Denmark as my country of
     residency, that women's economic independence is one of the visible contributions
     of Western feminism. The three assertions reveal a lack of knowledge of feminism
     on Öcalan's part. Had he acquainted himself with feminism, he would also have been
     familiar with postcolonial contributions such as that of Saba Mahmood (2001, 2005),
     where Mahmood criticizes Western feminism for being blind to its own embedding
     in a liberal culture that prioritizes the individual and its striving for individual
     freedom from the norms of the collective. Here, Mahmood criticizes Western
     feminism for refusing to recognize as feminist the collectivist women's movements
     in, for example, the Islamic cultural area, where women's struggle is concerned
     with securing the freedom of the community (Mahmood 2001: 208). Mahmood's
     and other postcolonial feminists' insistence on collectivist contributions has a lot
     in common with the PKK's view of community and women's role in securing the
     freedom of the community.

26   Cf. Öcalan 1992: 282.

27   Cf. Öcalan 2012: 277.

28   Cf. Öcalan 2012: 161.

29   Cf. Öcalan 1992: 85–98.

30   Cf. Öcalan 1992: 89.

31   Cf. Öcalan 1992: 55.

32   Cf. Öcalan 1998: 238.

33   Cf. Öcalan 1992: 56.

34   Cf. Öcalan 1992: 30.

35   Cf. Öcalan 1992: 20. Öcalan does not address the male physique or physiology when
     he suggests that the first meeting between woman and man was unproblematic and
     based on mutual understanding. It is hard to imagine such a 'natural' and 'equal'

meeting. Man's physical strength, which produced better survival opportunities for him, is likely to have produced certain advantages in the relationship with the woman. The man and woman certainly needed each other for reproduction and survival, but man's physical superiority meant that he could always get his way, by force if need be.

36 Cf. Öcalan 1998: 233.
37 Cf. Öcalan 2004: 25.
38 The women fighters hold that the conspiracy led by Osman Öcalan was intended to prevent women from having more influence within the movement. The conspiracy explains why women within the movement hastened to organize themselves separately. I will elaborate on the perception of Osman Öcalan's conspiracy in Chapter 4.
39 With the application of 'homosociality' among women, I am referring to Eve Kosofsky Sedgwick's notion of how an 'intelligible continuum of aims, emotions, and valuations links lesbianism with the other forms of women's attention to women: the bond between mother and daughter, for instance, the bond of sister and sister, women's friendship, "networking," and the active struggles of feminism' (Sedgwick 1985: 2).
40 Cf. Çağlayan 2007: 113.
41 Cf. Düzel 2018: 139–45.
42 Cf. Öcalan 1992: 198.
43 Cf. Sloterdijk 2013: 32–9.
44 Cf. Foucault 1982: 783–4.
45 Cf. Käser 2021: 22.
46 Cf. Foucault 1979: 100.
47 For a similar point, see Käser 2021: 9–10.

Chapter 4

1   YJA-STAR (Free Women's Units STAR) & PAJK (Kurdistan Women's Liberation Party).
2   Cf. Foucault 1979: 100.
3   Cf. Öcalan 1998: 233.
4   Cf. Foucault 1995: 97.
5   Cf. Çağlayan 2007: 110–17.
6   Cf. Öcalan 2013: 52.
7   Cf. Dirik 2022: 93.
8   Cf. Cansız 2015: 103.
9   I refer to the Women's High Council as the Kurdish women's movement, because it is better known by that name.
10 http://www.kjk-online.org/hakkimizda/?lang=en. Accessed 13.04.2018.
11 Cf. Cansız 2014a: 289.
12 The women fighters were not specific about the countries in the world where they thought women had failed to maintain their rights and opportunities for action after the struggle. However, I think they may have been drawing on examples such as Eritrea, where, despite accounting for a third of the militant movement associated with the liberation struggle, women were nevertheless forced to be wives and mothers

after the revolution (Hale 2000). Similar examples can be found in Latin America and in Sri Lanka. For more on this, see Kampwirth 2002; Stack-O'Connor 2007; Parashar 2014; Tripp 2015; Darhour & Dahlerup 2020.

13　Cf. Öcalan 1992: 34.

14　Cf. Öcalan 1992: 35.

15　Cf. Öcalan 2004: 135.

16　Cf. Cansız 2015: 94.

17　I have chosen to anonymize the time and place for the platform.

18　'Feminist figurations' is a concept applied by Haraway in her introduction of the 'cyborg' as a figuration. The cyborg is a figurative description of a blend of human and non-human elements, including technology and discourse, together constituting a subject. The configuration was developed to avoid universal, essentialist assumptions, including the dualism between nature and culture, subject and object (Haraway 1992: 297).

19　Öcalan is critical of the positivist mindset and rejects Auguste Comte's three-stage understanding of the history of humankind's mental development, in which each step is more advanced than the previous one. The three phases are the religious stage, the metaphysical stage and the positive stage. Comte compares this process to a person's transition from childhood to adulthood. Öcalan criticizes positivism both for its linear understanding of development and for its ideology, which states that there is only one reality. Öcalan also emphasizes that positivism as a science contributes to the power dominance of the nation state and to the development of capitalism (Öcalan 2009: 19).

20　Here, Delal was indirectly criticizing the sociological timeline developed by Marx, according to which the pre-communal society was the first period in which primitive humans lived. It was followed by the slavery society, feudal society and capitalist society in that order, and the future, according to Marxism, will be communist. Delal's critique is based on Öcalan's analysis in which he is critical of the dialectical mindset, which is the foundation of Marxism and positivism. The dialectical mindset implies the epistemological method that consists of exchanges between thesis and antithesis, resulting in a synthesis of interweavings. Öcalan is against this chronological division and stresses that society does not evolve in 'social phases' based on advances that every society must go through (Öcalan 1993: 55; 2004: 53).

21　It is important here to point out the similarity with Saba Mahmood's point as mentioned in Section 3.3.4. Mahmood criticizes Western feminism for being based on some fixed concepts as a template for understanding other cultures and hence not recognizing as feminist the collectivist women's movements in those cultures (Mahmood 2001: 208). Like Mahmood, I argue that the women of the PKK use the Neolithic woman not to enable liberation of the individual woman in a liberal, Western feminist way, but that their figuration is part of a collectivist discourse that aims at securing the freedom of the community. Still, like Western feminist figurations, the PKK women's figuration exerts the same function as the Western feminist figuration of mobilizing and generating new horizons.

22　Cf. Al-Ali & Käser 2022; Dirik 2022.

23　Cf. Barad 1998: 106.

24　Cf. Beauvoir 2010: 30.

25　Like Berivan's account, Jo-Ann Owusu's article 'Menstruation and the Holocaust' (2009) on female Holocaust victims, based on their oral testimony and memoirs, shows that women were at first ashamed of their menstruation and found it embarrassing to talk to each other about their menstruation during their time in the concentration camps. Despite this, they persisted in bringing up the subject and overcoming the stigma associated with the shame. In the most dire and extreme of circumstances, the subject became a kind of rallying point for the women, bringing a feeling of solidarity and community. Being able to have periods under utterly merciless conditions came to be perceived as a symbol of their freedom as it reminded them of their womanhood.

26   According to another woman fighter, Delal, this acceptance is mainly due to Öcalan. Öcalan has decreed that no one in the movement is to make Cihan's sexual identity a subject for discussion, as he is to be respected as he is and must be left in peace to carry out his political and musical activities (fieldnote, 15.6.2017).

27   Cf. Butler 1990: 134–41.

28   Cf. Çağlayan 2007: 112.

Chapter 5

1   Cf. Van Bruinessen 1992.

2   Cf. Tezcür 2019.

3   See also Section 1.5 for more information on Şemdin Sakık, who was often described by the women fighters as a good example of the 'male mentality'. As a former high-ranking leader in the PKK, Şemdin Sakık is particularly known for his crimes against women fighters while he was part of the movement.

4   See Section 3.4.1.

5   Düzel writes about the development of masculine militant femininities in the PKK as follows: 'The diaries and the interviews show a transcendental path for women's empowerment in three different forms of militant femininity. They were mostly positioned in a linear evolutionary path, yet connected to the war and intensity of the conflict, women's individual choices, and urbanization of the movement, these forms mixed and merged with each other. The first form was "masculine womanhood" (erkeksi kadınlık), transcendence of the previous Kurdish womanhood. It emerged at the initial stages of women's involvement (1984–1994). The second was "woman's color" (kadının rengi), transcendence of the (Kurdish) men and finding the feminine spirit. This form corresponds to the formation of women's councils and eventually a separate army in 1995. The third form was "goddessness," transcendence through/in death, which was expressed most strongly with Zeynep Kınacı's suicide attack act in 1996' (Düzel 2018: 143–4).

6   Cf. Öcalan 2004: 135.

7   Cf. Gergen 1997: 195.

8   Cf. Çağlayan 2007: 108; Düzel 2018: 144; Käser 2021: 9.

9   Cf. Öcalan 1999a: 85–6.

10   Cf. Sjoberg & Gentry 2007; Alison 2009.

11   Cf. Viterna 2013: 209.

12   Nazan Üstündağ (2016) writes that Öcalan's understanding of the use of violence is based on a Marxist analysis of capitalism. In other words, violence under capitalism is exertive in nature (attack), while in communism it is about defending oneself. In this context, Üstündağ claims that Öcalan's understanding of violence is not about attaining power or creating dominance over others but is a necessary tool for an oppressed population to achieve its freedom. Moreover, like Yuval-Davis (1997),

Üstündağ maintains that capitalism and nation states have created a monopoly on the use of violence and thereby privatized it, so that it is hard for movements like the PKK to legitimize their use of it (Üstündağ 2016: 1999).

13 Zilan left behind a letter defining the purpose of her act. Link to the full text of the letter: http://www.yjastar.com/tr/sehitlerimiz/37-zilan-zeynep-kinaci-arkadasin -mektubu. Accessed 17.4.2020.

14 When civilians attend the funerals of *fedai* in significant numbers, it may indicate that the Kurdish population approves of their actions. It becomes difficult for the PKK to get permission to carry out suicide missions if Kurdish society does not recognize their purpose, as one of the most important aims of these missions must be to attract more candidates to the missions by paying tribute to their self-sacrifice. When the PKK also praises martyrs as much as it does, especially individuals who carry out *fedai* actions, the aim is also to make them into exemplary personalities in their anti-colonial struggle. The aim of creating exemplary identities is to use these figurations to provoke the others and trigger a form of 'impersonal shame' in them. This shame is induced with the intention of provoking people into working more actively for the ideals adhered to by the exemplary personalities (Norval 2007: 195).

15 Cf. Çağlayan 2007: 222.

16 Cf. Käser 2021: 136.

17 Cf. Khalili 2007: 19.

18 Cf. Geerdink 2021: 197.

19 Cf. Weiss 2014: 163.

20 Peshmerga forces are the official military forces of the Kurdish autonomy in northern Iraq.

21 There have been several battles between Kurdish Peshmerga forces and PKK fighters in Iraq. These battles are known among Kurds as the 'brotherhood war' [Kurdish: birakuji], as it was internal fighting between Kurds that caused them to be weakened, which was also in the Turkish military's interest.

22 See http://www.yjastar.com/tr/sehitlerimiz/341-sema-yuece-yoldasn-mektuplar (accessed 18.01.2010). Not only PKK members use their bodies as a tool to proclaim a political message. Turkish military forces also send a message to the PKK by abusing the bodies of dead guerrillas. This is done by displaying on social media the abused bodies of dead guerrillas, often with the head severed from the body, male guerrillas in women's clothing, the genitals of women guerrillas and so on. By displaying assaults on the Kurds that connote a humiliation pertaining to gender and sex, also known as *death pornography*, it seems that Turkish soldiers arrogate to themselves the rights and power over the 'other', not only in life but also in death (Isik 2022). The Turkish soldiers thereby send a strong message to male PKK members: that they failed to protect their women, who were therefore abused. But, when Turkish military forces record pictures of dead bodies and their abuse of them, and share them on social media, partly to punish the women who take up arms against the male army, the aim is no different to what Foucault (1995: 14) calls executing the punishment by a theatrical ritual in order to spread fear and thus obtain obedience.

Chapter 6

1 A few works (e.g. Alkan 2012; Buldan 2004, Marcus 2007, Grojan 2008) have reflected on male ex-members' decision to leave the PKK, often focusing on their

criticism of the PKK's leadership and especially Öcalan's inclusion of women in the PKK. Given the women fighters' praise of Öcalan according to my interviews, especially as rendered in Chapter 4, it would have been interesting to find out if women ex-members of the PKK had changed their perspective on Öcalan, his leadership and the gender ideals of the movement.

2 Cf. Düzel 2018.

3 As I have described in Section 4.2., the Kurdish women's movement is officially organized under the name the Women's High Council (KJB), which is an umbrella organization including women and women's organizations from the four parts of Kurdistan. The women's movement in Rojava as part of KJB is organized under the name Kongra Star. Kongra Star describes itself to be based on the voluntary union of democratic organizations, institutions and democratic figures. It considers itself as a women's movement, but not a political party, which is responsible for the coordination, implementation and supervision of the decisions and policies of different institutions, organizations and canton assemblies.

4 Cf. Öcalan 2011: 16.

5 According to YPJ spokeswoman Nesrin Abdullah, the SDF, of which the YPJ is a part, has made a great sacrifice, with 24,000 wounded and 12,000 killed (fieldnote, 19.12.2019).

6 This corroborates the claim (Enloe 2000: 235–87) that the value placed on the mother or motherhood in a nationalist context is proportional to her son's contribution to the liberation of the respective nation. Roza's narrative shows, of course, that 'the son' can also be a daughter. Kurdish attempts to liberate various areas by drawing on women's contributions should change how national-liberational agency is defined.

7 For similar reflections on the normalization of a militarized life, see Enloe 2000; Saigol 2000.

8 From 9 October to 17 November 2019, the Turkish military (TSK), together with the Syrian National Army (SNA), which consists of Sunni Muslim jihadists, conducted a military operation against the Syrian Defence Forces that controlled Rojava. The TSK and SNA succeeded in invading a small part of Rojava. The aforementioned women's village of Jinwar was also temporarily evacuated during this invasion.

9 It is estimated by the UN that the Islamic State in Sinjar, Iraq, in 2014 killed at least 5,000 men and kidnapped 7,000 women and girls as slaves. The religiously motivated genocidal attacks have subsequently contributed to the Yezidi community in Sinjar starting to organize itself with its own military forces, as the community has not experienced that the Kurdish Peshmerga forces and the Iraqi army in the country did enough to protect them. Sinjar's self-defence military forces have been established with the support of the PKK and YPG/YPJ, which have also largely helped to support the Yezidi community's survival struggle. In this connection, the Êzîdxan Women's Units (*Yekinêyen Jinên Êzîdxan*, YJÊ) were established in 2015. Women fighters from YJÊ have subsequently been active in the recapture of Sinjar from the Islamic State and are still active in the defence of the autonomy. When I was in Iraq in 2018 and 2019, I intended to carry out fieldwork in Sinjar in order to have a better insight into YJÊ's organization and their struggle for survival, which has also been a source of inspiration for the other women in the region. However, for security reasons I could not enter Sinjar. I expect the YJÊ to hold similar ideals and organize like the YPJ, because the YJÊ considers Öcalan their leader and follows the concept of democratic confederalism.

10 Cf. Mohanty 1988: 79.

11   Cf. Yuval-Davis 1997: 95.
12   For a similar opinion, see Wood 2019: 6.

Conclusion

1   Cf. Yuval-Davis 1997: 95.
2   For a similar point, see Cockburn 2004: 31.
3   Cf. Yalçın-Heckman & Van Gelder 2000; Çağlayan 2007; Käser 2021.
4   Cf. Yuval-Davis 1977; Hipkins & Plain 2007; Karshenas et al. 2016.
5   Cf. Berger-Gluck 1997; Kampwirth 2002; Turshen 2002; Viterna 2013.
6   Cf. Mojab 2001; Bengio 2016; Fischer-Tahir 2012; Begikhan et al. 2015.
7   Cf. Al-Ali & Pratt 2009; Darhour & Dahlerup 2020.

REFERENCES

Açık, Necla (2002): 'Ulusal Mücadele, Kadın Mitosu ve Kadınların Harekete Geçirilmesi: Türkiye' Deki Çağdaş Kadın Dergilerinin Bir Analizi', in *National Struggle, the Myth of Woman and Mobilizing Women: An Analysis of the Contemporary Kurdish Women's Journals in Turkey*, Edited by Aksu Bora & Asena Günal'larda Türkiye'de Feminizm [Feminism in Turkey in the '90s], İstanbul: İletişim.

Açık, Necla (2013): 'Re-defining the Role of Women within the Kurdish National Movement in Turkey in the 1990s', in *The Kurdish Question in Turkey: New Perspectives on Conflict, Representation and Reconciliation*, Edited by Welat Zeydanlıoğlu & Cengiz Güneş, Oxon: Routledge Publishers.

Ahmed, Leila (2008): *Kvinder og Køn I Islam*, København: Forlaget Vandkunsten.

Ahmed, Sara (2004): *The Cultural Politics of Emotion*, Edinburgh: Edinburgh University Press.

Akınan, Serdar (2014): *İştar'ın Kızları: Silahlarin Gölgesinde Bir Kadın Hareketi*, İstanbul: Destek Yayınları.

Al-Ali, Nadje & Käser, Isabel (2022): 'Beyond Feminism? Jineolojî and the Kurdish Women's Freedom Movement', *Politics and Gender*, 18(1): 212–243.

Al-Ali, Nadje & Pratt, Nicola Christine, eds. (2009): *Women and War in the Middle East: Transnational Perspectives*, London: Zed Books.

Alexievich, Svetlana (2017/1985): *The Unwomanly Face of War*, London: Penguin Books.

Alison, Miranda (2004): 'Women as Agents of Political Violence: Gendering Security', *Security Dialogue*, 35(4): 447–63.

Alison, Miranda (2009): *Women and Political Violence: Female Combatants in Ethno-national Conflict*, New York: Routledge.

Alkan, Necati (2012): *PKK'da Semboller, Aktorler, Kadınlar*, Istanbul: Karakutu.

Ann, Adele (1993): *Women Fighters of Liberation Tigers*, London: LTTE International Secretariat.

Arakon, Maya (2015): 'Belonging to a Minority, Being Kurdish and a Woman: Kurdish Women's Struggle for Identity and Equality in Modern Turkey', *Alternatif Politika, Kürt Sorununu Yeniden Düşünmek: Yanlış Giden Neydi?, Bundan Sonra Nereye?*, 2(7): 309–91.

Aras, Ramazan (2013): *The Formation of Kurdishness in Turkey: Political Violence, Fear and Pain*, New York: Routledge.

Barad, Karen (1998): 'Getting Real: Technoscientific Practices and the Materialization of Reality', *Differences*, 10(2): 87–128.

Barad, Karen (2003): 'Posthumanist Performativity: Toward an Understanding of How Matter Comes to Matter', *Signs: Journal of Women in Culture and Society*, 28(3): 801–31.

Barad, Karen (2007): *Meeting the Universe Halfway: Quantum Physics and the Entanglement of Matter and Meaning*, Durham: Duke University Press.

Barker, Eileen (1984): *The Making of a Moonie: Choice or Brainwashing?*, Oxford: Blackwell.

Barkey, Henri J. & Fuller, Graham E. (1998): *Turkey's Kurdish Question*, Lanham, Oxford, Boulder & New York: Rowman, & Littlefield Publishers, Inc.

Barth, Fredrik (1969): *Ethnic Groups and Boundaries*, Bergen: Universitetsforlag.

Beauvoir, Simone de (2010): *The Second Sex*, New York: Random House.

Begikhani, Nazand, Gill, Aisha K. & Hague, Gill (2015): *Honour-Based Violence: Experiences and Counter-Strategies in Iraqi Kurdistan and the UK Kurdish Diaspora*, Burlington: Ashgate.

Bengio, Ofra (2016): 'Game Changers: Kurdish Women in Peace and War', *The Middle East Journal*, 70(1): 30–46.

Bennett, Olivia, Bexley, Jo & Warnock, Kitty (1995): *Arms to Fight, Arms to Protect: Women Speak Out about Conflict*, London: Panos.

Berger-Gluck, Sherna (1997): 'Shifting Sands: The Feminist-Nationalist Connection in the Palestinian Movement', in *Feminist Nationalism*, Edited by Lois A. West, New York & London: Routledge.

Beşikçi, İsmail (1991): *Tunceli Kanunu (1935) ve Dersim Jenosidi*, Bonn: Wesanên Rewşen.

Bookchin, Murray (1990): 'The Meaning of Confederalism', *Green Perspectives*, 20(3).

Bookchin, Murray (2015): *The Next Revolution-Popular Assemblies and the Promise of Direct Democracy*, New York: Verso.

Bozarslan, Hamit (2008): 'Kurds and the Turkish State', in *Turkey in the Modern World*, Edited by R. Kasaba, Cambridge: Cambridge University Press.

Buldan, Nejdet (2004): *PKK'de Kadin Olmak*, Istanbul: Doz Basim-Yayin.

Butler, Judith (1990): *Gender Trouble*, New York: Routledge.

Çağlayan, Handan (2007): *Analar, Yoldaşlar, Tanrıcalar: Kürt Hareketinde Kadınlar ve Kadın Kimliğinin Oluşumu*, Istanbul: İletişim Yayinlari.

Cansız, Sakine (2014): *Hep Kavgaydı Yaşamım*, Volume 1, Neus: Verlag und Vertriebs GmbH.

Cansız, Sakine (2014a): *Hep Kavgaydı Yaşamım*, Volume 2, Neus: Verlag und Vertriebs GmbH .

Cansız, Sakine (2015): *Hep Kavgaydı Yaşamım*, Volume 3, Neus: Verlag und Vertriebs GmbH.

Cederman, Lars-Erik, Wimmer, Andreas & Min, Brian (2010): 'Why Do Ethnic Groups Rebel? New Data and Analysis', *World Politics*, 62(1): 87–119.

Chase, Michelle (2015): *Revolution Within the Revolution, Women and Gender Politics in Cuba, 1950–1962*, Chapel Hill: The University of North Carolina Press.

Cizre, Ümit. & Üşür, Serpil (1989): *Latin Amerika`da Askeri Diktatorluk ve Kadın*, İstanbul: Belge Yayınları.

Cockburn, Cynthia (2004): 'The Continuum of Violence: A Gendered Perspective on War and Peace', in *Sites of Violence: Gender and Conflict Zones*, Edited by Wenona Giles and Jennifer Hyndman, Berkeley: University of California Press.

Cohen, Dara Kay (2016): *Rape During Civil War*, New York: Cornell University Press.

Cooke, Miriam (1993): 'WO-Man, Retelling the War Myth', in *Gendering War Talk*, Edited by Miriam Cooke & Angela Woollacott, Princeton: Princeton University Press.

Cudworth, Erika (1988): *Feminism and Non-Violence: A Relation in Theory, Herstory and Praxis*, MSc dissertation, London School of Economics.

Darhour, Hanane & Dahlerup, Drude, eds. (2020): *Double-Edged Politics on Women's Rights in the Mena Region*, London: Palgrave Macmillan.

Davies, Bronwyn & Harré, Rom (1990): 'Positioning: The Discursive Production of Selves', *Journal for the Theory of Social Behaviour*, 20(1): 43–63.

Dean, Valentina (2019): 'Kurdish Female Fighters: The Western Depiction of YPJ and Combatants in Rojava', *Glocalism: Journal of Culture, Politics and Innovation*, 1: 1–29.

Deleuze, Gilles (1998): *Spinoza. Practical Philosophy*, San Francisco: City Light.

Deleuze, Gilles (2000): *Proust and Signs*, Minneapolis: University of Minnesota Press.

Deleuze, Gilles & Guattari, Félix (1987): *A Thousand Plateaus: Capitalism and Schizophrenia*, Minneapolis & London: University of Minnesota Press.

Demir, Arzu (2014): *Savaşta Barışta Özgürlükte Aşkta Dağın Kadın Hali*, İstanbul: Ceylan Yayınları.

Dersimi, Mehmed Nuri (1988): *Kurdistan Tarihinde Dersim*, Cologne: KOMKAR.

Dirik, Dilar (2014): 'Western Fascination with "Badass" Kurdish Women', *Al Jazeera*, https://www.aljazeera.com/indepth/opinion/2014/10/westernfascination-with-badas -201410211241 0527736.html.

Dirik, Dilar (2018): 'Overcoming the Nation-State: Women's Autonomy and Radical Democracy in Kurdistan', in *Gendering Nationalism: Intersections of Nation, Gender and Sexuality*, Edited by Jon Mulholland et al., London: Palgrave Macmillan.

Dirik, Dilar (2022): *The Kurdish Women´s Movement: History, Theory, Practice*, London: Pluto Press.

Dirik, Dilar et al. (2016): *The Dare Imagining: Rojava Revolution*, Williamsburgh Station: Autonomedia.

Durakbaşa, Ayşe (1998): 'Kemalism as Identity Politics in Turkey', in *Deconstructing Images of the Turkish Woman*, Edited by Zehra Arat, New York: S. Martin's Press.

Düzel, Esin (2018): 'Fragile Goddesses: Moral Subjectivity and Militarized Agencies in Female Guerrilla Diaries and Memoirs', *International Feminist Journal of Politics*, 20(2): 137–52.

Engels, Frederich (2010/1884): 'Origin of the Family, Private Property and the State', *E-book*, Project Gutenberg.

Enloe, Cynthia (1983): *Does Khaki Become You*, London: Pluto Press.

Enloe, Cynthia (1989): *Bananas, Beaches and Bases: Making Feminist Sense of International Politics*, London: Pandora.

Enloe, Cynthia (1993): *The Morning After: Sexual Politics at the End of the Cold War*, Berkeley: University of California Press.

Enloe, Cynthia (2000): *Maneuvres: The International Politics of Militarizing Women's Lives*, Berkeley: University of California Press.

Ersöz, Gurbetelli (2015): *Gurbet'in Güncesi/Yüreğimi Dağlara Nakşettim*, Diyarbakır: Aram.

Fischer-Tahir, Andrea (2012): 'Gendered Memories and Masculinities: Kurdish Peshmerga and the Anfal Campaign in Iraq', *Journal of Middle East Women's Studies*, 8(1): 92–114.

Flach, Anja (2007): *Frauen in der Kurdischen Guerilla: Motivation, Identität und Geschlechterverhältnis*, Cologne: PapyRossa.

Foucault, Michel (1979): *The History of Sexuality, Vol. 1: An Introduction*, New York: Pantheon Books.

Foucault, Michel (1982): 'The Subject and Power', *Critical Inquiry*, 8(4): 777–95.

Foucault, Michel (1995): *Discipline and Punish: The Birth of the Prison*, New York: Vintage Books.

Fujii, Ann Lee (2009): *Killing Neighbors: Webs of Violence in Rwanda*, Ithaca & London: Cornell University Press.

Fujii, L. A. (2010): 'Shades of Truth and Lies: Interpreting Testimonies of War and Violence', *Journal of Peace Research*, 47(2): 231–41.

Geerdink, Fréderike (2021): *This Fire Never Dies: One Year With PKK*, New Delhi, New Delhi, LeftWord Books.

Gellner, Ernst (1983): *Nations and Nationalism*, Oxford: Basil Blackwell.

Gergen Kenneth, J. (1997): *Realities and Relations: Soundings in Social Constructions*, Cambridge, MA: Harvard University Press.

Ghanim, David (2009): *Gender and Violence in the Middle East*, Westport & London: Praeger.

Gilbert, Sandra (1983): 'Soldiers' Heart: Literary Men, Literary Women and the Great War', *Signs Special Issue on Women and Violence*, 8(3): 422–50.

Goldstein, Joshua S (2003): *War and Gender: How Gender Shapes the War System and Vice Versa*, Cambridge: Cambridge University Press.

Gonzalez-Perez, Margaret (2006): 'Guerrilleras in Latin America: Domestic and International Roles', *Journal of Peace Research*, 43(3): 313–29.

Goodwin, Jeff (2001): *No Other Way Out: States and Revolutionary Movements, 1945–1991*, New York: Cambridge University Press.

Grojean, Olivier (2008): 'La Production de l'Homme Nouveau au Sein du PKK', *European Journal of Turkish Studies*, 8: 95–117.

Grosz, Elisabeth (1993): 'A Thousand Riny Sexes: Feminism and Rhizomatics', *Topoi*, 12(2): 167–79.

Günel Tekin, Gülçiçek (2014): *Özgürleşen Ruhlar: Kürt Gerilla Hareketi*, İstanbul: Belge Yayınları.

Güneş, Cengiz (2012): *The Kurdish National Movement in Turkey: From Protest to Resistance*, London & New York: Routledge.

Güneş, Cengiz (2013): 'Explaining the PKK's Mobilization of the Kurds in Turkey: Hegemony, Myth and Violence', *Ethnopolitics*, 12(3): 247–67.

Gürer, Çetin (2015): *Demokratik Özerklik: Bir Yurttaşlık Heteropyası*, Ankara: NotaBene Yayınları.

Hale, Sondra (2000): 'The Soldier and the State: Post-liberation Women: The Case of Eritrea', in *Frontline Feminisms: Women, War, and Resistance Waller*, Edited by Marguerite R. Waller & Jennifer Rycenga, London: Routledge.

Hall, Suart (1991): 'Old and New Identities, Old and New Ethnicities', in *Culture, Globalization and the World System*, Edited by Anthony D. King, New York: Macmillan.

Haraway, Donna (1989): *Primate Visions. Gender, Race, and Nature in the World of Modern Science*, New York & London: Routledge.

Haraway, Donna (1991): *Simians, Cyborgs and Women, The Reinvention of Nature*, London: Free Association Books.

Haraway, Donna (1992): 'The Promises of Monsters: A Regenerative Politics for Inappropriate/d Others', in *Cultural Studies*, Edited by Lawrence Grossberg, Cary Nelson & Paula A. Treichler, New York: Routledge.

Hassanpour, Amir (2001): 'The (Re)Production of Partiarchy in the Kurdish Language', in *Women of a Non-state Nation/the Kurds*, Edited by Shahrzad Mojab, Costa Mesa, CA: Mazda Publishers.

Hill Collins, Patricia & Sirma, Bilge (2016): *Intersectionality*, Cambridge: Polity Press.

Hipkins, Danielle & Plain, Gill (2007): *War-Torn Tales: Literature, Film and Gender in the Aftermath of World War II*, Bern: Peter Lang AG.

Hobsbawm, Eric J. E. (1990): *Nations and Nationalism Since 1788*, Cambridge & New York: Cambridge University Press.

Humphreys, Macartan & Weinstein, Jeremy M. (2008): 'Who Fights? The Determinants of Participation in Civil War', *American Journal of Political Science*, 52(2): 436–55.

Isik, Ruken (2022): 'Claiming the Bodies of Kurdish: Women Kurdish Women's Funerals in Northern Kurdistan/Turkey', *HAU: Journal of Ethnographic Theory*, 12(1): 39–45.

Jayawardena, Kumari (1986): *Feminism and Nationalism in the Third World*, London: Zed.

Jenkins, Brian (1990): *Nationalism in France: Class and Nation Since 1789*, London: Routledge.

Jongerden, Joost & Akkaya, Ahmet Hamdi (2012): 'Reassembling the Political: The PKK and the Project of Radical Democracy', *European Journal of Turkish Studies*, 14: 33–51.

Jongerden, Joost & Akkaya, Ahmet Hamdi (2015): *PKK Üzerine Yazilar*, Istanbul: Vate.

Joseph, Suad (1999a): 'Brother-Sister Relationships, Connectivity, Love and Power in the Reproduction of Patriarchy in Lebanon', in *Intimate Selving in Arab Families, Gender, Self, and Identity*, Edited by Suad Joseph, Syracuse: Syracuse University Press.

Joseph, Suad (1999b): 'Introduction, Theories and Dynamics of Gender, Self, and Identity in Arab Families', in *Intimate Selving in Arab Families, Gender, Self, and Identity*, Edited by Suad Joseph, Syracuse: Syracuse University Press.

Jowkar, Forouz (1986): 'Honor and Shame: A Feminist View from Within', *Feminist Issues*, 6(1): 45–65.

Kampwirth, Karen (2002): *Women and Guerrilla Movements*, Nicaragua, El Salvador, Chiapas & Cuba: Penn State Press.

Kandiyoti, Deniz (1989): 'Women and the Turkish State: Political Actors or Symbolic Pawns?', in *Woman-Nation-State*, Edited by Nira Yuval-Davis & Floya Anthias, London: Macmillan.

Kandiyoti, Deniz (1991): 'Identity and Its Discontents: Women and the Nation Millennium', *Journal of International Studies*, 20(3): 429–43.

Karpat, K. H. (1988): 'The Ottoman and Confessional Legacy in the Middle East, I', in *Ethnicity, Pluralism, and the State in the Middle East*, Edited by Milton J. Esman & Itamar Rabinovich, Ithaca and London: Cornell University Press.

Karshenas, M., Moghadam, V. M. & Chamlou, N. (2016): 'Women, Work and Welfare in the Middle East and North Africa: Introduction and Overview', in *Women, Work and Welfare in the Middle East and North Africa*, Edited by N. Chamlou & M. Karshenas, London: Imperial College Press.

Käser, Isabel (2019): 'Mountain Life Is Difficult but Beautiful!: The Gendered Process of Becoming "Free"', in *PKK Education Kurds in Turkey: Ethnographies of Heterogeneous Experiences*, Edited by Lucie Drechselová & Adnan Celik, London: Lexington Books.

Käser, Isabel (2021): *The Kurdish Women's Freedom Movement: Gender, Body Politics and Militant Femininities*, Cambridge: Cambridge University Press.

Kedourie, Elie (1993): *Nationalism (1960)*, Cambridge: Blackwell.

Khalili, Laleh (2007): *Heroes and Martyrs of Palestine: The Politics of National Commemoration*, Cambridge: Cambridge University Press.

Kinnane, Derk (1964): *The Kurds and Kurdistan*, London & New York: Oxford University.

Kirisci, Kemal & Winrow, Gareth M. (1997): *Kürt Sorunu: Kökeni ve Gelişimi*, İstanbul: Tarih Vakfı Yurt Yayınları.

Knapp, Michael & Jongerden, Joost (2016): 'Communal Democracy: The Social Contract and Confederalism in Rojava', *Comparative Islamic Studies*, 10(1): 87–109.

Knapp, Michael et al. (2016): *Revolution in Rojava, Democratic Autonomy and Women's Liberation in Syrian Kurdistan*, London: Pluto Press.

Koefoed, Minoo (2019): 'Autonomous Spaces and Constructive Resistance in Northern Kurdistan: The Kurdish Movement and Its Experiments with Democratic Autonomy', in *Kurds in Turkey: Ethnographies of Heterogeneous Experiences*, Edited by Lucie Drechselová & Adnan Celik, London: Lexington Books.

Kristeva, Julia (1982): *Powers of Horror: An Essay on Abjection*, New York: Columbia University Press.

Laura, Sjoberg & Gentry Caron, E. (2007): *Mothers, Monsters, Whores: Women's Violence in Global Politics*, London & New York: Zed.

Levitt, Peggy & Schiller, N. G. (2004): 'Conceptualizing Simultaneity: A Transnational Social Field Perspective on Society', *International Migration Review*, 38(3): 1002–39.

Luciak, Ilya A. (2001): *After the Revolution: Gender and Democracy in El Salvador, Nicaragua, and Guatemala*, Baltimore: JHU Press.

Lykke, Nina (2010): *Feminist Studies: A Guide to Intersectional Theory, Methodology and Writing*, New York & London: Routledge.

Mahmood, Saba (2001): 'Feminist Theory, Embodiment, and the Docile Agent: Some Reflections on the Egyptian Islamic Revival', *Cultural Anthropology*, 16(2): 202–36.

Mahmood, Saba (2005): *Politics of Piety: The Islamic Revival and the Feminist Subject*, Princeton & Oxford: Princeton University Press.

Marcus, Aliza (2007): *Blood and Belief: The PKK and the Kurdish Fight for Independence*, New York: New York University Press.

Marx, Karl & Engels, Frederick (1973): *Det Kommunistiske Manifest, 12. Oplag*, København: Forlaget Tiden.

Marx, Karl & Engels, Friedrich (1988): *Collected Works, Vol. 43, Letters: 1868–1870*, New York: Lawrence & Wishart.

Matur, Mejan (2011): *Dağın Ardına Bakmak Looking Behind the Mountain*, İstanbul: Timaş Publishing.

McDowall, David (1996): *A Modern History of the Kurds*, New York & London: I. B. Taurus.

Moghadam, Valentine M. (1993): *Modernizing Women Gender and Social Change in the Middle East*, Boulder & London: Lynne Rienner Publishers.

Mohanty, Chandra T. (1988): 'Under Western Eyes: Feminist Scholarship and Colonial Discourses', *Feminist Review*, 30(1): 61–88.

Mojab, Shahrzad (2001): *Women of a Non-State Nation, The Kurds*, Costa Mesa, CA: Mazda Publishers.

Norval, Aletta J. (2007): *Aversive Democracy: Inheritance and Originality in the Democratic Tradition*, Cambridge: Cambridge University Press.

Nush, June (2005): 'Introduction: Social Movements and Global Processes', in *Social Movements: An Anthropological Reader*, Edited by June Nush, USA, UK and Australia: Blackwell Publishing.

Öcalan, Abdullah (1992): *Kadın ve Aile Sorunu*, İstanbul: Melsa Yayınları.

Öcalan, Abdullah (1993): *Kürdistan Devriminin Yolu*, Cologne: Agri Verlag.

Öcalan, Abdullah (1997): *Tarih Günümüzde Gizli Ve Biz Tarihin Başlangıcında Gizliyiz* (place of publication unknown and publisher unknown).

Öcalan, Abdullah (1998): *Aşkın Kanunları, Savaş Kanunlarından Daha Zordur, Ocak 1998 Çözümlemeleri, Parti Merkez Okulu Yayınları*, (place of publication unknown and publisher unknown).

Öcalan, Abdullah (1999a): *Kürt Aşkı*, İstanbul: Aram.

Öcalan, Abdullah (1999b): *Kürt Sorununda Çözüm ve Çözümsüzlük İkilemi, Ek Savunma*, Istanbul: Mem Yayıları.

Öcalan, Abdullah (1999c): *Savunma: Kürt Sorununda Demokratik Çözüm Bildirgesi*, İstanbul: Mem Yayınları.

Öcalan, Abdullah (2004): *Bir Halkı Savunmak*, İstanbul: Çetin Yayınları.

Öcalan, Abdullah (2008): *War and Peace in Kurdistan*, Cologne: International Initiative Freedom for Öcalan – Peace in Kurdistan.

Öcalan, Abdullah (2009): *Kapitalist Uygarlık. Maskesiz Tanrılar ve Çıplak Krallar*, Çağı, Diyarbakır: Aram Yayınları.

Öcalan, Abdullah (2011): *Democratic Confederalism*, London: Transmedia Publishing Ltd.

Öcalan, Abdullah (2012): *Kürt Sorunu ve Demokratik Ulus Çözümü: Kültürel Soykırım Kıskacında Kürtleri Savunmak*, Neuss: Mezopotamya Yayınları.

Öcalan, Abdullah (2013): *Liberating Life: Woman's Revolution*, Cologne: International Initiative Edition & Mesepotamian Publishers.

Öcalan, Abdullah (2016): *Hakikat Aşktır, Aşk Özgür Yaşamdır, Jineloji Tartişmalari*, Neuss: Weşanen Mezopotamya.

Oldfield, Sybil (1989): *Women Against the Iron Fist: Alternatives to Militarism, 1990–1989*, Oxford: Basil Blacwell.

Owusus, Jo-Ann (2009): 'Menstruation and the Holocaust', *History Today*, 69(5): 18–33.

Özbudun, Sibel (2012): *Latin Amerika'da Yerli Hareketleri*, Ankara: Dipnot Yayınları.

Özcan, Ali Kemal (2006): *Turkey's Kurds. A Theoretical Analysis of the PKK and Abdullah Öcalan*, Oxon & New York: Routledge.

Özcan, Ali Nihat (1999): *PKK (Kürdistan İşçi Partisi) Tarihi, Ideolojisi, Yöntemi*, Ankara: ASAM.

Özsoy, Hisyar (2010): *Between Gift and Taboo: Death and the Negotiation of National Identity and Sovereignty in the Kurdish Conflict in Turkey*, PhD thesis, University of Texas.

Parashar, Swati (2014): *Women and Militant Wars, the Politics of Injury*, London: Routledge.

Parkinson, Sarah Elizabeth (2013): 'Organizing Rebellion: Rethinking High-Risk Mobilization and Social Networks in War', *American Political Science Review*, 107(3): 418–32.

Petersen, Roger D. (2001): *Resistance and Rebellion: Lessons from Eastern Europe*, New York: Cambridge University Press.

Romano, David (2006): *The Kurdish Nationalist Movement: Opportunity, Mobilization and Identity*, New York: Cambridge University Press.

Roulston, Carmel (1997): 'Women on the Margin: The Women's Movements in Northern Ireland 1973–1995', in *Feminist Nationalism*, Edited by Lois A. West, New York & London: Routledge.

Saigol, Rubina (2000): 'Militarizasyon, Ulus ve Toplumsal Cinsiyet: Şiddetli Çatışma Alanları Olarak Kadın Bedenleri', in *Vatan Millet, Kadınlar*, Edited by Ayşegül Altınay, İstanbul: İletişim.

Sancar, Serpil (2001a): 'Türkler/Kürtler, Anneler ve Siyasaet: Savaşta Çocuklarını Kaybetmiş Türk ve Kürt Anneleri Üzerine Bir Yorum', *Toplum ve Bilim*, 90: 22–40.

Sancar, Serpil (2011b): *Türkiye'de Kadın Hareketinin Politiği: Tarihsel Bağlam, Politik Gündem ve Özgünlükler, Birkaç Arpa Boyu . . . 21. Yüzyila Girerken Türkiye'de Feminist Çalişmalar*, Istanbul: Koç Üniversitesi Yayınları.

Scalbert, Clémence & Le Ray, Marie (2006): 'Power, Ideology, Knowledge – Deconstructing Kurdish Studies', *European Journal of Turkish Studies*, 5: 3–43.

Schmidinger, Thomas (2018): *Rojava: Revolution, War and the Future of Syria's Kurds*, London: Pluto Press.

Sedgwick, Eve Kosofsky (1985): *Between Men: English Literature and Male Homosocial Desire*, New York: Columbia University Press.

Shesterinina, Anastasia (2016): 'Collective Threat Framing and Mobilization in Civil War', *American Political Science Review*, 110(3): 411–27.

Sloterdijk, Peter (2013): *You Must Change Your Life*, Cambridge & Malden: Polity Press.

Smith, Anthony D. (1995): *Nations and Nationalism in a Global Era*, London: Duckworth.

Spivak, Gatyatri Chakravorty (1988): 'Can the Subaltern Speak', in *Marxism and the Interpretation of Culture*, Edited by Cary Nelson & Lawrence Grossberg, London: Macmillan Education.

Stack-O'Connor, Aliza (2007): 'Lions, Tigers, and Freedom Birds: How and Why the Liberation Tigers of Tamil Eelam Employs Women', *Terrorism and Political Violence*, 19(1): 43–63.

Tezcür, G. M. (2009): 'Kurdish Nationalism and Identity in Turkey: A Conceptual Reinterpretation', *European Journal of Turkish Studies*, 10(10): 20–38.

Tezcür, Murat Güneş (2019): 'A Path Out of Patriarchy? Political Agency and Social Identity of Women Fighters', *Perspectives on Politics*, 18(3): 722–39.

Toivanen, Mari & Baser, Bahar (2016): 'Gender in the Representations of an Armed Conflict: Female Kurdish Combatants in French and British Media', *Middle East Journal of Culture and Communication*, 9(3): 294–314.

Topal, Mustafa Kemal (2008): *Ægteskabsmigration, En undersøgelse af kvinders perspektiver på transnationale ægteskaber og statens Intervention*, Master thesis, Roskilde: Roskilde University.

Tripp, Aili Mari (2015): *Women and Power in Postconflict Africa*, Cambridge: Cambridge University Press.

Turshen, Meredeth (2002): 'Algerian Women in the Liberation Struggle and the Civil War: From Active Participants to Passive Victims?', *Social Research: An International Quarterly*, 69(3): 889–911.

Üstündağ, Nazan (2007): 'Kürt Hareketinde Kadınlar ve Kadın Kimliğinin Oluşumu', *Tiroj Dergisi*, 27.

Üstündağ, Nazan (2016): 'Self-Defense as a Revolutionary Practice in Rojava, or How to Unmake the State', *South Atlantic Quarterly*, 115(1): 197, 210.

Üstündağ, Nazan (2019): 'Mother, Politician, and Guerilla: The Emergence of a New Political Imagination in Kurdistan through Women's Bodies and Speech', *D i f f e r e n c e s: A Journal of Feminist Cultural Studies*, 30(2): 115, 145.

Van Bruinessen, Martin van (1992): *Agha, Shaikh, and State: The Social and Political Structures of Kurdistan*, London: Zed Books Ltd.

Viterna, Jocelyn (2013): *Women in War: The Micro-processes of Mobilization in El Salvador*, New York: Oxford University Press.

Walby, Sylvia (2000): 'Kadın ve Ulus', in *Vatan Millet Kadınlar*, Edited by Ayşegül Altınay, İstanbul: İletişim.

Watts, Nicole F. (2010): *Activists in Office: Kurdish Politics and Protest in Turkey*, Seattle: University of Washington Press.

Weinstein, Jeremy M. (2007): *Inside Rebellion: The Politics of Insurgent Violence*, New York: Cambridge University Press.

Weiss, Nerina (2014): 'The Power of Dead Bodies', in *Histories of Victimhood*, Edited by Steffen Jensen & Henrik Rønsbo, Philadelphia: University of Pennsylvania Press.

West, Lois A. (1997): *Feminist Nationalism*, New York & London: Routledge.

Westrheim, Kariane (2008): *Education in a Political Context, A Study of Knowledge Processes and Learning Sites in the PKK*, PhD thesis, Bergen: University of Bergen.

White, Paul (2000): *Primitive Rebels or Revolutionary Modernizers? The Kurdish National Movement in Turkey*, London & New York: Zed Books.

Wood, Elisabeth J. (2003): *Insurgent Collective Action and Civil War in El Salvador*, New York: Cambridge University Press.

Wood, Reed M. (2019): *Female Fighters: Why Rebel Groups Recruit Women for War*, New York: Colombia University Press.

Wood, Reed M. & Thomas, J. L. (2017): 'Women on the Frontline: Rebel Group Ideology and Women's Participation in Violent Rebellion', *Journal of Peace Research*, 54(1): 31–46.

Yalçın-Heckman, Lale (2002): *Kürtlerde Aşiret Ve Akrabalık İlişkileri*, İstanbul: İletişim.

Yalçın-Heckman, Lale & Van Gelder, Pauline (2000), '90'larda Türkiye'de Siyasal Söylemin Dönüşümü Çerçevesinde Kürt Kadınların İmajı: Bazı Eleştirel Değerlendirmeler' [The Image of Kurdish Women in the Framework of the Transformation of the Political Discourse in Turkey in the 1990s: Some Critical Evaluations], in *Vatan Millet, Kadınlar*, Edited by Ayşegül Altınay, İstanbul: İletişim.

Yeğen, Mesut (1999): *Devlet Söyleminde Kürt Sorunu*, İstanbul: İletişim.

Yeğen, Mesut (2006): *Müstakbel Türk'ten Sözde Vatandasa: Kürtler ve Cumhuriyet* [From Prospective Turks to so Called Citizenship: Republic and Kurds], Istanbul: Iletisim Yayinlari.

Yüksel, Metin (2006): 'The Encounter of Kurdish Women with Nationalism in Turkey', *Middle Eastern Studies*, 42(5): 777–802.

Yuval-Davis, Nira (1985): 'Front and Rear: The Sexual Division of Labor in the Israeli Army', *Feminist Studies*, 11(3): 649–76.

Yuval-Davis, Nira (1991): 'The Gendered Gulf War: Women's Citizenship and Modern Warfare', in *The Gulf War and the New World Order*, Edited by Haim Bresheeth & Nira Yuval-Davis, London: Zed.

Yuval-Davis, Nira (1997): *Gender and Nation*, London: Sage.

Yuval-Davis, Nira & Anthias, Floya (1989): *Woman-Nation-State*, London: Macmillan.

Zerai, Worku (1994): *Women in the Eritrean Military, Paper for Gender and Nation Fag*, Lahey: Institute of Social Studies.

INDEX